To Call Myself Beloved

A STORY OF HOPE, HEALING, AND COMING HOME

To Call Myself Beloved: A Story of Hope, Healing, and Coming Home
YGTMama Media Co. Press Trade Paperback Edition.
ISBN trade paperback: 978-1-989716-03-8
eBook: 978-1-989716-04-5

The publisher is not responsible for websites (or their content) that are not owned by the publisher.
Published in Canada, for Global Distribution by YGTMama Media Co.
www.ygtmama.com/publishing
To order additional copies of this book: publishing@ygtmama.com

Edited by Christine Stock
Cover design by Letitia Calver
Interior design & typesetting by Doris Chung
Illustration by Lucky Jackson, artist, from her Childwood Series. luckyjackson.ca
Cover photography by Emily Doukogiannis emilydphotography.com
Author photography p378 by Sara Tanner

For Mia, Grey, and Clara
Thank you for teaching me what
unconditional love feels like.

If you want to be a writer, you're going to need something to write about.

~ My dad, when I was sixteen

To Call Myself Beloved

A STORY OF HOPE, HEALING, AND COMING HOME

LEISSE WILCOX

YOTNAMA MEDIA CO.

TORONTO

Did you get what you wanted in this life?
I did.
And what was it that you wanted?
To call myself beloved; to feel myself beloved on the earth.

~"Late Fragment" by Raymond Carver

Contents

PROLOGUE

The chaos of becoming

"Even when it's not pretty or perfect. Even when it's more real than you want it to be. Your story is what you have, what you will always have. It is something to own."

~Michelle Obama

When you go out to eat at a restaurant, your food is brought to you as a beautiful, nourishing, pleasurable package. It's admired, coveted, shared, enjoyed. It's joy, which is exactly what you see and feel.

What you don't see or feel is HOW that joy came to be what it is—you don't see the fire, blade, blood that got it there; the burning, cutting, bleeding that brought it there. The mad dash around the kitchen of bodies in motion, shouting, scraping, slicing. The drama, the hustle, the natural unfolding process of everything getting where it needs to be, the demanding to know where the hell the scallop is for table eight.

Pouring acid, hitting it with salt, bringing out the balance and the flavor that leaves you wanting more. The tenderness and care that goes into chilling things cold, and keeping things warm, with an exacting, patient, and final wipe of the plate to ensure perfection before the presentation.

You only feel the joy, not the chaos of becoming.

In each of our lives we have this "kitchen phase." The agony and ecstasy of heartache is just the prep. The uncharted course of unexpected expectations is the mad dash of reorganizing your mind. The near reckless state of emotional highs and lows that have brought tears of joy and tears of longing is the seasoning to give you your unique flavor. And those final details that seem to be taking forever to resolve the last and tender motions of the presentation—all before this course of delicious perfection and joy is revealed for you to enjoy.

This is the chaos of becoming.

When we expect ourselves to succeed overall, we expect that things work out, and we expect that the game is rigged in our favor, this amazing thing happens: the game starts to be rigged in our favor, things start to work out, and we experience our success overall. We have to start with that as our foregone conclusion, that things will work out for us in each aspect of our lives in due time.

Maybe it doesn't work out in the short term. Maybe it doesn't work out in our predicted timeline, and maybe it doesn't work out along the identical way we anticipated. Even if that is the case, there is a beauty in coming to know and accept that all of it is working out:

sometimes it's just a more circuitous, lesson-filled, and yes, annoying path to discovering "Oh, hey! It actually DID work out—just not in the way I imagined."

Picasso said, "Every act of creation is first an act of destruction," and you, lovely, are no exception.

Can you love yourself enough to take the time, cultivate patience, and teach yourself to see the big picture as a sum of its moving parts?

Yes, you fucking can.

INTRO

The rebellious act of being yourself

THIS IS A STORY OF COMING HOME TO YOURSELF.

*T*o *Call Myself Beloved* offers the permission you've been looking for to simply be yourself, and to accept that with courage, pride, and grace. It really is that simple, even if it is that complicated. Too many of us are living with the feeling that we need to look outside ourselves to feel whole and loved, that we need to keep "the mask" on and hide who we really are; we read book after book, see therapist after therapist, and take course after course, all with the intent to "fix what's broken."

The secret is that we aren't broken—we are healing. We are learning to sort through the messages of what we've been told versus what we believe, and we are figuring out how it aligns with what we want out of our life. The quest to continuously solve a problem that isn't real with a solution that doesn't exist leaves us dissatisfied and constantly wanting more.

Leisse Wilcox

To Call Myself Beloved is informed by lessons learned through navigating the most cataclysmic events of one woman's life and realizing throughout each one that *I am still okay. We are still okay. This is still okay, unfolding somewhat differently than I had expected, but overall, okay.*

Let this book guide *you*, lovely, through the process of adulting: finding clarity in what you want, confidence in who you are, and the courage to stay true to both—even if that means making big changes in mindset and behavior simply through the rebellious act of being yourself.

Can you love yourself enough to come home to yourself and learn to call yourself beloved?

Yes, you fucking can.

Why this book

In 2015 I was lying on my family room floor, playing with my three baby girls. My then-husband and I owned a stunning seven-bedroom century home in a small town, six blocks from the lake. We had renovated it to include bathrooms with heated floors, an entire kids' wing, a natural outdoor playground, and a private patio with a hot tub. It had new paint and artwork, custom lighting installations, and a swank kitchen with exposed brick, subway tile, white cabinetry with a rolling "appliance garage" to hide clutter, a stand-alone ice maker, custom-built steel shelving to artfully display a rainbow of fresh fruit, seamless audio from room to room, and sixty-square feet of Carrera marble kitchen counters.

It was beautiful.
It was perfect.

I looked around at my beautiful and *perfect* family, my beautiful and *perfect* house, my beautiful and *perfect* life, and I couldn't shake the feeling that *this wasn't enough for me.* I had a sickening feeling that if this wasn't enough for me, then what the hell was wrong with me?

That's when I woke up.

That's when I woke up from a lifetime slumber of avoiding my real feelings at any cost, and from making decisions based on what I thought was expected of me to make everyone else happy. I realized that no matter what picture I painted of my life on the outside, it was my life on the inside that was screaming for help.

This wasn't "enough" for me because I wasn't enough for me.

I was drowning inside, slowly suffocating as I accumulated more and more and more, while simultaneously becoming further detached from what really mattered.

And what really mattered was my own level of internal happiness and peace.

I didn't yet have the words or emotional awareness at the time to know that that was what was missing, but I did have the wherewithal to make some incredibly difficult and life-altering decisions that set a brand new path of self-discovery in motion.

Until that "aha!" moment of clarity, I had spent most of my life searching and feeling "less than." Every bad decision I made, I made from a place of low self-worth, hoping that *this* would be "the thing" that would make me feel loved and respected. *This* would be the thing that made my relentless feelings of irrelevance and anxiety go away. It wasn't until that moment of waking up that I knew on a visceral, intuitive level that *the only way I would ever feel loved and respected would be to first love myself.* And respect myself enough to act on that wake-up.

This realization felt earth-shattering. Maybe it was possible that I had everything I needed—independent of what anyone else thought of or gave to me, and I just needed to get clear on how to accept it: accept all those parts and experiences that shaped me; accept the anger and resentment and decisions made along the way. Maybe it was possible to love those parts of me I'd found completely unlovable and to forgive the people from the past who I felt had made it so difficult to feel lovable and accepted.

This was the beginning of a complete shift in my mindset: how I saw myself, how I defined "family," how I gave and received love—including to and from whom I gave or received it—and how I would choose to live my life going forward.

I was desperate for some kind of a guide book, some kind of instruction manual that would make me feel less alone and more "normal" in my quest to essentially become *me* again; I wanted a guide book on how to safely feel my feelings and process them in a way that made sense without feeling constantly overwhelmed by the roller coaster I'd been riding in years past.

I spent tens of thousands of dollars in courses, coaches, books, retreats, vacations, vintage jackets, tacos, margaritas, and self-soothing healing modalities only to realize that I'd had what I needed inside me all along—the simple and authentic ability to just be myself and to be both fiercely proud of and at peace with that.

To Call Myself Beloved is the book that I was looking for: an honest, open account of "a regular person" living a life and learning to figure it out along the way. It's a guide to shed a lot of light and share insights on the human experience we're all having, even if it feels like we're painfully alone in having it. It's a manual to validate that you are, in fact, enough as you are, and anything you're feeling isn't wrong, just unattended to.

Because our feelings are always feedback, giving us valuable insights as to what still needs to be healed.

The intention behind this book is to share my story—relatable to so many women—in a way that makes you feel like you are not alone (because you aren't). That you have everything you need inside of you (because you do). And that if *I* can go through the process of learning to call myself beloved (through childhood trauma, divorce, cancer . . .), then *so can you.*

To Call Myself Beloved is the permission I was so desperately searching for to just be myself and for that to be *enough*; it is my personal mandate to share this simple and profound truth with hundreds of thousands of women just like *you.*

Can you love yourself enough to dig into this truth and expand your emotional awareness?

Yes, you fucking can.

Why I am the one to write it

I am a professional human and real-life adult. My entire experience has been about coming home to my truest self and to call myself *beloved*. My work and life purpose is built around helping women find the confidence in being who they are, the clarity to find what they want, and the courage to stay true to both.

Through lots of life lessons learned firsthand—*including facing and overcoming the heartbreak of childhood trauma, death of a sibling, divorce, and breast cancer*—I can tell you very honestly that I have had *a lot* of life lessons. And through each one—each *intense* one—I taught myself to turn something ugly into something beautiful.

I call it *Emotional Alchemy*.

"I've experienced a lot in my life" feels like an understatement. And despite it all, I continue to embrace a positive mindset, outlook, and perspective and describe myself as genuinely "happy." In fact, it was

the conscious choice to embrace those states of mind that enabled me to cope so well through the rapid succession of major life changes.

IT TOOK THE EXPERIENCES OF (IN A TEN-YEAR WINDOW):

- Homeownership and renovation x 3
- Relocation from a big city to a small town
- Marriage
- Loss of my twenty-one-year-old sister
- Birth of my three kids in two years, including a set of twins
- Miscarriage
- Divorce
- Reconnecting with my biological mother—whom I hadn't heard from since I was seven
- Transitioning from being a stay-at-home mom to an entrepreneur (almost overnight)
- Working for a megalomaniac who never paid me—but who ran off with money I'd lent
- Confronting an abusive stepparent and healing old childhood trauma
- Navigating the confusing world of adult female friendship
- Breast cancer, the treatment for which included chemotherapy and a double mastectomy
- Being single and solo parenting for much, much longer than I had anticipated

I am not alone in my pain; every single person experiences pain, adversity, and some degree of suffering. There is a relatability to the human narratives throughout *To Call Myself Beloved*. I know from my experience as a coach, friend, and keen observer of the human condition that even for the most seemingly well-put-together people who look like they have it all figured out, all you have to do is scratch the surface and realize that *everyone* is figuring this out, everyone has doubts, and everyone has moments or years of having absolutely no idea what they are doing or how to do it.

We are all having the same human experience, but we feel like we're having that experience in isolation, which leads to *exacerbated* feelings of isolation as we try to hide what it is we're truly feeling.

It's accepting this realization with the attitude of "learning through living" that moves us toward figuring it out, with grace. And if I can do this, and share the story of *how, specifically* I did this, I know there are hundreds of thousands of other women just itching to be inspired to make the same changes I made—and feel held while doing so.

With a career that began in Montessori education and taught me so much about the concept of human development (from childhood well into adulthood), I found myself at home with three kids under two and no one to talk to, no one to effectively communicate all the knowledge and information circulating around my head. So I started writing a "Practical Parenting" column for a local newspaper.

In preparation to impress a group of women at a "women in media" lunch I was invited to (as a plus one), I turned that column into a website and blog and back-filled it with my column content. Because I wanted people to read my blog, I learned how to use my voice on social media to establish a clear and authentic presence that encouraged women to read that blog. When some peers in my area started a music festival and asked me to be their PR person, I cemented my social media and copywriting skills for a much wider audience.

Fresh off the success of that experience, a partner and I started a boutique creative agency together, with the intent to hijack small to medium business clients' Instagram feeds to tell their story visually. This was just as Instagram was becoming a thing, and well before anyone really caught on to the value of social media marketing and the subsequent value in hiring someone to run their social platforms for them.

My business partner and I were BUSY—not only with the six kids under six between us, but with a full client roster that included predominantly female entrepreneurs. Every single time we worked with a client the conversation came down to "I'm not sure if I can do this. My mom said I could never be creative. My husband thinks this is just a hobby and is getting tired of me trying new things that don't work. I've always wanted to be an artist but don't think I have any original ideas. I know I have something to say, but I have no idea how to get people to listen. I really want to do this and make a difference—but I am *terrified* of failure."

Without knowing or intending it, I had started a coaching practice for women, and I was *really* good at it.

When my marriage officially ended a couple months later, yes, it felt necessary, and it also felt like life as I knew it had imploded. Running my own business seemed overwhelming suddenly. So we shuttered the creative agency, and I started working for "Christopher," an ad agency consultant specializing in pitch strategy. I found myself with no "real" experience, no formal marketing education, no idea what the hell I was doing, but *holding court* in meetings with agency CEO/CFO/strategy teams—with clients in Toronto and New York—and pulling it off.

There is a moment burned indelibly into my brain. I was sitting in a meeting (without my boss who had stayed home with a hangover or was sleeping with his most recent waitress) with the CEO of a global ad agency and her director of marketing strategy *offering up ideas* of my own for their upcoming client pitch—a *mega* retail giant. I thought I was going to faint through most of it and was 99 percent sure there would be a team in hazmat suits busting in and yelling "IMPOSTER" before hauling me away.

Neither of those scenarios happened.

Instead? The CEO and strategy guy looked at me and said, "Wow, Leisse, that's a *great* idea." That was a moment of a *massive* shift—that I, contrary to the toxic and abusive messaging I grew up with at home, was bright. Talented. Capable. Worthy of being heard. It was one of those "one small step, one giant leap" moments in my own process of becoming and was worth all the rest of the crap Christopher put me through.

Being a single mom of three and working from 6:00 a.m. to 2:00 a.m. for a manipulative megalomaniac boss with a silver tongue, who had every intention of taking advantage of my kindness and naivety and zero intention of *ever* paying me (think: the Fyre Festival of advertising), proved to be just too much after a year, so I quit. Well, I lent him a few grand to pay our interns first (face palm), and *then* I quit.

I started freelance writing and social media strategizing for an influencer marketing agency and online magazine for women, while also writing daily messages of empowerment and inspiration and building my own brand the whole time.

One day people started reaching out via direct message on Instagram asking if I would coach them, and I realized that I had been doing it all along without even knowing it. Their requests gave legs to a formal coaching practice, and I pursued training as a Master Neuro-Linguistic Programming (NLP) Coach and Practitioner. I launched an online self-study course and sold it out—all with a list of under 100 subscribers, and all while being on my own with three kids in my custody 80 percent of the time.

Even more momentum grew after I announced my breast cancer diagnosis, and subsequent treatment, all while handling the grit with much, much grace. This was the moment that really felt as if I had captured people's attention, more than any other time. I've always prided myself in writing from an authentic place, but the ability to convey the juxtaposed integration of my tender vulnerability with steel-like strength really proved to my audience that I was legit.

And that is the place of power from which this book is being written—it is *Emotional Alchemy* in its truest sense: to take something dark, ugly, and unwanted, and turn it into something beautiful, golden, and uniquely your own. That is the entire premise behind *To Call Myself Beloved* and is true to the process I've used to get here.

Will this process be the same for you?
Probably not.

"Uh-oh," you're thinking. "Why am I reading this?"

Because even while the process looks and unfolds a little differently, there is one universal truth that does not cease to amaze: we are all having a profoundly similar experience—the experience of simply being human.

And all we need is a little perspective to show that exactly where we are is exactly where we're supposed to be.

Our lives may seem radically different than anyone else's we know, and still, if people are being honest? There is a shared experience in feeling a lack of belonging juxtaposed against the desire to connect. There is a pervasive feeling of being an imposter juxtaposed against the reality that not one single person has it all figured out; therefore, to a certain extent, we are all faking it—and some of us are just better at faking it than others.

Loneliness. Worthiness. Lovability. The deep desire to connect and serve while quietly feeling a little angry that most people don't live up to your expectations.

It's as if we're each a forest full of falling trees, each one making a sound we're not quite convinced that anyone else can hear.

And that's why this book matters.

I've outlined the tools I have used in my own life and have taught thousands of others to use as well, in their own way. Think of these tools as emotional scaffolding: this book is the structure; now that you know it's built, all you have to do is climb it.

Can you love yourself enough to do this foundational emotional work?

Yes, you fucking can.

Why you are the one to read it

Understanding child development is familiar for most of us, particularly if you're a parent, but even if you aren't, it's easy to see how children are expected to meet certain milestones and go through certain phases of their life at fairly predictable times. There is a fallacy that this development ends when those kids turn nineteen: it can feel like "Okay, phew! We did it; we raised and launched them."

One of the best-kept secrets of our lives is that—not only will we spend a solid 30 percent of our time finding and resetting our online passwords—*we never stop developing.* We are in a constant state of growth, change, evolution, iterating throughout our adult years that have *equally predictable* timed phases and characteristics of development. So when we feel like we're feeling listless, restless, directionless in isolation, chances are we're in our thirties.

It's a profound moment of clarity to realize and appreciate that through all that change, all that relentless reiterating, you're not going crazy, or losing your mind, or "hormonal," you're simply living your adult life.

This book came together after a pretty epic reflection of the "first half" of my own life, moving through the transition of daughter/child to parent/wife and beyond. It speaks to anyone who has that gut-dropping moment of clarity, asking "What the hell just happened? This many years later, and who the hell am I? Why am I still hurting from something that happened ten, twenty, thirty years ago? What am I doing here?"

It speaks to navigating the experiences we have as we are figuring it all out, through decades of massive change, and to coming to terms with accepting ourselves as we are—that period through which we come to call ourselves beloved.

The content is all a human narrative and is framed within the context of speaking directly to women and calling up familiar tales of childhood, adulthood, making mistakes, living through misdirection, and learning all the lessons through it all. The goal is to evoke that feeling of "I feel like she was reading my mind and saying everything I felt but didn't know how to say."

You'll see that each section of the book starts with "Personally Speaking," which is an intimate look at the events of my own life that prompted the radical changes I chose to pursue: an emotionally abusive childhood, a painful divorce that triggered the Complex Post-Traumatic Stress Disorder (C-PTSD) I'd experienced from childhood, a breast cancer diagnosis (and the aggressive treatment thereof) at thirty-six years old. Is it my intention to write a tell-all book? Heck no.

In fact, I was inclined to not say anything about my own story because hey—it's mine. But you know what? I am super contextual, and I love to know (and appreciate knowing) where someone is coming from when they're sharing information about how they made the changes they made. Plus, if they ever make a movie about my life, not only will it have a killer soundtrack, but this book will act as a good place to start (especially if they foreshadow my future by casting Ben Affleck as the leading man . . .).

I am sharing my story simply to frame the context of how I navigated where I came from, to where I am, to where I am going.

And wildly? Although my story is my own, I am ever aware and constantly surprised by how when you just scratch the surface of someone's life, you find all kinds of skeletons, wounds, and traumas among the love, joy, and hope. From my experience, I know we tend to self-select into two camps: those who focus on the pain and those who focus on the hope.

You can say we are all wounded, or you can say we are all healing.

I say we are all healing, and the only way we can properly heal is to keep doing that, keep focusing on the hope.

That is what makes this book specifically worthwhile for you: *It gives a voice to so much internal processing we all experience and invites it to come to the surface.* It invites the opportunity to open up the conversation that stops the feeling of isolation in its tracks and strips away the shame of feeling "I thought I was the only one."

Through my current writing (both short- and long-form content on my own platforms and those for which I've guest written and spoken), THIS is the "super-power" quality I have: to go into our darkest places and bravely turn on the light.

Can you love yourself enough to trust me to guide you through that process?

Yes, you fucking can.

How to get the most out of this book

L ife is meant to be joyful. Peaceful. Pleasurable.

And even so, as we make the decisions that bring us joy, create peace, and pursue pleasure, there are rocky spots and rough patches along the way. Inevitably, the stuff that shapes you the most and teaches you how to get comfortable with being uncomfortable.

It can be tempting to avoid those rough patches because they don't feel good. They feel uncomfortable. It can seem a lot more appealing to circumvent them entirely and go the other way when we come across one. You know the one: an icky conversation we can feel creeping up, the end of an unhealthy or otherwise stagnant relationship, a departure from something known to move on to the unknown, or a decision that you know is right but is also going to piss off a lot of people.

We are pleasure seekers and pain avoiders—particularly on an emotional and spiritual level. The irony is that for most growth work, we need to experience at least a little bit of pain to get to where we're going:

1. Pain that comes from breaking free and detaching from old patterns, narratives, and habits and transitioning over to adopt new ones.
2. Pain that comes from releasing toxic relationships and the grief that follows in order to receive healthy loving people in your life.
3. Pain that comes from the emotional or mental struggle of not getting what you (thought you) wanted.

If you want to grow and expand—and chances are if you are here in this moment, you do want to grow and expand—this kind of discomfort is inevitable. Do you think it feels good for the snake to shed an entire layer of skin? Doubtful, but it is still necessary for the snake to shed that skin to *be* a snake. And the same is true of our own shedding of the old and adapting to the new. It isn't necessarily going to feel great at first, but it is still necessary in order for us to *be* who we are. They're called growing pains for a reason.

And this, like anything, gets easier with practice and more familiar over time.

Once you are familiar with acknowledging "I know what this feeling is" and owning it, you can sink into it for what it is because you know that you're strong enough to get through it as well. Inch by inch, day by day, conversation by conversation. When we name what we're feeling, we don't have to *shame* what we're feeling; we give ourselves the space just to feel it and then move through it in a healthy way.

After enough practice it doesn't feel as scary, and the urge to cut and run might not even come up anymore—you know you're brave, courageous, and tenacious enough to handle it with grace and ease.

Treat the discomfort as part of the flow of the changes you're making. Learn to be comfortable with being uncomfortable, so when you come to the part of your path that feels a little rocky, you're more mentally ready to just keep going and move through it with the knowledge that you've done this before and you can do it again, emerging stronger than you were before. This is the guidebook to navigating that process I wish I'd had. The answer to my prayers when I was silently screaming, "Yeah, but how the HELL do I DO this?" This is the forgiveness, the compassion, the comfort, the permission to just be myself—and feel comfortable feeling that *that* was enough—that I was desperate to find. And eventually, through my own processes and multitude of healing modalities, I found it. I wrote this, and I'm giving it to you.

Allow yourself to feel into it, to see yourself in a shared experience and to hold space for that; allow yourself to find the forgiveness, the compassion, the comfort, the permission to just be *your*self and know that that is enough.

Make this experience your own; appreciate the hard truth that there is no magic end point of arrival. Throughout our whole lives we are constantly adapting and evolving. This transformation is what makes us a work in progress and work of art at the exact same time.

Come home to yourself and call yourself beloved.

Can you love yourself enough to make this your own?

Yes, you fucking can.

Part 1

ORIGIN STORY

Understanding where you've come from

"We are all children of children."

LW

PERSONALLY SPEAKING

I spent the first thirty years of my life feeling terrified and sad.
I was riddled with doubt, self-loathing, and a pervasive feeling of loneliness no matter how many people were around.

I came by those feelings honestly; my mom left our family when I was three. Well, technically she left when I was an infant, just before my dad's final medical exams to become a physician, but then she came back.

We relocated from Ottawa (where I was born) to Stratford, Ontario (where Justin Bieber was born), as a family, and yes, when I was three, she left . . . for real this time.

Cue the insecure attachment wound.

My dad had full custody of me, which was amazing. We had a nanny stay with me, who felt more like a live-in grandmother; we even called her Grandma Helen. My life felt pretty sweet. Although my dad was (freaking) busy building his career as a young MD, setting up a practice in a small town, he somehow always managed to carve out time for me. He was an amazing, present, engaged, funny, loving father.

I remember the feeling of going skating with my class at the public rink and having my dad show up as a surprise, just coming up behind me, sweeping me up into his arms, and carrying me princess-style around the rink. I remember my dad coming into my class to read aloud to us all as a parent volunteer; I got my love of language and books from him for sure—and the fact that he always used different voices to act out different characters helped. He was so funny and so charming, and from the few old photos I have and the stories my aunts and uncles have told me, I know he was by my side.

It felt like we were a team.

Each year he took me to Disney World, rented a red T-Bird, and let me eat Twinkies and drink SunnyD. It was the best. He also paid for Grandma Helen to visit her family in Texas every year, which I knew even as a kid was a class act. He sent me roses at school for Valentine's Day and took me to work with him on the weekends whenever possible.

I would do "rounds" at the hospital with him on Saturday mornings, trying desperately to keep up with his six-foot-three self by taking steps two at a time, talking to patients in the ICU, and learning how to read echocardiograms, all while wearing his stethoscope. I also remember him bringing donuts home some weekends after he'd made rounds on his own when I had stayed home with Grandma Helen.

One of my greatest memories of my dad, though, was going on house calls with him. Because I grew up in southwestern Ontario, there were several Mennonite farms around us; one of my dad's patients was a seven-year-old girl named "Julie," and because she was on dialysis—and her Mennonite family didn't have a car (or phone, or radio, or television . . .)—my dad made specific trips to the country to see her. While he did his medical visit inside the house, I went to the barn with Julie's siblings and looked at animals, held the piglets, then visited inside with Julie and her mom when the medical stuff was done. On the way home, my dad would stop for cheese curds, chocolate milk, and apple butter for us.

It was really lovely.

Another bonus of living with my dad 98 percent of the time—and him being second oldest of the bunch—was our family gatherings at our beautiful home with a pool and a wraparound porch. We have a huge extended family, with eight siblings on my dad's side alone. My aunts and uncles would come and visit for a weekend, and it was just so much fun. Laughing, splashing, joking; I felt bright and loved. A normal kid. The age gap was so big between my dad and some of his younger siblings that in many ways it felt like they were my older brothers and sisters, not my uncles and aunts.

It was such a wonderful, low-key, easy, and peaceful existence together—even in the face of effectively losing one parent, I knew I was safe, and I felt grounded and loved.

For the next few years, I visited my mom in Toronto on certain weekends. My parents would meet halfway in the parking lot of the Mohawk Inn to do the "great kid exchange." Often, just before those weekends, my mom would cancel; other times, she would make pretty bad decisions while I was there with her. I have a memory of being kissed on the lips by one of her creepy boyfriends, for example. Being held up and over an apartment balcony (by another creepy boyfriend) "as a joke" comes to mind, as does waking up one morning to a silent, empty apartment in The Beaches and believing adamantly that she had left for good. I wondered how the hell I was going to get home to my dad, two hours away, at age six (this was before cell phones were a thing). It turns out she had gone out for croissants, but that fear was real, and I vividly remember that fear of being abandoned—again—to this day.

There were some happy memories too, like watching *Beaches* with my mom and her friend at the movie theater, going to Lick's (a classic burger joint) at their original Queen Street East location (back when the kitchen guys would sing your order back to you: "plain hot dog, cheese and pickles, one chocolate shaaaake"), and learning to ride my bike on the boardwalk by Lake Ontario. My mom always dressed well, smelled good, and taught me that lipstick counted as sunscreen, and to this day I think this is where my obsession with having bold lipstick comes from.

The problem was that the good stuff was overshadowed by the not-so-good: the "yes, I can come to your dance recital" then choosing last minute not to. The "I just really want to talk to my dad and need to call home" and being physically restrained and restricted from making that call.

It didn't feel great. Over and over again.

Once, my mom dropped me off at home, back with my dad, and my parents got into an *epic* fight at the door during drop-off. My dad was pretty conflict-averse, and I *never* saw my parents fight, or even argue, so this was already very disorienting. I was six. So what happened next became a truly formative and life-changing moment in how my childhood would be forever and indelibly different from that point forward.

My mom and I had gone shopping during our visit and bought me a silk, emerald-green dress with black velvet polka dots (because it was the 80s, and because one of my aunts was getting married soon). I knew my dad had unwittingly paid for it, and I knew it had been expensive. I was proudly wearing the dress to show my dad, and that's when things just fell apart.

My parents were shouting at each other, and because they *never* shouted at each other, I assumed that it was the dress—ergo, moi— who was the real source of the anger. I remember crying and saying, "I'll take it off, we can take it back!" and feeling very deeply that this fight was, without question, my fault.

And then I remember my dad shepherding me inside where a woman I had never met was sitting on our living room couch while two springer spaniel dogs walked around our house. The woman introduced herself—I'm pretty sure she said she was my stepmom (but admittedly that is a little foggy)—and then *she had me join her on the couch* within complete and total earshot and eyeshot of my parents' row.

She sat and watched and listened to every single angry and cursing word exchanged at the door between them while I sat with her, doe-eyed, wanting to be protected from what was happening but not knowing what the hell to do.

Even at such a young age, I was aware that it seemed as if she *wanted* to sit there and watch (and relish in?) the fight that was happening instead of doing what I think any other human would do: *protect this little girl and distract her in any way possible.*

Where was the "Let's go find a snack! Want to show me your room? Hey, let's read a book together. Have you met my dogs? Let's take them outside." None of it. None of the normal, empathetic, compassionate actions that any sane, kind human would offer up. She chose to sit there, with me, and bear witness to a fight I thought I had caused.

This memory was so painful that I buried and suppressed it until many decades later, well into my thirties; in hindsight, this precise moment was the very rocky beginning of my *Life 2.0: A Cinderella Story.*

This woman indeed (and overnight) became my stepmother, though I was never allowed to call her that or introduce her as such because she didn't like the "negative connotation that came with the title." Irony at its finest. I physically could not stomach calling her "mom," so I just called her by her first name: "Dani."

Again, Dani literally *showed up* one day without any notice, discussion, preparation, or warning from my dad that he was even *in* a relationship. She just appeared overnight, with her two dogs, apparently intent on staying. She was, to say it lightly, not my biggest fan, and she wasn't exactly "shy" about letting me know that.

If I had to guess, knowing what I know now about the human experience and how we process or repress our emotions, I would say Dani "had her own shit" she was too afraid to deal with, and so she took it out on me. Who knows what that was, what her own wounds from childhood were like, or what the unhealed trauma was for her that enabled her to be so callous as a stepmother.

In hindsight, it felt like an intense jealousy she had. I think she, in some way, felt threatened by me or my relationship with my dad and didn't have the coping skills to deal with that properly or healthfully, so instead acted in ways—that I'm sure had decent intentions—but were, in practice, highly emotionally and extremely psychologically abusive.

In short, what that felt like was feeling ashamed of my very existence.

Children who grow up in families where their sexuality is rejected will talk about the feeling of having to "repress" their sexuality and minimize that part of themselves to feel like they belong. For me, it wasn't one quality or aspect of mine that was rejected—it was just *me*. Period.

In order to survive emotionally, I had to repress *all* of me. Minimize my existence, *entirely*. It was like my very presence was an extreme burden on her; that I had ruined her life by being there . . . even though I was there first. It decimated my self-worth, which I came to realize in adulthood would snake its tendrils into literally every aspect of my life, including my relationships, career choices, and sexual self, because that shame became mine to carry—until I chose much later to do the work required to finally let it go.

It was such a painful existence from age six to nineteen years old (when I moved out) that even now as I write this book, I am aware that there are still layers of wounds in the process of healing.

I could probably fill a book with the experience of growing up with narcissistic emotional abuse, and a parental guardian who openly hates you and not so subtly sets you up to fail, but this isn't about that:

this is about learning to heal from literally anything, including severe Stockholm-Syndrome-style trauma that led to an actual diagnosis of Complex Post-Traumatic Stress Disorder (C-PTSD) that taught me to doubt/hate/endlessly critique myself.

Because I am living proof that this kind of healing *is* possible.

It cost me about $50,000 and almost twenty years to figure that out, hence the "why" behind this book: a Coles Notes on how to have hope, heal, and come home to *yourself*. And while I am not a therapist, I can share with you, for educational and community purposes, the techniques I learned personally and then professionally that allowed me to overcome a painful and abusive childhood.

Using NLP coaching techniques and tons and tons of reading (followed by endless hours on the phone with my very supportive aunt), I was able to process my past with Eye Movement Desensitization and Reprocessing (EMDR) therapy and integrate the experience into my present, enabling me to prepare for my future, with everything laid out in this book.

If you are at all familiar with the dynamics of abuse, you'll know it is basically an imbalanced power differential. Step one of maintaining that power differential—the first and essential strategy—is for the abuser to teach the abusee they are crazy. Like, batshit. The goal is to make the abusee think they are going absolutely bonkers so that whatever it is they are feeling is immediately negated under the guise of being crazy. "This can't possibly be happening; I'm sure she didn't mean it. I must have done something to deserve this. She's right. I am a failure. I'll just have to try harder and be better."

In the biz we call that "gaslighting," and it feels like psychological warfare—not feeling safe enough to even trust your own thoughts . . . and sanity.

Step two is isolation. The abuser cuts off pretty much all connection and contact with the abusee's outside world so that in the event step one is unsuccessful and the abusee finds the courage to reach for help, there is *no one there* to help.

Dani was a master of both these steps.

Step two was particularly impressive as she somehow managed to cut almost all contact with Grandma Helen, my primary caregiver, and our extended family who—just weeks before—had been strong, cohesive, and involved. All those tightly knit connections with my aunts and uncles . . . poof! Gone. Overnight. Except for rare and obligatory all-family events.

One of my amazing aunts has later recounted (after we reconnected several years later) a story in which she remembers driving away from our house in tears, and with the knowing feeling that she would never see me again. It was incredibly manipulative, calculating, and toxic behavior.

Dani was able to convince those closest to me that she knew what she was doing and that she was there to "save" me from the rocky start with virtually no mom.

Including my dad.

Whenever there is a rescue narrative in a relationship, trust me, it is a major red flag to *run*, not walk, away. If you find yourself saying or thinking "this person saved me," or "I rescued this person," it is a major warning bell that a codependent relationship is being formed. And that codependency all but requires the continuity of that symbiotic relationship for it to feel complete.

And so it perpetuates over and over again the feeling of "I owe it all to this person who came along and rescued me from my own life."

The solid relationship my dad and I had, our amazing bond, was totally and completely obliterated. Gone. It was as if the father I knew and loved *died*, instantly, never to return . . . despite my best efforts as a child and again later as an adult. There was a pervasive theme of how he, too, had been rescued by Dani, and she was the reason for anything good in his life. Therefore, it seemed to me that to act in opposition to anything she said, thought, or did would be a violation of the gratitude he had for having been "rescued" by her.

Barf.

She also somehow managed to convince me that the best way to protect myself from getting hurt or disappointed by my mom was to cut off all contact with her, full stop. More barf. I have no idea how this decision became mine to make—at age seven—or if Dani ever discussed it with my dad or just told him, falsely, that this was a decision I had made.

Again, I was seven. All I know is that this was exactly what happened.

Because Dani arranged it so that there were no other adults I could trust around me, and that she would be there all the time, in order to survive, I felt the relentless need to please her, earn her affection, and prove my value and love. I remember at each one of her birthdays, and every Mother's Day, I wrote her a lengthy card telling her "this will be the year I change, do better, turn over a new leaf. I'll be a brand new me! Please don't give up on me." Each one she *accepted*, with a terse smile. Frankly, even my *(totally unnecessary)* apologies *(for having the audacity to be me)* seemed like they fell short of her "expectations."

Per Dani's instructions, and per my desperate need to feel loved, any time a call came in from my mom, I was "busy." Any time a letter or package came in the mail, I was—in my own writing (for dramatic effect)—to cross out the address and write *return to sender*. Thinking about the psychology of this, from the perspective of Dani, me, and my mother, still shocks me to this day. The damaging ripple effect this ritual had, at such a tender age, is almost incomprehensible.

What's even more incomprehensible? After a few returned letters and packages, a few missed phone calls, my mom stopped sending them and stopped calling. Once, shortly thereafter, she did try to pick me up from school, but Dani had warned me that my mother would one day—as a reaction to me returning all her letters—try and kidnap me. So when I saw her gray Buick pull up curbside at my public school, I literally ran screaming in the other direction.

You can imagine, at age seven, already feeling insecure that my mom had left, my dad had turned his back, my nanny had gotten fired, my aunts and uncles were being kept at bay (and demonized for reasons unknown to me to this day, just a part of the "everyone else but me is bad for you" culture Dani was adamant to implement), and at a very tender age, I had been instructed to cut contact with my allegedly criminal mother.

My inner world felt like an actual war zone, and emotionally, it was. It was a completely unsafe place to be, a place where anyone important to you, anyone who is supposed to be there looking out for you, will just disappear without a trace, at any moment, and there will be nothing you can do about it. (This is a wound I still am highly sensitive to, even as a grown-ass woman.)

And the one constant? The one person who was continuously there? Dani.

There she was, the only person who would "stick around long enough to care about me . . ." yet constantly tell me what a disappointment and failure I was. There to ensure I knew I wasn't special. There to announce that everything I did was wrong and that I was too stupid to notice—and that I should be grateful she was there to tell me.

And still—she was the only adult there. And I really needed her to love me.

Boom: Stockholm.

Enter the subconscious (and limiting) belief that love is having to prove yourself over and over, and earn affection, and be met with endless rejection . . . fighting to demonstrate your value to someone who will actually never value you.

Dani and my dad went on to have two children together, and the astounding thing to me then, and now, was that she was an amazing, engaged, loving, *supportive* mother to both of them; she was and is their biggest champion and advocate. So much so that when we circle back to step one of the abuse dynamic (convince abusee they are nuts), both my half sisters were looped into that. They, too, alongside my father, believed I was cuckoo and never had any idea about what my problem was with Dani. To them, she was an awesome mom for whom I should be grateful.

It's kind of fascinating when you step back and observe it from a behavioral perspective, that two simultaneous and opposing truths can exist at the same time—and both be right. It's very "Schrodinger's Cat."

Perspective truly is everything.

Everyone in our family drank the Kool-Aid, but I was the only one who seemed to be dying a slow and painful death.

From where I stood, I could never do anything right. That was my truth as it was told and reinforced to me over and over again. All my natural talents, gifts, and abilities were chastised, criticized, told they held no value, told they didn't really "count" as gifts or talents because they just weren't worth anything.

For example, I'm a pretty good singer. I'm not like Taylor Swift good, but I easily win-second-place-in-a-karaoke-competition good. As a kid and into my teens, I was in an auditioned choir. One year I was given a solo. Dream! My solo was to be performed at not only our concert but at our national vocal competition. I was so happy and so proud. When Dani found out, she said they would not be attending, and that I'd have to go to the concert on my own because "it wasn't for [them], it was for [me]" and if I had any hopes of flying with the choir to the west coast to perform said solo, I was going to have to sell a lot of chocolate bars because hey, "that's what fundraising is for."

Shortly thereafter, I heard Dani on the phone with a friend talking about another kid my age who was playing a show in his band. Dani, knowing I was standing in the room, said, "If I had a kid with real talent, I just don't know what I'd do. Everything it took to support them, I guess."

The subtext—and foundational narrative I learned and committed to memory here—was that:

I held no value; I could not be loved. I was not worth anything. No matter what.

Moreover, if I *did* want to achieve something, if I *did* want to feel loved and feel like I *did have* value, I would have to radically change my personality to do so—and so I began faking it. I began trying to live up to the expectation that who I am was nowhere near good enough, and I attempted to be the person they wanted me to be—which (spoiler) was still never enough.

I grew up feeling like I was walking on eggshells, holding my breath, doing my best not to be noticed around our house. I remember actively closing cabinet doors without making a sound, leaving everything exactly as I found it, avoiding the squeaky floorboards or rustling the plastic bag of a cracker box because I was so conscious about making it seem like I didn't exist.

I was told—and subsequently learned—to second-guess everything I did. That I was stupid, a disappointment, not creative, a constant failure, a big fake. At one point I remember my dad telling me at the dinner table to do the exact opposite of what my gut told me to do when making decisions and instead think to myself, "What would Dani do?" From that moment, until about age thirty-two, I learned to actively ignore my intuition.

Sometimes my childhood feels like a highlight reel, or more accurately, a *low*light reel of a slow-motion video. Thanks to a lot of EMDR therapy, and every single coaching method and healing modality laid out in the pages of this book, I can now remember and watch the events of that video (that led to having C-PTSD) without the anxiety attacks and hives I used to experience, but rather with total neutrality.

Even the very extreme memories, like, for example, how I wasn't allowed to dispose of tampons or pads in our family bathroom. My half sisters were a lot younger than me, and Dani didn't want them to know about periods yet (red flag: decades of sexual shame to follow). So instead, knowing I couldn't throw out these used hygiene products in our family bathroom, *I hid them in my room.*

I hid bags and bags and bags of them in my room, tucked away in my bedroom cupboards. To make matters worse, the physiological tension in our house was so intense that my body went into adrenal overdrive, and from the time I got my first period at age twelve until my early thirties, I had a reversed cycle in which I bled *heavily* for three weeks and had one week off.

Needless to say, my cupboards were quite full. And, being full of what is essentially human waste, eventually this collection of used feminine hygiene products really started to smell. Bad.

One day Dani must have been investigating where this foul smell was coming from and found the hidden stash of period shame and freaked out. She punished me and asked what the hell was *wrong with me* for hiding it all in my room. I responded with doe eyes, unable to talk or basically breathe. Again.

But one of my most poignant memories is the day I stopped writing.

As a kid, I wrote for pleasure. I was born with a love of and gift for language and the creative arts. I learned to read at age four and haven't stopped since. At school I turned everything I did into an art project whenever possible, making posters, songs, plays, and advertisements for any assignment we were given. I was in choirs and school plays as often as I could be, and growing up in Stratford with an extremely well-read father, I had access to much live (and mostly Shakespearean) theater, for which my dad had us *read* the play before we *watched* the play.

My parents were active supporters of the arts and had their names published as donors to the theater. Additionally, they took anyone who came to visit us *to* the theater and made a big deal of it.

So I couldn't figure out why they didn't support my own natural affinity for and love of language and the arts. In grade school I wrote short stories and even "published" them in bound books with covers we made out of wallpaper. I wrote plays and acted them out with paper-mâché puppets, and art directed every playdate I had. I basically instructed my friends on what to say while playing Barbie or My Little Pony.

Halfway through high school, I went to see the guidance counselor to get, you know, *guidance* on my future. After some conversation and some tests, she passionately told me that my gifts in the arts were so strong that I should focus exclusively on every single art/language/drama course I could get my hands on, that I should only take the bare essentials of science and math needed to graduate, and that I really should start to hone my abilities in what I was naturally gifted in.

I skipped home and joyfully shared that news with Dani who—without a word of a lie—told me that since I was "already good at that stuff, it didn't make any sense to pursue it." And instead, since I clearly was not as good in science and math, that's where I should hone my skill set.

After all, she pointed out, "there's no value in the arts. Anyone can do it, and if you want to do something with your life, you need to focus on the stuff you're not good at."

Quote unquote.

When I told my parents emphatically that I wanted to be a writer and that I needed to focus on developing those skills, they told me I was wrong. Dani, with her classic head-shaking, arms-folded-across-chest stance, looked at my dad and said, "Tell her!" My dad looked at me and said, "If you want to be a writer, you're going to need something to write about."

This comment started a much larger crack in my belief about myself, which was already sitting on a shaky foundation. I had felt the sting of my parents not supporting me in my singing, even though they went to every single horse show and competition my half sisters went to and recorded their performance to play back and watch together. If my sisters lost, it was *obviously* because of bias on the part of the judge, not their own ability.

But somehow it felt like it was getting worse. I was actually prohibited from taking any course at school that made me feel alive, successful, engaged, or joyful. Instead, Dani chose my courses for me—including my first year at university—which found me taking only the required English classes I needed to graduate. No arts, just chemistry, math, biology, and physics.

My marks were *not* good. Shocker. This stuff made my brain hurt, and not in a good way. It made me feel like I was failing all the time. And in some classes I almost was.

When the choral director of my high school came to me privately and said, "Listen, we are doing *Joseph* for the spring musical and I want to give you the lead—without auditioning," I skipped home to share the good news. I felt so much joy, but I was promptly told without question, NO. *Why?*

Because my grades weren't good enough.

I was constantly being set up to fail, a theme that echoed across several tests Dani manufactured for me. She would say, after "another" one of my great failures, "This was a test, Leisse, and you failed." Over and over.

I was encouraged to repress every single part of me that made me who I was and was instead forced to focus on who I wasn't. And then, when I couldn't deliver the results that were expected of me (for being a person I absolutely was not), I was punished for failing and repeatedly told what a disappointment I was for not living up to my potential.

I often cut the grass at home, and one day I noticed the lawnmower had something stuck in its underbelly. Halfway between the front yard and the backyard, I turned it over on its side on our wooden deck to have a look. I guess some of the gasoline from the lawnmower tank leaked onto the deck, staining it. Dani freaked out. Like *freaked* out.

She sent me to my room (I was sixteen) and demanded I write her an essay on lawnmower maintenance. So I did. In writing these words now, I can't even believe this was a real story, but I assure you it was. Very real.

I am sure the essay I wrote, though, was mostly made up because I don't remember being allowed to leave to go to the library, I don't remember having a lot of books on "lawnmower maintenance" in our home library collection, and the Internet wasn't really a household thing yet.

So when I submitted this essay to her, she skimmed it and wrote a giant red "C" on it, telling me to go back inside and do it again. And I did. And I failed it, again. I remember writing it three times before she got bored of reading, I guess, and that was the end of that.

This is just a trivial example of the weird and totally irrational behavior that was common in the dynamic between her and me.

She'd say jump.

I'd say how high.

She'd say figure it out! What the hell is wrong with you that you can't figure this out?

And so I'd jump.

And she'd say no not like that. God, seriously, are you that stupid? You don't even know how to jump?

I'd ask her if maybe she could show me how to jump.

And she'd say I shouldn't have to ask, I should just know. Pathetic that I didn't even know how to jump. She was the high record holder of jumping at her high school—still after all these years no one has ever beat me. And you. You don't even know how. God, you are lazy.

Each and every circumstance was unwinnable for me, and it started to add up. Back in the 90s we didn't really have terms like mental and emotional health, but looking back, it's fair to say mine were both gravely endangered.

The final nail in the coffin was when I was writing for pleasure one weekend when I was a teenager. I had been experiencing friendship problems at school, and after talking to one of my aunts about it, I turned that pain into a lovely little metaphor of a short story based on her own life experience with the same feeling. I remember how good that felt, how cathartic it was to know I wasn't alone and that maybe my own life story could have a happy ending too, so I wrote it that way. I was really proud of it.

Dani stood over me, reading quietly, and as I pressed Save she said to me, again with the head shaking, arms folded: "This is shit. No one wants to read this, ever; do not ever write anything like this again."

So I didn't. I fully abandoned writing until my early thirties.

It was such a sore spot that I didn't wish to revisit. Dani had told me other things over the years including, "You aren't actually creative—you just steal other people's ideas and say they are your own. You don't have any original thoughts." And eventually, it just hurt so much that it felt easier to finally believe her and to finally concede:

I am not good enough. I am not smart. I am not creative. I have no original thought. I will never be lovable on my own. If I want to be loved, I will have to prove to someone that I am not who I really am, and I will have to keep proving that I am good enough, over and over. And even still, they will leave me as soon as they get a better offer.

These thoughts became my absolute truth.

It affected the relationships I chose, the decisions I made, and the way I showed up in the world. It has taken years of emotional work, years of therapy and coaching, tens of thousands of dollars, and relentless, conscious, focused, intentional effort to undo this "truth" and replace it with what *is* my current reality: *I alone am enough.*

Ironically, and here is the wild truth of it all—the insane, isolating, and abusive mindfuck of a childhood I had *shaped* me into who I am today.

Kaboom.

Read that again: all that pain and suffering *shaped the woman, coach, partner, and mother* I am today. My resiliency, courage, strength, vulnerability, authenticity, tenacity, and lovability all stem from the experiences that led me *here*. They prompted all the inner work I had to do—that I share with you in these pages—to truly become who I was meant to be and call myself beloved.

That's the simple significance of this book: *it's a testament to our human ability to overcome.*

If I spent the first thirty years of my life feeling terrified and sad, I can safely say with 100 percent confidence that I will spend the next sixty years feeling joyful, loved, grateful, and whole. If I was at first riddled with doubt, self-loathing, and a pervasive feeling of loneliness no matter how many people were around, I can say with absolute certainty that I am now filled with self-love, grace, and a pervasive feeling of peace.

If I can do this inner work and experience such a radical healing and transformation of self, my lovely, you can too.

Can you love yourself enough to believe that this kind of healing is possible for you?

Yes, you fucking can.

CHAPTER 1

The vine story

A few years ago I bought a house—on my own. A beautiful 1930's home with Spanish archways, natural sunlight, a huge yard, and enough space for my three girls, two cats, and me to really settle in and make it our own. This house had been in the same family since it was built—we were the first to own it outside that bloodline, and you could immediately feel the energy of a well-loved family home when you first stepped foot inside.

So make it our own we did: We took down cabinets and replaced them with subway tile and open shelving, we added feature walls of yellow and pink roses, gold chrysanthemums, and painted everything white. We ripped out knob and tube wiring and stripped away the old brown tile, replacing it with new wiring, air conditioning, and super Instagrammable flooring. Apartment Therapy, HGTV, Design Mom, and Dwellosophy did home tours when the renovations were finished, and the consensus was the same: a house of BoHo good vibes that looked like the lovechild of Gloria Steinem and *Domino Magazine*.

The inside was easy, the outside . . . not as much.

Along the fence delineating my property from my neighbor's was a vine. A mega vine. A monster vine. A vine growing so rampant that I was warned by another neighbor about its ferocity. Left unattended, it was growing onto the side of the house and lifting siding. It was creeping thirty feet away from its origin, crawling along gutters and staircases, showing no signs of relenting.

Every now and then I would get a surge of homeowner energy and go outside to rip out sections of it or cut some back—with kitchen scissors. It would feel good at the time, and then without fail, after a few days had passed, that vine was back in action, taking over everything in its sight. This pattern went on for two full seasons, the out-of-control and untamed vine against me, my (now dull) kitchen scissors, and a general apathy to actually solving the problem. I just got used to it as it was, even if it was icky and annoying

My kids and I went away for a weekend, a weekend that had the perfect summer storm of a lot of rain followed by even more sunshine. When we came home, this vine had fully taken over the deck. No joke, it had all but swallowed up my vintage picnic table, sliding door, and even the string lights I'd strung across the patio as a faux ceiling.

And I knew something had to be done, for real this time.

I asked the guy I was paying to cut my grass to figure out what we needed to do about this mother of a vine usurping my outdoor living space. He took each tendril of vine and followed it back to its origin. He climbed under the deck into a tight, dark, and uncomfortable space, and traced every single manifestation of the vine back to the root, and at the root, he hacked away at it until it was dead.

Two hours and forty dollars later, the problem was solved. He'd started at one leafy end of the vine and followed it back to its root. He did the uncomfortable task of following it back under staircases and deck boards until he found the point of origin and hacked it out.

It got me thinking that our emotional health and wellness is a lot like that vine: We watch as seemingly unrelated patterns, relationships, and events appear in our lives, leaving us to wonder where the hell that came from. We casually pick away at each one on a very surface level, avoiding the real work—the messy and uncomfortable work—at almost all costs. Maybe we're afraid of the scope of work, maybe we're afraid of what we'll find, maybe we're afraid that our lives are supposed to have these constant frustrations holding us back from enjoying the beauty of our own emotional backyard.

But I can tell you with a great degree of certainty that when we allow ourselves to get real with finding the root of what keeps holding us back in our business, life, and love, we find clarity in what we want, confidence in who we are, and the courage to stay true to both.

Consider learning to confront our emotions and feelings to be the exact same process as learning to confront this vine: when we bandage over what we're feeling, and avoid doing the real work of finding out where this comes from and how to heal it, we can keep swatting it away for temporary relief—we have a drink, buy a dress, sleep with someone we thought was a good fit at the time, have a second helping, step out for a smoke . . . all in the subtle name of not dealing with what is really bothering us and just relieving that pain, temporary measure by temporary measure.

But then it comes back. And it keeps coming back, stronger than before, until we can find the time and strength and tenacity to get under the deck, find the root of what is bothering us, and kill it dead.

This process can feel intimidating or scary, like it will take too long, cost too much, and not be worth the effort. The reality is, however, that *very seldom is anything as intimidating or scary as it seems.* It often takes less time and costs less money than we think, and ultimately, when we look back in hindsight, it would have been worth *any* time and *any* cost to feel the freedom we feel on the other side of what was holding us back.

Take a minute and ask yourself *where your own vine starts. Where does it end? In what ways has it appeared, maybe subtly at first, then overwhelmingly, in your own life? What is the root? Are you ready to deal with this properly, once and for all?*

You are in complete control of taking it upon yourself to deal with it *right now*, solve what's been hurting you for so long, and finally come to peace with it.

And when you do? You get the satisfaction of sitting outside, basking in the fresh air and light, so happy with the monumental simplicity of what you've just achieved.

And that is always, always worth the effort.

Can you love yourself enough to try?

Yes, you fucking can.

CHAPTER 2

A quick lesson in pop psychology

BEHAVIOR CHANGE IS HARD.

If you've ever tried to lose weight, drink more water, exercise, stop the daily take-out coffee, eat more greens, quit over-thinking, quit over-texting . . . you know it's a very hard thing to do.

Changing behavior is hard for our habits, and it's really hard for our thoughts. Because our thoughts and behaviors aren't just our thoughts and behaviors: they're a direct extension of our deep subconscious beliefs. So when we try to change a thought or behavior without looking at the belief it's so strongly connected to, we set ourselves up to fail. Over and over again.

Changing behavior starts with changing our subconscious beliefs. And the rub? Because they're subconscious, we might not even know consciously or rationally what they are. For example, you could think to yourself, "I am ready for love!" Your action/behavior might then look like opening a dating app or letting your friends and family know you're ready to be set up. Really "putting yourself out there."

But if somewhere in your subconscious is an old, outdated belief that you are not lovable, that real love is a joke, that most marriages end in divorce, that all the good ones are taken, that you are destined to be hurt again, that everyone leaves, etc., then your subconscious mind actually *sets you up* to fail—even if your thoughts and behaviors are aligned with what you want.

Your core values and subconscious beliefs must be aligned in order to truly make the change you intend. Why? Because the unconscious mind is designed specifically to protect you. Your subconscious is a gift designed to warn you about danger in your environment. When there is a bear following you down a forest path, or the vibe is sketchy as hell at a bar, or the cab driver gives you the willies, you can thank your subconscious mind for perceiving danger in your environment. It is alerting you with the feeling of fear and enabling you to react with a flight, fight, or freeze response.

See what I mean? A gift. It's like a bodyguard or personal security system built into your brain. It's truly wonderful.

Like anything and everything, there is a paradox here. While this ability to sense, perceive, and *react to* a dangerous environment protects us in so many ways, it also kinda jumps the shark by perceiving things that are not in any way dangerous or threatening as highly dangerous and threatening, thus giving those MAYDAY MAYDAY messages about stuff that poses *literally* no threat to your physical danger.

Your subconscious gives zero fucks about the difference between your physical safety and emotional safety. Therefore, "Holy fucking shit, there is an enormous bear chasing me!" and "Today I need to deliver a presentation that makes me feel vulnerable and like I might be judged by my peers" carries the same weight and gives the same fear response (flight, fight, or freeze) if your subconscious mind is primed to believe that you are not enough / lovable as you are / smart/ worthy/talented/capable/the real deal.

You can spot the design flaw here. You can observe and consciously process that "bear attacks" and "public speaking" are *radically* different from one another, but again, if there is a subconscious belief that something is true, then sweetheart, that is your truth, which is why behavior change is so hard. For a lot of us, our self-talk is incredibly negative. "I'm just not good enough, and I never will be. Someone will always do this better. Be better, thinner, prettier, funnier. I just can't compete; I just don't belong here. They might like me now, but once they get to know me, they'll leave. They always do."

And that negative thought pattern? You guessed it; it's rooted in really dark, painful subconscious beliefs that "I am worthless. Unlovable. Kinda dumb. Incapable. Undeserving. A big fake."

Ouch.

And even ouchier? Another character flaw of the subconscious mind is to keep the status quo, which means once a belief is there (and consequently, the related thoughts and actions are in place), the mind wants it to *stay* there. Once we believe something is true, our brain will do whatever it takes for that to *remain* true. Ergo, whenever something happens to *threaten* that truth, the brain kicks into overdrive (cough, sabotage mode) to preserve the truth it's always known.

It does so lovingly, because again, its job is simply to protect you. And because it values homeostasis and same-ness, it perceives change to be a massive threat and gets all **mama bear** to protect you from that threat. And also? It wants to do so in the easiest way possible, so even when a change seems like it might actually be okay (after say, much self-investment in very good coaching), it still wants to do things the way they've always been done.

So yeah. Behavior change is *hard*.

Where the heck do these beliefs come from?
Is it *ever* possible to change them?
Are we all fucked?

Excellent questions. In short?

Childhood.
Absolutely.
Absolutely *not*.

Imagine the brain as a freshly fallen sheet of snow, the kind you can't wait to get out and play in. When we're in our early years, playing in that "snow" is effortless! We run around, making new pathways to follow without even knowing we're doing it.

And then, around the time we turn seven, it's as if there is a flash freeze and those effortless patterns we made are frozen into place. The next time we "go outside," yes, we *can* make new pathways, but it's really hard; it's really hard to crunch through the ice and create a new trail. So even if we don't particularly like the pathways we've created, we keep following them because it's easy and it's what we've always done before.

This analogy is true for our own patterns of behavior rooted in our own beliefs we adopt before the "flash freeze" of the second phase of childhood. We spend most of our adult lives even following those old patterns and pathways *until we decide not to*. Until we decide to do the work it takes to create new paths for ourselves that lead us to new people and places.

The next question then is *how*. How do we do this?

Well, reading this book is an excellent start. So there's that.

Very simply, what we must do to change our behavior and change our thoughts is to do the work of changing our subconscious beliefs. And there are many strategies outlined in this book, but the Mack Daddy? Prove our subconscious beliefs/truths to be false and replace them with a new truth—one that is tender, loving, and serves our purpose and forward-moving intentions.

Can you love yourself enough to get started?

Yes, you fucking can.

CHAPTER 3

Changing the lens

Remember we talked about how our subconscious mind is basically solely responsible for our perception of truth and reality? Well, the very cool thing is that while this is true, it is also true that we can engage our conscious mind to work in conjunction with our subconscious mind to teach it a new truth.

Let me explain.

What we're talking about here—which is a lot simpler than you might think—is basically gaming our own system. If our subconscious mind believes the world is flat because of a whole bunch of wacky messages from people (well-intentioned or otherwise) in our early childhood, then yes, our belief is that the world is flat. But having the gift of a conscious mind, and a physical body that can explore the boundaries of this truth (thus capitalizing on our natural human drive *to* explore), we can start to look for proof of a new truth. In doing so, looking for a new reality, we can disprove the old and substitute the new.

This, too, is kind of an awesome design.

Practically, you can think of it like this: Imagine your subconscious mind as a lens you are looking through to see the world. You know in your own real life that if you change the prescription of your glasses, or even put on 3D glasses at the movies, that what you see / the way you see it is wildly different when you switch up that lens.

So, for example, if you really want to experience love and partnership but the lens your subconscious currently uses shows you that "love is hard, no one is trustworthy, all marriages are faking happiness, and most end in divorce," then you have to switch that lens to see what you want to be true in order to make it true. You have to consciously look for examples of what you want to be true to disprove that icky, old, negative programming. Tune out stories of people who are unhappy and tune into stories of people who are genuinely in love. Start looking for couples who are very much in love, are affectionate, and are shining examples of loving and healthy relationships.

You can start by looking at examples you don't even know personally. Look at famous couples first, or people you see when you're out and about. Deliberately look for people who express tender love and affection and allow yourself to receive the message that true love exists.

DO THE SAME FOR ANY EXAMPLE SPECIFIC TO YOUR OWN LIFE:

- Think you can't run a successful business? *Look for examples of "regular people" running a successful business.*
- Think that overweight women aren't attractive? *Look for examples of overweight women who are indeed attractive.*
- Think you can't be confident? *Look for examples of people who were incredibly shy but overcame it by adopting their inner confidence.*

Watch TED Talks, go to conferences and workshops, watch biographical documentaries, and read the same style of books (oh, hey, look at *you* getting a head start on this one!). Teach yourself to appreciate that we are all just people living our lives in the way that feels good to us—in the way we *choose* for it to feel good for us.

This advice is one of *the* most valuable mindset hacks I can give you and for you to adopt in empowering your own perspective and reality. Right now.

There are actual *millions* of examples and inspiring stories of people who've done what you want to do, who have what you want to have, and who are being who you want to be who got there simply by *deciding* to. Pay attention to those real-life examples of the kind of success you dream of, then reverse engineer it and let it lead you to where you already know you want to be.

For now, think of everything we experience in a given moment. Through our sense and our energy fields, we consume literally millions of pieces of information every single second. If we were physically able to process each and every piece of information we have access to and are exposed to, our heads would probably explode.

Cue the subconscious mind and its amazing ability to filter out that information based on the lens it's wearing at the time. And now that you understand that the mind wants to keep you safe, and also keep everything the same as it's ever been, you can understand that the lens will only take in messages that confirm what you know to be true, to be true. And further, you can understand that if you want what is true to not be true anymore, you can hack your mind to deliberately look for new messaging that you want to be true until it becomes true.

It's easier than it sounds. Pinky swear.

You've probably already experienced this without even knowing it. You know when a new restaurant opens and you make a mental note to go there? And then it seems like everywhere you go people are talking about this place? You pick up the paper and there's a review; you walk down the street and overhear a conversation about the same restaurant. Over and over again, there it is.

Or maybe you've decided you might be ready to get a dog, say a nice apricot mini Goldendoodle. You start researching the breed, and where to get it, and gradually you notice the exact same dog you've been dreaming of around you every time you leave the house.

It feels almost disorienting, like "is the universe reading my mind?" Kind of.

What's really happening is that you've polished that subconscious lens and have primed it to see certain things. And when you've primed it to see certain things, you start seeing *more* of those things. It's beautiful. And it's even more beautiful when you realize you can channel that process into becoming your own and deliberately curate what you see to align with what you believe. Before you know it, you'll find yourself inundated with more and expanding examples of what you *want* to be true, to be true.

That's hella powerful. It just takes a little bit of work.

Sometimes, depending on what the "programming" of your early years was like, this requires more work. If you've experienced severe trauma (like an untimely death, emotional/physical/sexual abuse, or repeated exposure to highly negative images or events), you will more than likely need the help of a therapist (trained in EMDR therapy) to start clearing out those beliefs in a safe way so that you can do this daily life work. Sometimes it isn't the trauma we experience, it's the inability to talk about it in a safe place that leads to further complications.

Depending on what your experiences have been so far, you may be able to work with an NLP-trained coach to help identify what the old subconscious beliefs are, release them, and move forward with an *awareness* of what your baseline triggers and vulnerabilities are. You can then process new information in a safe, healthy, and forward-moving way.

Know that this concept of looking through a new lens is fundamental in how we literally and metaphorically see our world, and that yes, we absolutely have the ability (and the ability to learn the skills) to change it when we want to.

How great is that?

Can you love yourself enough to see things differently?

Yes, you fucking can.

CHAPTER 4

Are You My Mother?

Remember that book by P.D. Eastman from when you were growing up called *Are You My Mother?* It's about a little bird that is separated from the nest and wanders around asking the dog, the cat, the cow—hell, even the *bulldozer*—"Are you my mother?" Searching, searching for the love of his mother.

We are each like that little bird because we each have a deep need for human affection, and our attachment bonds are formed in our earliest years. When we're lucky, we establish secure, loving attachments with our parents. A lot of us—and I mean a *lot*—don't get that attachment and affection and spend many years learning a lot of lessons while we seek out to create that connection we didn't necessarily get as teeny tiny humans.

I personally did not. My mother left our "nest" early on, and while she flew back and forth for a little while, she ultimately was not present in my childhood, period. Worse, when a new bird flew into the nest my dad and I had built—which was cozy, loving, supportive, and strong— she took over the rule of our roost and made it pretty uncomfortable . . . to put it lightly.

I spent a good deal of my life feeling just like that little bird, and I know intimately what it feels like to search for someone to make you feel whole and grounded and accepted. When we don't get love and affection or the unconditional acceptance and sense of belonging we need, we often jump through all kinds of twisted hoops to find it. We will go to all the wrong people and all the wrong places if it seems even remotely possible that we might find even the crumbs of what we are looking for.

Some of us are born into families who love and appreciate us unconditionally, but many of us are not. We are seen as extensions of our parents, or maybe even inconveniences, and often we are the vehicles for our parents to live vicariously through us. Sometimes we are born into truly loving families but experience the loss of one or both parents at a tragically young age.

The impact of our parents/guardians is formative—huge. And our need for secure attachment and unconditional love is so powerful that we do anything and everything we can to make our parents—even in our minds—the people we need them to be.

In an effort to reconcile that lack of attachment and create a sense of belonging, we look for friends, their parents, boyfriends, girlfriends, teachers, aunts, uncles, thought leaders (whomever) to be surrogate mothers, thus seeking out comfort in the world around us.

Can you love yourself enough to give yourself that kind of unconditional love and acceptance, tenderness and affection?

Yes, you fucking can.

CHAPTER 5

Children of children

HARD TRUTH: SOMETIMES WE DON'T GET THE PARENTS WE WANT.

So we look and look for someone to provide what we need for us. Eventually, over time, if the desire is strong enough, we ultimately learn instead to *be* the parent we need.

Right here, right now though, it's essential to understand the fallacy that our parents know what they're doing. Because (spoiler alert) they don't. If you are a parent, you can attest to this claim: we're figuring it out every day, learning new things about our kids and about ourselves, piecing it together as we go and doing the best we can with what we have at the time.

There is a startling realization that each of us has at some point in adulthood of "oh my gosh, I need to tell a grown-up about this and get help." You then look around and realize that—oh shit—*you* are the grown-up.

I have a theory that we never really grow up but rather stay some child version of ourselves, faking it through adulthood in an unedited, extended, director's cut game of house.

Sure, they give us mortgages and driver's licenses and let us book our own vacations and eat ten Oreos before dinner and expect us to work at jobs with tremendous amounts of responsibility, but at our core, we are still kids just playing house as this adult version of ourselves.

Our own parents are no exception to this rule.

While we may look (or have looked) up to them as the experts, the reality is that they, too, were and are just figuring it out. Yes, they've learned their own encyclopedic collection of wisdom and life experiences, but that's exactly what it is: *learned.*

Knowing what you now know about how the subconscious mind works, you can start to see another design flaw here: we're being raised not by experts in life or children or parenting, we're being raised by regular people, who were raised by regular people, who were raised by regular people . . . all figuring it out as they went.

What's more? Just a generation or two ago, *all these people* were raised during a war or were raised as a by-product of war. Think of the messaging that goes along with it: The world is a scary, scary place. Resources are scarce. Working hard and keeping your head down is the only way to survive. Trust is a commodity that can be bartered at any time. You should be grateful for what you have, even if what you have is what you don't like, because hey, you're alive. You. Are always. In danger.

Our generation, our cultural context in this moment, in this specific geography and demographic, is experiencing the luxury of existential crisis of consciousness. We are experiencing peak anxiety and a pervasive leveling up of the collective conscious, *because we can.* For many of us, we have been blessed without knowing the horrors that our parents/grandparents/great-grandparents experienced through world wars and a global economic depression.[1]

We are lucky as hell.

And it is our responsibility to have compassion for the ones who raised us, and yes, even for the ones who hurt us, because they didn't know any better / didn't have their own healthy tools and coping mechanisms to do better. I understand intimately that this responsibility can be a bitter pill to swallow, especially for those of us who were *really* hurt—and I mean really hurt—by the ones who were supposed to protect and love us.

A huge focus and purpose of this book is the underlying concept that the job of forgiveness is ours—even if the one who hurt us hasn't apologized or isn't even sorry. Ugh, I know. But forgiveness is the only way to truly move forward and have this next-level sense of compassion for how hurt he or she must have been to hurt us the way he or she did.

It is that simple, and it is that complicated: hurt people, hurt people. And while it may be a part of our experience to experience that, it is also our choice to process it in a healthy way (using Emotional Alchemy) and ultimately let it go. I'll break this process down step by step in Part 3.

---

1 The manuscript for this book went to my publisher one week—ONE week—before the WHO declared COVID-19 a global pandemic. At the time of editing, we are in the middle of what is proving to be a defining moment of our generation, and we do not yet know what impact the lasting ripple effects will have.

We are all children of children.

There is no expert. There is no guidebook. There is only a biological need to procreate, followed by a relentless and never-ending learning curve of figuring it out.

Take a big breath and understand that even if this is where you've come from, it doesn't have to be where you're going or where you'll end up. You are already taking the big, brave step of being here, reading this, and turning all your learning and all your pain and experiences into healthy, informed, inspired action to move forward in the way that feels good to you, and to treat every single person you come into contact with in the way you wish to be treated and in the way you treat yourself.

Can you love yourself enough to treat yourself with loving kindness, respect, and adoration?
Can you love yourself enough to be the parent you really wanted?

Yes, you fucking can.

CHAPTER 6

Crumbs

How many of us identify or have identified ourselves as people-pleasers? Sometimes (cough, much of the time) we learn quickly to meet other people's needs at the expense of our own, to develop what feels—at the time—like a secure attachment by proving our love to someone else. If we are searching for that unconditional love and acceptance from people or places external to us, we develop a "foolproof" formula to find it:

1. Work your ass off to be perfect
2. Prove to the one you're trying to win over that you're worthy of their affection
3. Change yourself as necessary to better meet their needs and expectations of you
4. Suppress and repress any part of you that doesn't sit well with the person from whom you're trying to earn love
5. Repeat

This formula creates the framework by which we measure every other relationship in our lives—does it feel like I am walking on eggshells with the looming fear that I may disappoint them at any moment? Perfect! It feels like it's always felt! Does it feel like I am grateful that they are even talking to me and that anything that goes wrong must be entirely my fault? Excellent! This dynamic is exactly what I'm used to.

This is how people-pleasers are born: learning to suppress our needs and meeting the needs of others by keeping the peace and doing what it takes to ensure stasis.

When love is scarce, when acceptance is conditional, when all the attention and affection that we are programmed at a biological level to seek out in order to preserve our species is withheld, we will do whatever it takes to get what we need.

We have to.

In the absence of having our needs readily met, our brain can't fully process the pain of not being loved, and so we figure out way after way after way of getting what we need, often at our own expense. Don't believe me? Take a minute and revisit the Psych 101 example of baby monkeys removed from the care of their mothers and placed instead with a sock tied onto a mesh cage. In the absence of a mother's love and affection, the baby monkeys will cuddle up to the SOCK in the same way they'd cuddle up to their mama. Look it up.

Now let's take a look at gang culture. In the absence of strong male role models, many kids find comfort and protection from obviously violent and illegal nefarious gangs. Our need to belong and feel love is so powerful that we can override compassion, forget empathy, and find acceptance while kicking the living hell out of someone else because we were told to by our gang leader—who "loves" us.

I am sure you can come up with more examples. Codependent

friendships come to mind right off the bat. Maybe even in your own romantic or employment history. And again, not to beat a dead horse here, but what our subconscious mind believes to be true is true and will repeatedly do whatever it takes to make it remain true. So if the message is "I find love by putting myself in abusive situations, so I will continue to put myself in abusive situations. Therefore, I will be loved." If the message is "I find acceptance by doing things that feel uncomfortable or wrong, so I will continue to do the things that feel uncomfortable or wrong because that's how I find acceptance."

Love and acceptance become associated with abuse. With toxicity. With discomfort. With that heavy, icky feeling of knowing it's not really right, but hey, it's the only dynamic I've ever known and therefore it must be right . . . *right?* It is such a deeply flawed part of our design, even though it comes with the best of intentions. And we keep repeating/reliving/attracting/being drawn to that dynamic over and over again because it's what we've always known.

It's like you learn to live off the crumbs of "love" someone is showing you by begging at the table and waiting until they throw it our way. But you also know that you can never feel full by simply eating crumbs.

And so you continue to go back and repeat the behavior with the hopes that maybe there will be enough this time. It's a shocking dynamic to observe when you're no longer in it, and one that most people can intimately identify with.

Consider this: Imagine there is a coffee shop with a pizzeria by its side. You walk into the pizzeria and order a latte. They tell you, "Sorry, sis, this here's a pizza joint. You'll have to go next door to get your coffee." And so? You go next door to get your coffee. Likewise, if you walk into the coffee shop expecting pizza, you'll be politely told that to get what you're looking for you'll have to go next door.

HERE'S WHAT DOESN'T HAPPEN:

> You don't demand pizza from the coffee shop.
> You don't demand coffee from the pizzeria.
> You don't expect one to be what they're not.
> Neither the pizzeria nor the coffee shop compromises what makes them special and unique to give you something that they don't make.

> And still somehow in our own lives we go to the ends of the earth to serve coffee from our proverbial pizzeria and start slingin' pies from our tiny coffee shop, all with the intention to be loved. "Well, I've never made a latte before, and I don't have any of the ingredients on hand, but you know what? We have a customer. A customer! Not the customer we want or need, but hey, it's a customer nonetheless. Maybe I can convince this customer that I am exactly what he's looking for. Watch now as I abandon every part of my business I know to be true in order to meet the needs of this one person instead of staying true to my own values and mission statement."

It doesn't happen. Usually.

(Keep reading to find out what happens when it does . . .)

Can you love yourself enough to find yourself in these pages?

Yes, you fucking can.

CHAPTER 7

Let them eat tacos

I love tacos. LOVE them.

They are simple and comforting, great for snacks and for parties, the great unifier of bringing family and friends together. Bonus? You can eat them with your hands.

In every city I've been to I inevitably find or source legit tacos, which means I can tell you a great taco place in each of the great American cities, any neighborhood in Toronto, a few joints across both the Atlantic and Pacific shores of Mexico, and anywhere up the coast of California between L.A. and Seattle. They are, in short, a perfect food and a quirky but genuine expression of my identity and who I am.

I really love food in general. It brings people together, is a beautiful expression of love and care, and brings so much joy in the preparation and consumption of it around the family table with music, children, friends, and cocktails. The only food (two foods really) that I don't like—abhor, actually—are lamb and salmon. I've tried them many times, and there's something about each of them that just gets me the wrong way, like they hit me in the wrong part of my mouth and tongue and make me wince just thinking about eating them.

You know what I served for dinner at my first wedding? *Lamb and salmon.*

And you know why? *Because I thought other people would like it.*

Cringe.

I thought other people would respect and value and thank and love me for serving lamb and salmon at my first wedding. The caterers did them both beautifully—a gorgeously dressed and roasted leg of lamb and a spectacular whole poached salmon with cucumber scales, artfully arranged, served alongside a mango salsa.

And I didn't have one bite of either dish.

Why? Because I think that lamb and salmon are really, really gross, frankly, and find both to be entirely unappealing and inedible. And do you know who I told about my disdain for both dishes?

No one.

I kept it to myself, served both on my plate and then did that trick from when I was a kid where you kind of mash it up a bit with your fork and spread it around the plate to trick your parents into thinking you've given it a solid try. But I didn't eat any of it.

At.

My.

Wedding.

Think about that: the perfect dinner, the perfect food, the one thing I deliberately have traveled out of my way for and have ordered in different languages, the staple I have shared countless first dates with, share every Tuesday like religion with my children, the thing I have posters and keychains and pennant flags dedicated to around my house, the series of memes other people send to me and tag me in—the thing I love and that brings me joy that would have been a beautiful, fun, engaging, and above all an authentic expression of me—I hid out of sight on what was at that point in my life the most epic dinner party I'd ever thrown in favor of what I thought someone else would find valuable and love and appreciate me for.

And you know what?

It didn't work. Actually, it was kind of a disaster.

People complained, vegetarians were upset, Dani got really, *really* drunk by 4:30 p.m. and made it known that she thought I had used politically incorrect meat as a statement on her presence at my wedding, and some people were downright scared and too grossed out to try either.

So instead, they ate all the salads.

And then we ran out of salad. The caterers had to go back to the restaurant to make and get more salads to feed all the hangry guests who hadn't eaten yet. It was like a scene out of a Woody Allen movie.

Lamb and salmon didn't please people, didn't make people love me or value me or appreciate me or thank me—lamb and salmon, in all their inauthenticity running perpendicular to my natural self, made people upset.

And instead of feeling seen, valued, appreciated, and full, I felt like I was walking on eggshells once again.

Also, I felt super hungry.

This one example perfectly describes an entire thirty years of how and why I made decisions: I took whatever I wanted and thought was best, wrapped it in a little bow, and pushed it aside to make space for what I thought other people would like, and particularly what other people would like from me.

Nobody (outright) asked me to do it, it was a decision I made over and over and over again based on patterning I created from what I thought other people wanted from and expected of me that had given me the illusion of safety in my childhood.

My point is that sometimes you just need to let them eat tacos.

In fact, if you are lucky enough to know that tacos are what make you happy and nourished and playful and joy-filled—eat them! Share them! Share your love of tacos with the world, because whatever that taco equivalent is for you, it IS you. And whatever IS you deserves to be celebrated, appreciated, and valued and thanked and loved and honored for being as perfect as it is—just the way you are.

Can you love yourself enough to just be you?

Yes, you fucking can.

CHAPTER 8

Imposter syndrome (part one)

If you can relate to that feeling of needing to feel loved and accepted by someone external to you and doing whatever it takes to get that love and acceptance, you probably also know firsthand that you spend most of your life feeling like a fake.

In our highly Instagrammed, falsely positive, not-many-people-really-know-what-they're-talking-about world, we get a lot of messaging around imposter syndrome as being rooted in lack of confidence. That the feeling like a big phony comes from not knowing or appreciating our true value and worth or what unique skills we bring to the table.

And sometimes, this is exactly true. Most of the time, though?

We feel like a big fake because we've been faking it for the past thirty years of our lives.

Sorry, not sorry. This is another hard truth.

For many people who have learned—with good and innocent intentions—that the only way they will find love and acceptance is to not be who they really are, they spend most of their lives learning how to put on the mask, then put on another mask when the first mask isn't working so well anymore.

When you keep putting on layers and layers of security masks, yes, babe, you're going to feel some dissonance. Because no matter how adept you become at learning how to please other people, how to put on that mask and put on the show in order to seek outside acceptance, love, approval, and validation, there will always be your soul calling out to you that this is not who you are.

There comes a certain point in your life (usually early to mid-thirties) when that voice starts calling. Some of us learn to listen to what it has to say and start the process of removing the masks we've worked so hard to put on, and some of us keep tuning it out. We tune it out by reaching for more success, more booze, more online shopping, more empty sex, more drugs, more food, more false control, more more more of everything that is wrong for us and contributes massively to the person we are not.

But that voice doesn't quit; it gets louder, and harder to tune out, and our drug of choice becomes less effective. And we really start to feel the icky, awful feeling of being trapped in a life that isn't ours.

If we grow up feeling punished or excluded or unloved for being ourselves, we learn quickly to become someone else, and at a certain point, after faking it for so long, wearing masks and meeting other people's needs in lieu of our own, something starts to crack. Feelings of emotional exhaustion, anxiety, anger, reaching for substances, imposter syndrome . . . it all happens here.

Removing these masks and learning to come home to ourselves is big work. And you're doing it, right here and right now, just by reading this book. High five yourself because that is awesome. When you do this big, brave work of removing the masks and coming home to yourself, it's amazing. You start to feel like *you*. You feel more balanced, less anxious. More at ease, less unsure. More peaceful, less dramatic. More grounded, less roller coaster-y.

More loved, less judged.

Our feelings are just feedback; they provide incredibly valuable insights on what it is we're feeling and what has yet to be healed, and they invite us in to heal that. So if "faking it" is one of those icky feelings you're having, take it as a sign to investigate it. Part 2 of this book will help a lot. If you feel like you're faking it, and like you don't belong, and that nobody sees the real you, or that if they *do* see the real you they'll reject you, then it's time to take great note of that.

We place so much importance on how we will be accepted by those around us and, as I've alluded to earlier, it's in our DNA to do so. We are essentially animals, and pack animals at that. We know, deep in the genetic fiber that makes us human, that our survival is dependent on being accepted as part of the group. It is less true in the world we live in, and even less true when we are grown-ups, but still, it's an evolutionary trait built into us that we must find acceptance in order to live.

That subconscious security system is alive and well.

But what we ultimately have to get comfortable with is that while we understand our programming, the only person we really need to please, the only person we truly need to love and accept and validate and belong to, the only opinion that really matters about how we choose to live our lives and must listen to is that of the person looking back at you from the mirror.

And this is where the real work begins.

Ready?

Can you love yourself enough to say yes?

Yes, you fucking can.

Part 2

Making peace with where you are

"We have two lives, and the second begins when we realize we only have one."

~Confucius

PERSONALLY SPEAKING

When I think about divorce, I have a visual of two people sitting on the couch in their living room, when suddenly they notice a crack in the ceiling that wasn't there before. "That's weird," they say. So they get out the putty and plaster and paint to fix it up, then carry on with their lives.

A few weeks later, they notice a new crack, in a new room, and do the same thing: slap a quick and easy fix over it.

They carry on like this for a few months, maybe even years, plastering over every new crack that pops up, until they notice that in addition to the errant cracks, there's a cluster of little leaks and drips happening all over the house. There are ants coming in through the windowsill, there's a wasp nest under the basement stairs, and the hot water tank is puking water out into the basement with unprecedented force.

The couple looks at each other, frantically tries to keep up with every little accident happening by slapping quick Band-Aid fixes on each and every one, until it hits them:

There's a crack in the foundation.

That is the real source of the problem needing to be addressed if they want to keep living in this house; they either repair the cracked foundation . . . or they jump ship, sell the thing, and move on.

THAT is what the very beginning of divorce feels like: going through the emotional bargaining of what it looks like if you stay, and what it looks like if you go.

Do we have what it takes—and is it worth it—to work on and invest in our foundation, or do we cut our losses and start again?

For me, when it got to this point, it became crystal clear that we did not have what it took; in spite of what it may have looked like to the outside world looking in, we simply were not a good or compatible fit. That realization was crushing because it conflicted so *diametrically* with my own vision and values.

I believe in the institution of marriage, and when I got married, I intended to stay married. What I didn't realize at twenty-eight (that I realize all too well now) is that people grow and evolve over time. If you're lucky, you find a partner with whom you can grow and evolve at the same rate, or at least at a rate that supports the growth and evolution of one another.

Most of us, I would argue, don't find that partner in our twenties because we are not yet fully formed adults. We're still kids. Still figuring things out. And if, on top of that adolescence, you're still healing from past trauma (or in complete denial that there is even a *need* to heal from past trauma), you can't be in a long-term marriage with any success because it's more than likely that you are not yet *whole on your own*. And if you're not yet whole on your own, it's going to prove to be quite challenging to feel whole and loved as part of a couple—particularly if what you're lacking is the ability to even *feel* whole and loved on your own.

Divorce was harder than cancer.

Oh yeah, you read that right: not only did I have cancer—and chemo, total hair loss, and a couple of body-transforming surgeries (see Part 3)—but I lived to tell the tale as a single, self-employed woman with three kids.

And I assure you, *divorce was harder than cancer.*

Divorce was the end of life as I knew it and the beginning of life as I know it.

It was single-handedly the hardest and most emotionally grueling experience of my life, while also being a catalyst for *every single amazing, positive, healthy change* I made in my state of mind, my life, and the way I relate to myself and to other people. It also allowed the space and time I needed to process and heal the toxic patterning I had learned so early on.

It felt like—in having the courage to be honest about my feelings—I had detonated a bomb that caused *concentric rings of loss* in the life I had built and the family I had loved so dearly.

And still, divorce is what allowed me to rise like a phoenix and start over.

If you want to be a phoenix rising, sometimes you have to set yourself on fire. And for me, that fire was the traumatic event called "divorce." After realizing that no amount of therapy, vacations, *alcohol*, parties, couples' massages, or date nights could fix a broken foundation, I knew that I had to call time of death on the relationship. And it almost killed me to do so.

In staying true to myself, my values, and my beliefs that I was worthy of feeling good for being myself, having great sex, feeling loved without condition, experiencing mutual respect and adoration, laughing, and feeling seen and at ease with my partner, I had to do the thing that scared me most: walk away from my marriage.

And in doing so, I lost *so much*—the network of "friends" I had worked so hard to create, an extended family I married into that felt like home, the stability of being an at-home mom with kids and having someone else manage all the finances—literally *everything* in my life changed with the end of my marriage. I'm not exaggerating when I say I had to completely rebuild my life from the inside out.

Because of my background and early childhood trauma, I also had to contend with messages like: *These are the worst thing you can do to your kids. These are your hormones talking. You're giving up. You're only doing this because you think it's normal for people to leave. You're premenopausal. You will live to regret this; you're making a huge mistake. You'll never have what it takes to be financially comfortable; you will be poor for the rest of your life. You can't handle this. The least you can do is get a job at Tim Horton's. You're going to ruin your kids' lives.*

Each of the above statements were real conversations/emails/texts I received in the early days from some people I thought were closest to me at the time after announcing that I was exiting a fourteen-year relationship. And while every word felt like a knife going directly into my heart, I knew I was doing the right thing—and now had the added fuel to prove those people wrong.

As much negative feedback as I experienced,[2] I also had unwavering support from my extended family, one of my aunts in particular. Through every single wound and setback, terrible email, emotionally abusive text, heartbreaking conversation, and shocking realization, she was there as a rock, supporting me to do what felt like the right thing to do in my own heart, and always, always telling me it would get easier and that it wouldn't be this hard forever.

Even when it didn't feel like it, I hung on to those words and cultivated the hope that she was right, which was a good chunk of what allowed me to move forward and carry on with my own healing because that was a huge part of the foundational crack: *I was so wounded from my own past, I was not able to show up fully as myself in my marriage.*

That is painful to admit, but it's true. I couldn't love or be loved in the way I wanted to, by a person who was capable of doing so, partially because I wasn't yet able to love or be loved as myself. Instead, I chose to compromise my own wants, needs, and values in the never-ending quest to feel loved, juxtaposed against having found a relationship that felt like it had saved me.

---

2 For example, one friend began dating my ex-husband just months after we split (and other friends covered it up) until I found out during a car ride home after a concert we'd been to together. I spent the rest of the ride home coaching her through her guilt. No, we're not friends anymore.

Now, do not misread this: While divorce and the losses it incurred were devastating, and the grief has taken several *years* to process, I harbor no feelings of anger or resentment. Not only did that relationship bring our three *superlative* daughters into the world (and without question the *gift* of the world's *best* and most supportive, engaged, loving and lovable grandparents), it also had its fair share of really happy memories, adventures, and truly formative experiences in the woman I've become and the experiences I've had. Time is a great healer, and I am grateful to have experienced the healing effect time has had on so many of the relationships that were damaged in the process of divorce. I am hopeful that time continues to heal those wounds, many of which I know I played a part in causing.

As I was saying, I take responsibility for my role in the breakdown of the marriage. I remember one day going through a notebook I'd kept of all the "things we tried" to make our marriage work and being hit in the head with a profound realization: "I know what we need to do to save this marriage! All he has to do is radically change his personality, or I have to radically change mine!"

After a lifetime of *trying* to change my personality, I knew this belief was exactly what had been holding me back and was again hit on the head with the realization of what I needed to do next.

Oh shit.

I always laugh when I hear people recount the stories of other people's marriages "falling apart."

Honey.

It's not like one day someone wakes up and finally realizes how much seeing their partner's dirty socks on the floor drives them nuts, which then starts a cascade effect of other things that drive them nuts too. Marriages do not "fall" apart; they burn quietly, slowly, and hotly until the entire fucking building is on fire and everyone is screaming to get out while they still can.

I never intended to get divorced and frankly didn't believe it was even an option. I was the one walking around (before I got married) saying flippantly arrogant things like: "If I thought I was going to get divorced, I wouldn't be getting married in the first place." So while it came as a shock to almost everyone in my life at the time, it may have shocked *me* most of all.

After you hear that little inner voice start speaking to you, and you try tuning it out only to find it getting older and louder, you reach a breaking point when you know something has to change. That "change" for me meant ending the relationship and starting over. I remember in the weeks leading up to the official point of departure, our gas fireplace gave out. We were having it replaced, and I stood in the kitchen with a friend and said, "We always knew the flame would burn out and need to be replaced, we just didn't think it would happen so soon."

I don't really know if I had been talking about the fireplace or the marriage. Those little signs and winks and nudges were prevalent and became too much to ignore. I knew what I had to do, which meant calling a spade a spade that this marriage was done, and it meant starting over.

It was starting over and rebuilding my life from scratch that taught me to get clear on my past to see what I had learned, then go through the process of unlearning that past and rewiring my brain to believe what I wanted to believe, not what I had been told. It introduced me to

Neuro-Linguistic Programming, which is now central to my coaching practice and understanding of the human experience, and it allowed me to step into my own and genuine identity as a strong, confident, independent young woman who knows how to handle her shit and inspire others to do the same. It made me a healthy and present role model for my daughters, and it has allowed me to cultivate my grace and use it to show up with purpose, joy, and intention. It made space to create a deep and sacred relationship with the divinely unknown, and it allowed me to tap into an inner knowing I had been taught to ignore for so long.

All of this faith, mindset work, and reestablishing a sense of inner peace and security *because* I became so clear on my identity is also what allowed me to navigate breast cancer and its treatment as well as I did; this is an invaluable skill set I continue to use daily and believe emphatically I would not have learned had it not been for the excruciating pain of calling time of death on my marriage.

For me, this life-changing shift was mitigated by divorce, which is why I'm sharing that here. For you, it might also be that change in relationship that kick-starts the cascading events of inner change and growth. Or maybe it's another loss, like the death of a family member or a critical or chronic illness or other physical change beyond your control. Maybe it's being laid off, let go, or otherwise finding yourself at the crossroads of making a dramatic career change. Perhaps it's finding out that things weren't the way you thought they were in your childhood, and that discovery is so life altering it finds you altering your life as you know it now.

One thing remains the same: It doesn't matter what that mitigating event is. What matters is how you respond to it and how you use it to further shape your future rather than allowing it to define your past.

This is a huge difference: accepting the fact that while you cannot control most of the events that happen in your life, good or bad, you can always control your own reaction to them.

Ain't nobody coming to save you. The only person responsible for your peace, your happiness, your joy, your success, and your *life* is *you*, lovely.

Knowing that mic-dropper of a truth is an *empowering* truth because it enables you to be the person you want to be, regardless of circumstance, without waiting for someone to come and do it for you.

This is the juicy stuff, and it starts with how to get clarity in what you want.

Can you love yourself enough to find clarity in what you want?

Yes, you fucking can.

CHAPTER 9

Our emotional body, health, and wellness

I mentioned before that our feelings are simply feedback, and I will say it again. I will say it over and over to just about anyone who will listen, and again even if they won't. This is how passionately I feel about letting this truth be known: our feelings are simply feedback, and all this feedback offers valuable insights as to what still needs our attention and healing.

It is very rare that we receive education about our emotional well-being. Growing up, girls are (mostly) taught to be nice, play fair, share, dial back their emotions, say sorry even if they don't mean it, interpret unkindness from boys as a sign of interest, finish up their turn early if someone else wants what they have, not to brag, tone it down, sit down and be quiet. And boys, mostly, are taught to tough it out, it's okay to be wild and crazy—they are how they are, after all, suck it up, be a dude / little man, get dirty, be assertive, don't cry, get messy, run around.

This culture is shifting—slowly—but that is the pervasive and gendered messaging kids get. If not from parents, teachers, and coaches, then from the *abysmally* inappropriate content that is being produced "for" and marketed to kids.

Even the most well-intentioned of us inadvertently teach our kids to gloss over their feelings: "Don't cry, it's okay; I know you fell, but you're okay; Say sorry; Let them play with you; Share your things . . ." Even in trying to teach normal social rules of togetherness and getting along, we tend to lose the nuance of *validating the feelings* of little ones.

And it was even more exacerbated when our generation was growing up.

So there's no wonder (unless we had highly communicative, self-aware, ego-free adults in our lives growing up—see note on this being incredibly rare), that we received little to *no* education for our emotional body or its health and well-being. There's been a (welcome) shift in the past few years to open the conversation about mental health. Where people used to keep feelings of despair, anxiety, depression, disordered eating, body dysmorphia, etc. to themselves, we are now having more conversations that "normalize" that experience.

And even still, we have lumped these conditions under "mental health" without paying any real attention to "emotional health," and they are *very* different beings.

What about the many people who've been told for a lifetime that they are "too sensitive?" Or the ones who are told that they are "closed off" or "emotionally unavailable?" While the conversation about mental health is a good one and gets help to people in need (while stripping away perceived stigma and shame about legit illness of the mind and chemicals therein), it's only a fraction of the conversation.

We are never truly taught how to feel.

Nor are we taught what to do with those feelings when we have them; instead, we are often taught to ignore how we feel. If you are someone who identifies as "too sensitive" or even highly sensitive, it's a good sign that you've just never learned how to listen to your feelings, how to get your needs met, or even asked for what you want. Instead, you feel almost constantly overwhelmed with emotion.

Likewise, if you're someone who has never felt comfortable expressing emotion or talking about how you feel, it's a pretty good sign that you, too, have never truly been able to listen to your feelings, how to get your needs met, or even asked for what you want, and instead, you have learned to repress them for the sake of the "greater good" or to not draw attention to yourself.

This is where it gets really interesting.

Sometimes, when we are detached from how we truly feel and end up either overcompensating with regular floods of emotion or under compensating with invisible walls built so high around our hearts no one can possibly climb them, we lose sight of what it is we're actually feeling and it presents as something else.

You know how when you see the color green you process the fact that it is the color green? You seldom—if ever—stop to think, "Hey, there's the color green, which is made up of both yellow and blue." This fact is absolutely true, but it is rare for us to stop and break down what is already synthesized into the parts of its sum. We just experience it the way it seems and the way it has always seemed.

Feelings are like that too.

Sometimes we experience a feeling like sadness, and we take that for what it is: sadness. So then we try and treat "sadness." We do things that bring us joy, we try to laugh more, or we spend time with family or friends, but weirdly, we can't shake that pervasive feeling of sadness. Maybe it's not there *all* the time, but it's there enough of the time to make us think we're just going to feel sad for the rest of our lives. It's just the way it is.

Just like our ability to experience color, though, sometimes our feelings are the sum of more parts—*we are simply unaware of how to process what is really going on.*

Often, sadness is the combination of anger and rejection, but it manifests in our experience as sadness. So when we continually treat sadness, we're not actually addressing our true feelings of anger and rejection, and so we just keep feeling sad—and now frustrated, maybe a little scared that there is something wrong with us, or like we'll never know happiness on account of all this sadness.

We need to learn how to identify our feelings, individually, and give ourselves permission to feel them. Frankly, we need to feel them in order to heal them, but more often than not, we are rushed through any feeling of discomfort and ickiness—just like we've always been taught to do—and we ignore what it is we're truly feeling inside.

Our overly "memed" world of GOOD VIBES ONLY, LIVE HIGH-VIBE, NO BAD DAYS does not help, even if it's supposed to. If we want to truly feel good inside, we need to get very comfortable with identifying, feeling, and addressing what it is we're feeling at a given moment.

Healing is not linear; there is a widely accepted theory that our one Self is composed of several selves within it. So when we experience a trauma, regardless of what that trauma is (and while pain is relative, it is always our own pain to bear), it's fair to assume that more than one of our selves is affected by this trauma in its own unique way.

So let's say you go to therapy and heal a traumatic event from your past. Then later, maybe even years later, as you're parked at a red light or shopping in the cereal aisle at Walmart (true story), you get hit with a wave of sadness. "WTF?!" you think. "Didn't I already heal this shit?"

Yes, you did . . . and no, you didn't.

Once you heal one part of your Self, it's as if you've created a safe and stable environment to invite the other parts of your Self to heal too. So when you feel that wave of emotion, you now know that (because our feelings are simply feedback) it is giving you both insight and opportunity to go deeper with your healing and turn that love and attention to the next part of your Self that needs it.

Can you love yourself enough to listen to the parts of you that are calling out for that love and attention?

Yes, you fucking can.

CHAPTER 10

Inside wants out

We are born with an incredible affinity for language and communication, and if you ever find yourself bored one day, look up videos of babies in labs reacting to facial expressions across cultures. Our ability to perceive and learn language and communication is fundamental to our survival as tiny ones, and because this ability is so embedded into our very genetic fabric, it's probably worth paying attention to.

Because we are social pack animals, way down deep in our biology and DNA, we have an inherent drive to communicate. You likely already know this feeling well if you've ever traveled or been in the company of someone who doesn't speak the same language as you. You will smile and use gestures to act out what you want to say, all in an attempt to communicate.

Our natural state is to communicate—even if we don't learn how to do so properly or in a healthy way.

Inside wants out, and we *want* to be able to express ourselves. We *want* to be able to understand what others around us are saying. *This* is how we communicate, bond, develop empathy, find compassion, and both offer and seek out support in times of need.

It comes very naturally to us, and sometimes, even when we don't learn these skills early on, we can teach them to ourselves at a later time—we just need to teach our subconscious mind that it's okay for us to do so and that we're safe to share what's on our hearts.

When I was three and my mom left for good, my dad hired a full-time live-in nanny. I was very young, and he was a new doctor with a lot of responsibility and not a lot of time.

He hired this delicious, squishy, biscuits-and-gravy-fed older woman from a little country town nearby, and as I told you earlier, we called her Grandma Helen. There was nothing not to like about her: She was present, engaged, doughy, and constantly used expressions like "Well I see, said the blind man," and "What in the Sam Hill?" She made tuna casserole and playdough from scratch, let me watch *Leave It to Beaver* when I came home for lunch in kindergarten/grade one, and took me to see her daughter and friends at Gene's Chinese Restaurant every now and then so I could eat chicken wings and egg rolls while she chatted and knit. And every year on my birthday she took me to their Chinese buffet where I was allowed to have, like, *endless* Jell-O for dessert.

Grandma Helen was a marvelous and loving woman who showed me what love felt like during those malleable early years. When I first met her though, I didn't know any of this to be true.

I knew that my mom was gone, my dad was busy, and I was pissed off. I have a vivid memory of meeting Grandma Helen for the first time, her sitting in an emerald-green Tiffany wingback chair (hey, it was the 80s), me kinda lying on the ground at her feet, rolling around on our matching emerald-green wall-to-wall carpeting. And

I remember looking at her square in the eye and saying, "I don't like you, and I don't want you here."

She looked back at me, unfazed, and said something to the effect of "Well I sure like you, and I'd like for us to get to know each other better." And I remember just like that, I felt safe.

Just the simple act of her empathy, compassion, and holding space for my awkward and angry feelings during an awkward and angry time made me certain I could trust her deeply.

Fast forward thirty-four years to my initial breast cancer diagnosis. The first few weeks that followed the diagnosis were equally awkward and angry and full of appointments with experts who—while keeping my best interest in mind—handed me the card of the hospital social worker every time I started to have "a feeling."

When you're diagnosed with cancer at any age or stage of life, it's a lot to handle, but when you're young, single, self-employed, have three kids under seven and no family history, "a lot" doesn't quite describe the gravity of the diagnosis. So I think it's pretty natural to cry. Feel angry. Feel scared. And I felt all these things over and over. But every time I expressed one of these feelings, someone handed me the same business card, sympathy-head cocked to the side, and said, "Yeah, have you talked to our social worker?"

By the time the sixth person handed me this card (a nurse, who became one of my favorite nurses), I reverted back to that three-year-old self—this time with a thirty-seven-year-old vocabulary—and actually said out loud to her, "WHY THE FUCK WOULD I NEED A FUCKING SOCIAL WORKER? DO YOU HAVE ANY IDEA WHAT I DO FOR A LIVING? JUST LET ME FEEL MY FEELINGS AND STOP FUCKING REFERRING ME TO SOMEONE WHO OBVIOUSLY CANNOT HELP ME, FOR FUCK'S SAKE."

My nurse nodded compassionately and said, "I know it's hard," then let me cry it out while she held the space for me to do so and offered continued words of heartfelt empathy. And then I booked an appointment with the social worker because clearly, I needed someone within the system to talk to and get this off my chest.

When I saw the social worker the first time, I sat *in* her chair (not lying on the floor this time) with my arms folded and legs crossed, actively communicating that I was *not* open to receiving help. And as we started to talk, she said, "Leisse, I have a lot of respect for who you are and what you do, and I think I can also learn from you and your experience of this." My entire body and persona softened, and I knew once again that I could trust *her* deeply.

When I cried and swore and told her how crucial it was for me to not be a patient, to maintain a healthy state of mind, and to reframe all traditional language used in the medical system in a way that felt like cancer and chemo were happening with and for me not *to* me, she nodded emphatically and made really supportive comments.

This acknowledgment allowed me to be more open and free and more comfortable expressing that in the midst of all my strength and tenacity and courage that I was having moments of extreme doubt and intense fear. That physically needing to lie down after making lunches in the morning brought me great shame.

My kids never asked for their parents to divorce. They never asked for their mom to be single for the next hundred years. They never asked for their primary caregiver to be wiped out with fatigue at certain moments of the day while she handled cancer and its cure head on—oh yeah, and ran a business with *minimal* financial support in the meantime.

These were awkward, angry feelings that almost felt like a betrayal to me as I was feeling them, and as loving and beyond amazing as my supportive family and friends were, this was stuff I could not bear to let out yet could not bear to keep in. Interestingly, once I felt safe to communicate these dark and ugly fears, I no longer felt ashamed to have them—they weren't good or bad, they just *were*.

After I stripped away the shame of having them by feeling comfortable sharing them aloud with the social worker, I was able to make them my own and speak more openly about them with my family. And almost if by magic, they weren't so scary anymore. I was able to process them and heal them, and ultimately, they were no longer fears or overwhelming. They just melted away as I carried on.

That's the thing about feelings: you have to feel them to heal them. Your feelings *have to* come out in order for you to find peace within.

When we keep stuff to ourselves, it bubbles and ferments until it presents as something bigger and scarier than just a feeling. The raw and vulnerable act of sharing our darkest moments can feel scary, until it doesn't.

Can you love yourself enough to go into your dark and shadowy places and bravely turn on the light?

Yes, you fucking can.

CHAPTER 11

The paradox of positivity

I am a relentless optimist.

I vehemently believe that things work out, that there's always enough for everyone, that there is a silver lining (even if we can't see it), and that whatever it is we are experiencing has the capacity to push us forward in ways we never thought possible.

Having a positive outlook is, I believe, an actual secret to living a life that makes you feel full, satisfied, appreciative, loved, and connected. It's through positive thinking that we pause and give thanks for the simple pleasures of daily life and have the wherewithal to know, even in our darkest times, that this too shall pass. A positive mindset is essentially having a hopeful mindset and the tenacity to know that you have done hard things before so you can do this too.

But thinking positively isn't enough.

And I will tell you, as someone who believes in a real way that thoughts become things and that we are able to speak our soul's desires into existence, that just because we have taught ourselves to see the bright side *doesn't let us off the hook to feel the rest of our shit*. We can't ignore the big, deep, dark, negative feelings that come up.

When we ignore how we feel, we ignore our truth; we invalidate ourselves through denial or shame for having negativity come up. When we tune out the heaviness that can creep into our heads, hearts, and bodies, we dismiss the messages we are receiving from all three and pass up an incredible opportunity to learn, heal, and grow.

Having a positive outlook does not mean you get to tune out your shit: if you want to heal, you need to *feel*, even when that feels scary, threatening, uncomfortable, or just plain gross.

Remember when you were a kid and you'd wake up with growing pains in your legs? That achy, uncomfortable, "WTF is happening to my body right now" state? Our personal and emotional growth is like that too. The experiences and situations necessary for our growth— that we are constantly invited to attend to, work through, heal from and move on—will challenge us. They will put us through the ringer and make us want to squirm away from them (or hit them with a hammer) until they go away.

When we are brave, we can meet those challenges, those exercises in adversity, and yes, the negative feelings that come with them, head on. We can also coach ourselves to know that this is just a part of the process. These are just the growing pains that bring us closer to ourselves.

That's where we loop back to our positive mindset; it's what gives us the courage to see the bright side without being blinded by it or ignoring how we feel in the present moment.

In my darkest of days, the months (and frankly, years) when it felt like life was over and that there was no coming back, it did not serve me to dwell in the state of panic that was expected of and even encouraged for me by others. In order to make it through some of the stuff I personally have made it through, I had to be aware of what my truth was and triage it to varying degrees.

Okay, that's fear, I can address that right now. That's rejection—nope, can't handle that one yet. Oh, hey, there's despair . . . probably going to park you for a hot minute while I catch my breath. Oh—anger! Yes! Anger I feel ready to feel—maybe I will scream this out at the lake. And in the meantime, I know that everything happening is leading me in a better, healthier, more loving direction. So chin up, and off I go.

Know that if you're only feeling negativity, you are doing yourself a disservice—likewise, if you're ONLY feeling positivity and are using it as a comfort blanket instead of as a beacon for growth, you're also doing yourself a disservice.

Feel your feelings, have the courage to see the bright side, and don't allow yourself to get blinded by the light.

It's having the hope of a positive and healthy mindset that allows you to safely feel the shadow stuff and navigate through it in a peaceful, grounded, and secure way. Ignoring it doesn't work. Repressing it doesn't work. Dwelling in it really doesn't work.

If you want to truly feel at peace within your very being, you need to learn how to identify, name, and feel your feelings, then trace them back to where they're coming from and see what else still needs to be healed there.

Our emotions are just feedback, remember? It's only insight as to what still needs to be healed, and an invitation to do so, that lets us know we're ready to heal that at the next level.

Leisse Wilcox

Can you love yourself enough to take your healing to the next level?

Yes, you fucking can.

CHAPTER 12

How to feel your feelings

"Don't call yourself an expert" was one of the first and best pieces of professional advice I received when I started writing, and to date, it is something I stand fiercely behind. Right here, right now, as a one-time only kinda thing, however, I'm going to make an exception. Because if there's one area of life I am *definitely* an expert in, it's feelings.

Oh yes, darling, I am like a black belt, high priestess, Grandmaster Flash guru of feelings.

If you know me in real life, I all but guarantee you've seen me cry or at least tear up with feeling the moment, whatever that moment is. And if you've read or followed my Instagram posts or other writing, you know I'm pretty honest about exactly that. I will share with you that over the span of three-and-a-half decades, I think I may have felt it all: moments of joy, delight, despair, grief, agony, bewilderment, fear, anxiety, love, infatuation, jealousy, pride, nervousness, anticipation, giddiness, deep smit, disappointment, shock, awe, disbelief, inadequacy, adequacy, superiority, terror, confusion, hope, shame, pride, forgiveness, lack, abundance, sheer happiness, ecstasy, overwhelm, underwhelm (though ironically, never just plain "whelm"). The list is *long*, babe.

And that was just for Tuesday! (Kidding. Kind of.)

As a highly sensitive person (to people, places, energy, dynamics, environments, subtext . . . you name it), I have lots of practice in feeling the feels and learning to balance them with a healthy emotional regulation. When I was a kid, and even well into my twenties, I thought these sensitivities were a problem, to be very honest with you. At some point I know I was told they were a problem and consequently that nugget became a part of my story to be true—until I decided otherwise.

Later, as I grew up and matured and found better footing in being straight-up me, I realized that being this sensitive isn't a problem but a gift. A total gift. When I accepted, then embraced this ability to feel deeply (about pretty much everything), things changed for me. I started to see the strength in my vulnerability and the joy in feeling such active emotions in response to what was happening in and around me.

I also learned how to navigate these feelings in a healthy way so that when a particularly intense one came along, I could feel it, acknowledge it, and let it go.

Once, I received an email from a reader of my blog:

"You talk a lot about working through things and feeling shit. But how? Honestly, how do you actually do it? I feel like there's stuff I should probably deal with and confront, but I don't even know how or where to start."

"Whoa. Dude. Have YOU ever come to the right place," I thought. But instead of writing that, I wrote this: *How do you feel your feelings? Especially if they are the big-ass scary ones that, when they peek at you from around a corner in your mind, make you run screaming in the opposite direction instead of facing them?* Imma break it down for you.

1. NAME IT

To quote G.I. Joe, "knowing is half the battle," and identifying/naming your feelings is the first half of this battle. It might sound silly to you, but if you're one of the *many* people out there who has learned over time to repress or bury your feelings, suddenly this instruction isn't so basic.

Again, think back to when you were a kid and what language your parents, caregivers, and teachers used: "You're okay. That's enough. You'll be fine. No more crying. Boys don't cry. Be a big girl." Each of those seemingly innocent messages has a way of embedding themselves into our ether and setting up shop. This is true for women, and Oh Em Gee, so true for men.

The way we talk to boys tends to be so dismissive of their feelings it's shameful; it teaches them to bury everything, only for their girl-friends, wives, and therapists to encourage them years down the road to dig deep and get real with what they're feeling.

How do you know if you're repressing some shit? *You feel angry, anxious, or numb a disproportionate amount of your time.*

Did that get your attention? The truth is that anger and anxiety are generally considered to be manifestations of fear. And when you feel fear—as we all do—without identifying it as such, or without working through that fear, it presents itself as anger or anxiety or numbness (that "I feel nothing" feeling).

You've met these people, and chances are, as I say, you *are* these people. The people who are pissed off about everything. Cynical. Always have something to bring the conversation or occasion down a notch. Like a little black cloud is hanging over them as a security blanket, lest they feel what they are really feeling.

If that sounds familiar, I have a challenge for you: When you start to feel angry or anxious or realize you don't really feel anything, stop and identify it. Select whichever of these statements applies and really think it through:

"I feel angry because . . ."

Are you angry because the guy in front of you at the gas station is a "talentless ass clown" or because you are running late and are afraid of getting in shit at work? Or do you often feel like your time is undervalued and under-appreciated, and this little encounter just backs up that gross feeling you have way down deep?

"I feel anxious when . . ."

Notice your feelings after you leave an interaction with any environment or person. Do you feel lifted and recharged? Or drained, insecure, and spent? Are you trying to prove something to someone that just isn't authentically you? Are you engaging in activities in your life for the sake of pleasing others but leave you feeling untrue and unsatisfied?

"I don't feel anything right now; why is that?"

This is a tougher one, and one that might take some practice. But ask yourself why and then start to walk yourself through the absence of feelings to see what comes up. Pssst—"I just don't feel anything" means you're not there yet, toots. Keep going. If you need some help dragging this stuff out, an intense but super-effective trick is to find a quiet and private space, put on "that song that gets you every time" with headphones at full volume, and let whatever comes up wash over you. This trick is an almost surefire way to kick-start the process and invite anything that has been trained to stay down and not be felt, felt. Be very gentle with yourself afterward, as the intensity of this exercise might surprise you; leave time to rest and reflect for a while.

2. ACKNOWLEDGE IT

Once you've identified your feelings, i.e., "In this moment I feel angry that she didn't text me back, and I think I'm afraid that I might have fucked up another relationship," you have a couple options.

Option one is to say, "Freak that noise" and bury it back down where it came from.

Option two is to acknowledge what you are feeling and go from there. Can you guess which one is the healthy choice here?

I get it. Sometimes it's as complex as you not being ready or equipped to feel the big feels, especially if they're related to childhood or intimacy. Sometimes it's as simple as you standing in a crowded elevator with a group of strangers and getting that awful feeling of overwhelm, and you just can't deal with it at the moment. "At the moment" is key though, because cruelly, the only way through something is to actually *go through it*.

Any of those negative feelings you have and avoid and pack way back down where you can't feel them don't actually go away until you deal with them. And the kicker? The longer you avoid those feelings, the stronger and more powerful they become, and they come at you more and more fiercely until you own up and face them head on.

There's a Buddhist saying I love, which to paraphrase, says that you can acknowledge your feelings and let them in, but don't invite them to stay for tea. In my mind, I imagine a big family table full of emotions sitting around. Everyone gets to express how they feel, but nobody gets to monopolize the conversation. Some people will push you to "kick fear's ass!" or "tell your fear to fuck off!" and I think that reflects a gross misunderstanding of how our emotional bodies work.

We've talked at length about how fear is an incredible value feature of our subconscious mind and how our feelings of fear serve us now, and have served us in the past, to protect us. In psychology there is an understanding that under the umbrella of one "Self" we actually have many selves. In each stage of our lives, for each self we embody as a part of our larger Self, we feel things differently, experience things differently, and have different ways of meeting our different needs.

For some of those older selves (i.e., selves from childhood), it was fear that actually protected us and kept us safe. When we're older, have done more healing work, and have made peace with other parts of our past, it's incredibly self-disrespectful to flip that fear the bird; after all, it was there helping us survive for so long.

Rather, part of acknowledging our feelings is to embody this awareness that everything that came before this moment has served us in some way. So at this family table of emotions that I would encourage you to adopt, or reframe for your own imagination, "fear" absolutely gets a voice that is heard yet is not welcome to monopolize the conversation.

This is where we move on to Step 3.

3. ACCEPT IT

Step 3 is the most freeing of the steps.

Simply accepting how you feel, not questioning it, not shaming it, not blaming it, just effing accepting it. What does that look like?

"I feel lonely. I am scared I will be alone forever. I am afraid I will be the kind of father my father was. I think this marriage is dead. I think I am in the wrong career and am afraid to make the change. What if I can never get pregnant? I am uncomfortable in my body. I miss my mom. I regret not traveling and am worried I missed my window. I made a mistake and I don't know how to solve it. I am tired of feeling like I'm second best. I treated her like crap, and I don't know if I can ever make up for it. I'm worried I've taken on too much and I don't think I can handle it, but I don't know how to ask for help. I want and need a partner. I think I am in love, and I really don't want to mess it up this time. Okay. This is how I feel."

Whatever the feeling is, accept it. Period.

If we've learned to suppress things along the way, when they bubble up (as they always do—see Step 2), not only do we get the icky feeling itself, but we get it wrapped in a protective coating of shame. So now we have to deal not only with the feeling, but the feeling of shame just for feeling said feeling.

Make sense?

So instead, to free yourself, I am giving you permission to do this:

just feel it. It might be the most fucked up thought you've ever had. It might come from a place of weakness in which you thought you were strong. It might be painfully simple or wildly complex; it doesn't matter.

Just identify it ("This is fear that I'm feeling"), acknowledge it ("Oh, hey, fear of rejection. I see you, and I'm sorry for what you've experienced so far that has led you here. You're safe now"), and accept it ("Wow, I am afraid of being rejected. I've never admitted that before").

Let the feeling wash over you like a wave and hold on with the knowledge that as quickly as it came crashing in, it too will go.

Take a breath, have a glass of water, hug, cry, nap, and keep going.

4. HEAL IT

Healing is a lifetime process. It gets easier with time and really comes down to accepting your feelings and processing them in a healthy way.

One of the biggest human needs that we tend to overlook is the need to be seen and heard. A crucial part to resolution is talking it out, either with yourself (or with whomever it is that you involve spiritually in that conversation) via journaling, to a close friend or family member, or maybe even to a professional.

I've had very deep and intimate conversations with people I barely know, as if I came upon them at the right place and time for them to vent out and work through whatever is on their mind. I am a frequent recipient of "Wow. I can't believe I just told you that; I've never told anyone that before," and I love it. I love being the one who gets to *hear* people because I know how important and soothing it is to be heard. I am also grateful for the handful of people in my life who take the time to *listen* to me in that same way. Maybe not in line at the grocery or flower store, but whenever the time and place feels right for me.

Once you've allowed this shit to bubble up, you need to let it go to set it free, and a huge part of this process is resolving and healing it through being *heard*. If your dog is a willing and active listener, so be it. I'm not even kidding. Just talk it out to someone and notice the change in intensity, the increase in clarity, the decrease in overwhelm, and the upped confidence level in knowing exactly what to do.

And of course it goes without saying here that if the feelings that come up are bigger and more complicated than you thought, conversing with a great therapist is an excellent option to help move that mountain out of your way and carry on.

Can you love yourself enough to feel your feelings?

Yes, you fucking can.

CHAPTER 13

How to find clarity in what you want

Who do you think you are? Really and truly. When we're kids and someone asks us that question, it's usually pretty easy. "I love horses, I'm going to be an artist and a mermaid when I grow up, and I just love eating pizza with my family." Simple, clear, visionary.

When we're grown-ups and someone asks us that same question, we tend to answer it by defining who we are in relation to something or someone else: "I'm Angela from accounting, I'm Jackson's mom, I'm the founder of XYZ Company, I'm married to Phil who works in finance." Sometimes we even define ourselves by whom we *used* to be: "I used to be a runner, an athlete, a singer . . . and now I am a mom, work in insurance, help my husband with his business, take care of my parents."

It's wild—and wildly accepted—to abandon our own sense of self in favor of supporting everyone else's. Take a minute to pause and appreciate the loss that this is for us way down deep in our souls. Are any of those roles bad? Oh hell no, and truthfully, parts of us are certainly influenced if not defined by the supporting roles that we play for other people.

But we mustn't overlook the Academy Award we deserve for being our *own* leading lady and appreciate that in addition to the many hats we wear, we remain a whole person at our core. So I want to ask you again: Who do you think you are?

Personally? I had no idea who I was until I was about thirty-seven years old. By age thirty-four I could tell you who I wasn't, but not who I was. Remember I told you in Part 1 that while we study child development, we kinda forget to study and observe human development after childhood ends?

Well, that becomes very important here.

Human beings are constantly developing, growing, and evolving over their lifespan. The incredibly cool thing is that, just like the markers and milestones we use as metrics to chart our kids' development (when does baby hold her head up, when does baby roll over, when does he say his first word, when does she lose her first tooth, etc.), there are markers and milestones we can use as metrics in the cultivation and development of our adult selves too.

Many psychologists agree that our parenting style has changed so much in the last generation or so that it is safe to say that "adolescence" extends until about age twenty-nine, which means that we are *teenagers* until we turn thirty.

Kinda puts things into perspective, don't you think? Subsequently, we hit another milestone in our thirties, which is that "aha!" moment of waking up. For many women somewhere between the ages of thirty-two and thirty-eight (or so), there is a wild realization that "I have been somebody's daughter. I have been somebody's sister. I have been somebody's wife, mother, employee, boss, friend, confidant, and caretaker. Just when do I get to be *mine* in all of this? Where do the roles I play end . . . and the ones with the real me begin?"

It's staggering. And this is why around this age group (within our culture and context), you start to see a spike in divorces. It's the process of all those women who got married as "teens" in their twenties waking up and realizing the life they're living isn't their own.

Cue the near 50 percent divorce rate, with an estimated 60 percent of those divorces being initiated by women. Myself included.

Understanding who you are is fundamental to your success in moving on and both requires and is deserving of your full attention. Set aside at least an hour of your time; schedule it into your calendar now and treat it like a date with yourself free from any other distractions like people, phones, and Netflix. If you prefer, read through these exercises now and then commit to yourself to circle back and *actually* do them during the time you've carved out *to* do them.

Oh yes, I see you. And I'm talking to you. It's engaging in this kind of action that separates "being inspired" from "taking inspired action" and is the magic wand to make what you want happen, happen.

Now. It's time to take action to help you through this process of self-knowing and to show you how to embody it—i.e., "just how you think" instead of having to consciously think about it. We know behavior change is hard, and what I'm about to share with you is *how* you can start teaching yourself a new and healthy behavior that will eventually feel effortless as you adopt it and evolve your own self-awareness and emotional body to tap into *how to* feel your feelings.

Remember, this *is* the work, and we are digging into the tools that *enable* that work. Reading this book alone is not enough; you need to do the follow-up in order to embody the change as part of your lifestyle.

So get out your calendar and book a date to do this work. Your future self is already high-fiving you for taking this kind of insider action right now.

For the sheer delight of your inner child, I'm calling them "Taco Tivities." You know, activities that are as amazing as tacos. Everyone likes tacos, so therefore everyone likes these activities. If you're the one person who doesn't like tacos—gasp—call them Ice Cream Tivities, or whatever else feels good and kinda lights you up when you hear the word.

Great, now I'm hungry.

Therefore, in case you haven't already done so,, get out your calendar and book a date with yourself . . . and these *Taco Tivities*.

Can you love yourself enough to follow through?

Yes, you fucking can.

TACO TIVITY 1

What is your ideal day?

This task is best accomplished with a pen and paper. If you have (or have been wanting to have) a dream or vision journal, this is an excellent opportunity to use it. Put away your phone, your screen, your distractions, and just be here with me now, turning all your attention inward on you.

For the next few minutes, or as long as it takes, I want you to allow yourself to daydream.

I want you to think of all the times you've ever thought or said, "I wish. If only. Wouldn't it be nice. In a perfect world I would . . ."

This is your chance to get that all down on paper. Our feelings are always feedback, so if you're having a particularly strong feeling about something, this is your chance to learn a little more about what that feedback is.

Just allow yourself to sit and dream as I guide you through this exercise, right here, right now.

Take a deep breath in, all the way in, and allow yourself to let it go. Let yourself feel grounded in this moment, right here, right now, and just enjoy the feeling of being *here*. Take a nice, deep, *cleansing* breath in, all the way in, and let yourself release that cleansing breath out as you exhale, feeling completely safe and grounded in this moment.

I want you to imagine having an absolutely perfect day. An ideal day. I want you to imagine the day that would make you wake up every morning feeling excited about and would make you go to bed feeling excited about waking up again.

It can be as similar or as different from your current day as you like—after all, this is *your* dream. It belongs to you and no one else. This dream is sacredly your own to simply dream and enjoy.

I want you to imagine yourself at the very beginning of this day: What time is it? What do you see? What do you feel? Who is there with you, or are you completely on your own? What does your room look like; what do you see? What does your bed look like; how does it feel?

How do *you* feel as you wake up in this moment? What do you do? What are you doing?

And now I want you to imagine, what happens next?

Really feel into this moment—what is the next step of your day? What time is it, and what are you doing? Most importantly, how do you feel in this moment while you are doing it?

Okay, great. You're doing great.

I want you to keep this exercise going for every single thing that happens in your dream day, your ideal day: What is happening, what do you see, what time is it, and how do you *feel*?

Keep going through every point in your day asking yourself, "What happens next? How does it feel?"

And then, when the day is done and you are climbing back into bed, I want you to keenly observe how you feel at the end of this day, this perfect day, your *ideal* day, as you gently drift off to sleep.

Now take a deep breath in, all the way in, and allow yourself to let it go. How do you feel?

Write it down.

Next, I want you to think about your current day, or a typical day in your current life. Go through a similar exercise, moving through each moment of your current day, observing how you feel at each moment. Write it down.

When you're done, you will have two lists in front of you: one describes how you *would* spend an ideal day, and one describes how you *are* spending your current day.

How are they similar?

How are they different?

Here's the fascinating thing: In many (if not most) cases (in my experience working with clients one on one through this exact exercise), the two days are incredibly similar but with a few shifts. Often, we only need to make a few shifts to make our current day our *ideal* day.

The secret? **Focus on the feeling.**

Too often we chase after "things." We think that in order to feel happy, we need a million dollars, a glass of champagne in our hand, a yacht, and no responsibility. In reality, we don't want the "thing." We want the *feeling* we think the thing will bring us.

So go back to your ideal day: What is the overarching feeling you have living out that lucid daydream? And then turn your attention to *how to create more of that feeling* in your current day.

Want more freedom? How can you create more freedom in your life right now? Want more joy? How can you create more joy in your life right now?

Want more wealth? How do you create more of what you think that wealth will bring you in your life right now?

In order to truly feel whole and good, we need to constantly bring ourselves back to living in the present. Honoring where we've come from? Absolutely. Having a clear vision of where we're going? Essential!

And the action happens now, in this moment. When we fixate on "One day," "I wish," "I will have," "It would be amazing if," we are actually keeping those things at bay. Our subconscious thoughts only exist in the present, so if we are thinking of what *will* happen, we are effectively stopping ourselves from actually experiencing it now.

So what we want more of we need to cultivate now and let that create the magnet for more of what we've created to keep creating.

It really is this simple; it really is this complicated.

Here are two amazing examples from real-life women I have worked with:

Suzi: During her ideal day, this entrepreneur dreamed of having more time with her daughter. Her ideal day allowed her the time to walk her to school and allowed her the freedom to feel more peace / less chaos by not feeling enslaved to client and employee demands. Rather, it created space to just spend time with her little one as well as gave her an extra day to work from home without traveling.

I asked her, "If you had a magic wand, what would you do with it in your current day?" The solution was almost instant. For three days of the week she would deliberately schedule all her work commitments to start after she had—you guessed it—dropped her daughter off at school. She would intentionally plan one full day that was open to client demands, three that allowed her time to travel *after* she had walked her little one to school, and one full day of working from home to focus on the inner workings of her business and home without needing to travel for meetings.

In almost no time at all, with just a few simple shifts and adjustments, she created the freedom and peace that had thirty minutes prior felt entirely out of reach.

Anna: I love this example because when I was talking to Anna about how simple these shifts are to make, she called shade. She said, "Nope, sorry, I actually don't believe you. I mean, in my ideal day I have a private chef, and sorry, but hiring a private chef requires money, and a lot of it."

I asked Anna what the feeling was she hoped to experience in having a private chef. This question seemed to be a little blocked for her, so I prompted it: "When I hear private chef, I hear a desire to feel nourished, cared for, taken care of; I hear someone sharing the responsibilities of caring for a family as well as helping take care of you. Does that feel accurate?" Anna, a business owner, mom, and podcaster, got a little teary and said yes, that felt pretty accurate.

So the challenge was to figure out how to create the feeling of being nourished, cared for, and attended to right here, right now. Sure, it might seem like a million dollars would solve this problem and afford the opportunity to hire a chef, but the opportunity to create that feeling in her immediate life had many options of manifesting.

+ How could she comfortably share her feelings of overwhelm with her husband and family?

+ How could she effectively communicate her need for the right kind of help and support from her partner?

+ Would a meal delivery service (in which a recipe and its ingredients arrive, all chopped and measured and ready to be assembled) help take the weight off and make this part of the day feel easier and more attended to?

It didn't take long (and I mean like *ten minutes* long) to start shifting her awareness from "I couldn't have that until I am a millionaire, and I'm just going to have to hustle hard and suck it up until then" to "Hey, maybe there is an underlying problem I haven't felt safe or comfortable addressing yet; maybe I can just talk this out with my husband and share the fact that I feel drained and exhausted and need help sharing the load more evenly." She just had to identify the feeling first.

This is the shit that *lights me up* and gives me all kinds of chills because we are all capable of *having what we want* by *feeling how we want to feel.* That freedom is available to each of us through a number of different ways, starting with identifying first what the feeling is and then taking action to identify the feedback the feeling is giving us.

Even if resources are scarce and we don't yet have the people we want to support us, we can start within. If you want to feel respected, respect yourself. If you want to feel loved, love yourself. If you want to feel happy, choose to feel happy now by doing something that brings you joy.

Your ideal day is closer to you than you think. It is that simple; it is that complicated.

Can you love yourself enough to take the time to figure out the what and allow the how to come more easily to you?

Yes, you fucking can.

What are your values?

This task is best accomplished with a pen and paper. If you have (or have been wanting to have) a dream or vision journal, this is an excellent opportunity to use it. Put away your phone, your screen, your distractions, and just be here with me now, turning all your attention inward on you.

More often than not, when I ask somebody what their values are, they tell me they aren't really sure or haven't really thought about it. So when I ask you here, "Tell me, what are your core values?" and you feel on the spot thinking, "Oy, I'm not really sure; I haven't really thought about it," know that you are not alone.

We tend not to talk about our values anymore, and that's a shame because as you will soon see, they are kind of fundamental to our success as humans who feel good and aligned with living their best life. When you are living in alignment with your values, everything feels in flow, easy, possible, completely within your reach, joyful. And the flip side, of course, is that when you're living out of alignment with your values, things feel anxious, tense, friction-y, stuck, unpleasant, doomed.

Remember that our feelings are always feedback, and when we pause to observe what the feeling is, we can get some clarity on what feedback it's giving us about what needs our attention or what needs to be healed. And sometimes what needs our attention and what needs to be healed is coming back to alignment with our values.

You can see that if you have no idea what your values are, it can pose a challenge in coming into alignment with them. The great news is that your values aren't really yours to consciously determine: if you know that we have our behavior—which is dictated by our thoughts, which are dictated by our subconscious beliefs—you know that if one thing is out of whack, you have to recalibrate things at their root.

Values are even deeper than that, and I believe they are chosen at a deep soul level. Our values are what really guide us—from an inherent place—regardless of our experience. Think of your values as a set of parameters and guiding principles. If you are familiar with the concept of "human design," you can think of your values as being factory-implanted settings on your particular model of human being. Just like your cell phone comes with a specific operating system embedded that is unique to its core design, you also come born with a soul-driven set of parameters that shape your outlook and interpretation of the world around you and your experience within it.

Most of us, in my experience, have about five to ten core values, each of which feels fundamental to *who* we are.

Knowing that, *now* tell me, what are your core values?
Take your time and generate that list here and now.

Family? Freedom? Inner peace? Laughter? Creativity? Mutual respect? Trust?

Your values are your own, and again, are the core intricacies of what make you feel completely in flow.

If you need a boost, think of the best relationship you've ever had—intimate, friendship, family, or otherwise. How did you feel when you were with that person?

Further, think of when you feel, or have felt, the most joy in your life: What, specifically, were you doing, and how did it make you feel?

Get clear on what your values are, because when you are, they will prove to be incredibly valuable as a filter for everyday decision-making about relationships and opportunities.

But first, while you're here with your list of values in front of you, come up with some actionable things that align with each of those values that make you feel like you. Step Two is to *do those things*.

For example, here's what this Taco Tivity looks like for me:

Family—spending downtime with my kids, having family dinners, going to the cottage with our aunts and uncles, visiting family during the holidays, prioritizing time with my kids, creating low-pressure memories together doing things that make us feel good, designing our home to be 100 percent family friendly in its design and flow, cooking at home, low-key traditions like popcorn / pizza / movie night, creating traditions that meet all of our needs *together*, fostering the relationship between my kids and our extended family (aunts, uncles, grandparents, cousins)

Using my voice—singing in the car, making up song parodies with my kids, speaking to large audiences, speaking to small groups, being interviewed, going on podcasts, hosting my own podcast, writing, actively using Instagram as a platform for social change, filming videos, sharing my wisdom with others, being comfortable with my vulnerability

Freedom—using my time as my own, decorating my house the way I want to, driving with the windows down and the music up (and when it's cold, turning up the seat warmers and opening the moon roof), having a plan for my free time to use it wisely, napping on the couch, listening to my body and doing what feels right/purposeful in the moment, taking downtime when I need it, building my business in the way that feels right to me (NOT in the way that has worked for other entrepreneurs), using my own judgment above all else to make decisions, keeping a lot of my life private, making decisions that feel good to me rather than what I "should" do, going to a matinee, going out for brunch

Solitude—spending time by myself at home, being selective about opportunities and commitments I say yes to, honoring my introverted needs to recharge after being around large groups of people, going for regular walks by the lake or in the woods, getting into nature, sitting on my couch and looking out the window with coffee in my hand, taking time to just be, allowing myself to think things through

Peace—keeping a calm home environment, making decisions on how I respond based on "who this will serve," being mindful of my own sensitivities / vulnerabilities / trigger points and being gentle with myself when they come up, being very clear on what I need in the moment and saying yes or no accordingly, only spending time with people who align with my values

Exploration—trying new things that are beyond my comfort zone, saying yes to things that sound scary if they feel like they could be good opportunities, going on road trips and solo traveling, visiting classic American cities for a weekend and living in one neighborhood like a local, learning new things, driving to one specific place to try a new donut or taco, waiting in a line outside a niche food place (like Korean waffles) for the experience of being a part of the hype, ordering only what the serving staff suggests as recommendations without looking at the menu, hiking

Beauty—making my internal and external environments places I feel comfortable and love spending time in, wearing lipstick, getting tattoos, having fresh flowers on our dining table, knowing the story and energy of every item that comes into our home, spending time outside, making every touch point of my life artistic, creating, giving themes to days (like Taco Tuesday) and parties, investing in original artwork and getting to know the artist personally, listening to my vinyl collection, drinking out of vintage glassware, owning carpets with history and texture, washing and moisturizing my face, treating mundane things with a sense of occasion and purpose

Joy—taking pleasure in simple, everyday moments, laughing, being with people who make me laugh, watching TV that makes me laugh, laughing out loud in the movie theater, making song parodies with my kids, taking photos, eating ice cream or tacos, going on road trips, singing, dancing in my kitchen, making my kids laugh, singing in the car, swimming, watching the waves, being at camp, sitting around the fire in any season, being at the cottage, sharing my joy, helping people improve their lives and feel like themselves again, petting cute and well-behaved dogs, being with my family

Once you are clear on your values and find ways to act on those values or put those values into action, you can see how you really start to carve out time for who you are. This task is foundational in the work of coming home to yourself because it honors and celebrates exactly who you are as you are. Further, when you're trying to make a decision (about a relationship or opportunity), you just go through the list and ask "does this align with my value of ___? Does it align with my value of ___?" It's like a Cosmo quiz: when you get to the bottom of the evaluation, if it's aligned with your values it's a hell yes, and if it isn't aligned, it becomes *so clear* that it's not for you—and you move on.

Can you love yourself enough to discover your core values?

Yes, you fucking can.

TACO TIVITY 3

What's the story you're telling yourself?

I am about to share with you the ten little words that will forever change your life, if you let them:

The story I'm telling myself is . . .

And after you know what the story is, ask:

Is that story true?

Here's why this activity is so powerful: If you've read this book in chronological order, you've learned that the people and circumstances in our earliest years (including while we're still in the womb) have a massive impact on shaping our "reality." We absorb all the images, messages, unspoken words, and emotional energy around us effortlessly and without filter or pause. We just soak it all in. And what we soak in has the tendency to become what we believe (even if we don't ever remember consciously learning it). We are significantly affected by what we pick up.

And you've probably also learned by now that until we decide to change that "reality," it remains our reality, even if it's a negative, toxic, or otherwise untruth that we don't even want to believe.

So often, when we react or respond in a particular way, especially if it's something in our lives that feels like it's triggering an inappropriate response, we are reacting based on the stories we've been taught to believe, even if those stories are the ones that do not serve us in any way, shape, or form.

A huge part of cultivating our emotional awareness and developing our emotional intelligence is taking the time to pause when we have an adverse reaction and asking those magic words: "The story I'm telling myself is . . ."

For example, let's say you are someone who is terrified of public speaking and you are asked to give a speech at a wedding. Giving a speech at a wedding is a wonderful thing to do, and probably aligns with your values (of respect, joy, and family), but still, the idea of speaking in front of a room full of people just makes you want to throw up.

Ask: "The story I'm telling myself is . . ."
And answer: "I am terrified of making this speech."

Ask again: "The story I'm telling myself is . . ."
And answer: "No one will care what I have to say. I will mess up and make a fool of myself. People will judge me."

Ask again: "The story I'm telling myself is . . ."

And answer: "Everyone will see I'm not perfect, and they will reject me. I will feel rejected."

Now ask: "Is that story true? Are people going to reject me for not making a perfect speech?"

And answer: "No. People make mistakes all the time and are still included in and loved by our family."

Kaboom. Fear = gone. Once we puncture a hole in "the reality" of what you're afraid of, we get to the real feedback of the feeling: fear of rejection.

So we can "heal" that fear of rejection by appreciating that "we make mistakes all the time" and finding real proof to satiate our subconscious need to know. We can then dispel that subconscious-perceived fear of rejection.

Once again, this has nothing to do with public speaking and everything to do with a feeling of being rejected. Maybe there was a time in your early life when you spoke up, or voiced your opinion, or made a mistake in a public place and felt the sting of rejection; your subconscious mind's duty is to keep you safe and protect you from feeling unsafe, physically or emotionally, ever again. So this gets anchored into our minds as "speaking up and making mistakes = rejection."

We get hung up on "the thing" but overlook the feeling the thing is giving us.

You now have the resources to do this activity in your own life. Whenever you're feeling fear, or anger (which is fear), or jealousy (which is fear), or resentment (which is fear), or scarcity (which is, you guessed it, fear), pause, then take yourself on this "emotional elevator": keep asking what the story is and go deeper and deeper with your questioning until you get to the root of the fear. And once you're there, ask yourself if it is true.

It is that simple; it is that complicated.

> *Can you love yourself enough to observe and question the story you're telling yourself?*

Yes, you fucking can.

***

You can see how this all starts to work in tandem. Sometimes these concepts are challenging to grasp at first because we're kind of working with four-dimensional, nonlinear concepts but only have the means to communicate with language, which is itself linear. The more you read about this though, you'll see the more connected everything is and how it all layers up and overlaps, and you can start to see how healing one thing is actually the beginning of healing everything.

Here's a quick summary of how to put this all together in a cogent, integrated way:

Let's say your "ideal day" activity reveals that you would love to have more time for yourself in the day. Your values reveal that "time to yourself" is, in fact, integral to who you are as a person. You discover, however, that when you think about taking time for yourself, you start to feel an overwhelming feeling of guilt. Because you are a student of your own self-love and are keen to increase your emotional intelligence by expanding your emotional awareness, you pause, noticing that this feeling of guilt is trying to tell you something and get your attention that there is something inside that needs tenderness and healing.

When you ask what the story is that you're telling yourself, you come to discover that you remember your own mother and grandmother working all the time. You remember watching them cooking, cleaning, ironing, dealing with the washing machine repair guy, making dinner from scratch every night and never, ever complaining about it. You love your mom and grandma so much that somewhere along the lines you associated "never-ending work" with "this is what a good mother is."

You realize that the story you're telling yourself is that "good mothers are always busy." Therefore, if you are taking a break, you must not be a good mother. You also realize that "family" is one of your core values and there's an inner conflict telling you "if I love my family, I must be a good mother, and being a good mother means never, ever resting. Therefore, if I am resting, I am not being a good mother or even loving my family."

You take a breath and suddenly appreciate where all that guilt and anxiety is coming from. You ask, "Is that story true?" and very carefully, very gently, you allow yourself to answer very honestly that "that was a different time with different expectations; it may have seemed like they were always busy without complaint, but I can only imagine how much they would have loved to have had the chance to just take off once in a while. I know that in order to *be* the good mother I know I am and truly be present for and engaged with my family, I require time to myself. So I'm going to plan out what that looks like in the way that feels good for me and allows me to honor exactly what my needs are including ensuring that my family is attended to in a way that also feels good for me."

Zowie.

All that guilt, all that tension, all that stress melts away simply because you had the discipline to take an hour and check in about what you want.

Can you love yourself enough to now find confidence in who you are?

Yes, you fucking can.

CHAPTER 14

How to find confidence in who you are

Go back and look over your ideal day. Visualize what feels most true for your dream life. Revisit your core values and think about how they've shaped your experience so far and how they can continue to lead you to a rich life of love and gratitude simply by existing as your guiding light.

Give yourself the space and time to really use these thought starters to get very clear on what you want and *why* you want it. Write it down and visualize over and over the feeling you get from it, especially first thing in the morning and as you're falling asleep. Create a vision that feels so real of what it is that you want—big or small, simple or complex—that it feels like an absolute truth that it's already yours.

Next: Now that you know what you want, it's time to find confidence in who you are. Not in what you are, but truly who you are as a person.

You are a person of value.
You alone are enough.
You already have everything you need.

Sometimes you're the only one who needs to be convinced of these statements. You know how you can look around and see all the good in the people around you? When someone comes to you with an idea and you believe in their ability to follow through and make it a success? When your friend tells you a relationship falls through or a job opportunity doesn't work out and you say "their loss" and mean it?

Well, all this belief in others, all these votes of confidence, all these hype-squad abilities you have for others? It's time to turn that inward toward yourself.

It's all well and good to be a champion for others; it's great, actually, to be a loving and supportive person. It's so great, in fact, that the number one person you need to champion is (and has been) staring back at you from the mirror since the day you were born.

It is time to find confidence in who you are.
Love yourself enough to start here.

Remember, cultivating your natural confidence is also fundamental to your success in moving on, and it both requires and is deserving of your full attention.

Anyway, in case you didn't do it when I suggested it a minute ago, get out your calendar and book a date with yourself . . . and these Taco Tivities.

TACO TIVITY 4

Positive self-talk

Today is literally the first day of the rest of your life. And today is the day you begin the self-reflective process of identifying patterns of thinking, digging deep to find out where they are coming from, and finding the courage to challenge and change them. Yes, these are exercises to implement into your week, and yes, these are actually the formative exercises that you will adopt as a practice throughout the course of your life because they are new and healthy patterns of thinking and of shaping your mindset to work for you in a way that feels tenderly authentic.

Every night before you go to bed, and every morning when you wake up, I want you to look in the mirror and talk to yourself about your day. Yes, you will definitely feel crazy at first, but I want you to push through and carry on. If it helps, talk to the child inside of you. Ask her how her day was. What was the best part? What would she do over if she had the chance? Tell her what you love about her, how proud you are of something she did today, how much you admire one of her best qualities. Tell her about her beautiful eyes or smile, tell her you are so happy to know her and have the chance to spend so much time with her. Do this activity every single day and indulge in the pleasure of telling yourself everything you want to hear. This is the beginning of cultivating a beautiful and loving friendship with yourself.

Connect with your inner child

Getting comfortable with this work and developing a connection with your inner child is a gift.

I'm a big believer that none of us ever really grows up; sure, they give us driver's licenses and mortgages and let us go to work and vote and have families. But really? We're all just big kids.

Somewhere along the lines though, we learn to tune out those child selves and their needs, especially if you've had a hard past or had to grow up quickly or had to care for someone else (or had to face any number of things that happen in our lifetime). We learn to ignore our true needs, which really are connected to the needs of our childhood.

When you pause and entertain the idea that there is a deeper and younger part of you that still exists and still has needs that need to get met, you can start to be the one to meet them. And when you do? You will feel more whole, more connected, more joyful and playful; you'll feel happier.

The work is so simple: just ask.

Ask that little person inside you, "What would you like to do? What would you like to eat? What do you need in this moment to feel loved?"

Then ask for the answer. This simple practice is an excellent way to start meeting your own needs and meeting them in an incredibly authentic way.

CHAPTER 15

Stop apologizing for how you feel

O nce, I went to a Dolly Parton tribute show at a local dive bar. When one lovely singer covered "Down from Dover," there were many tears coming from many eyes around me—and almost immediately, people started apologizing for those tears.

Why does that happen? Why do we do this? Why do we apologize for feeling how we feel?

I apologized relentlessly for how I felt for years, and for years I heard phrases like: "You're just too sensitive." "You're just overly emotional." "Oooh, *some*body's hormonal." "Aren't you overreacting?" "Why are you still sad about that?"

I accepted what other people told me about myself to be true, and accepted that yeah, I guess I was too sensitive. I guess I was just too emotional. I guess maybe I was overreacting or not seeing things for what they were. And in doing so, in accepting other people's versions of me as my own truth, I did myself an incredible disservice—I taught myself not to trust myself, my gut, or my intuition.

It took me years to undo that level of damage, the kind of damage that is cultivated over decades and leaves you thinking, "It must be me who's crazy. It must be me who's seeing this wrong." The kind of damage that cuts deep into your self-worth and confidence as you start to believe in a visceral way that you and your feelings and your perceptions are wrong and that somebody else knows better. The kind of damage that teaches you to ignore all kinds of red flags while accepting all kinds of bad behavior and toxic patterning.

All because I had learned to stop listening to myself and what I KNEW to be true.

We often apologize for how we feel because we don't want to make others feel uncomfortable.

The root of the above statement means that *we* are uncomfortable with how we feel. Does that sound familiar? I would ask, "Why?" Why do your own feelings make you feel discomfort? What's hiding under those feelings that is making you feel awkward?

If you feel like you're "too sensitive," it might be time to look at the trapped emotions that feel overwhelming to you because they've never had the chance to safely come out, be expressed, be processed and then be allowed to move on. Go back through the last couple chapters and reread how to feel your feelings so that you are finally free to *heal* those feelings.

Stop apologizing for how you feel. For what you think. For the way in which you see the world.

Start being ultra-honest with yourself about what is true for you— even if it's unpopular with whomever it is you think you're trying to please—and choose to show up for yourself from a place of love and authenticity. Ignoring how we feel, refusing to acknowledge our feelings, or even apologizing for them is to ignore and dishonor our-*selves*. Living from a place of internal dishonesty or shame drives us to more complicated and unhealthy feelings that "what" and "who" we are is not enough and that we must be changed if we are to be accepted and loved.

Can you love yourself enough to stop apologizing for how you feel?

Yes, you fucking can.

CHAPTER 16

Mirror, mirror

"We don't see things as they are, we see them as we are."

~Anaïs Nin

I t's not about you.

Get out your pen and underline this empowering truth:

It.

Is not.

About.

You.

One of the greatest lessons in this life is that we are a reflection for others and others are a reflection for us—we see things as we are, at our given moment in life, reflected back to us. When you see something in someone you really like? It's a quality you possess, one that you really like, being reflected back to you.

And when someone really irks you or rubs you the wrong way? You guessed it. It's a quality you possess, one that you really *don't* like, being reflected back to you.

Further, it means that you are also a mirror for everyone around you, and when they see things in you that they love about themselves, they respond favorably, and when they see something in you reflected back to them that they don't like or that makes them uncomfortable about themselves, they tend to react *less* favorably.

Remember that kernel of playground wisdom from the jerk-face in grade three? "I'm rubber, you're glue; whatever you say bounces off of me and sticks onto you."

Turns out that jerk-face in grade three had a point. Often, when people criticize us for something, it's because we reflect a quality back to them that they're not sure they like. Conversely, when people share our joy and enthusiasm, it's usually because we reflect a quality back to them that appeals to them and that they are drawn to.

Let's say you are making a major life decision like quitting your job and starting your own business—basically, any of the things that can happen as a natural extension of adulthood, especially the part of adulthood that finds you "waking up" to wanting to find your own truth and not the one someone told you to be true for the first half of your life.

You think it through, weigh all your options, do your research, run the numbers and are confident that you are doing the right thing. You may be nervous or a little scared of the newness, sure, but you are certain that this is the exact right thing for you.

Proudly, you start to tell people about your decision, expecting that they will see your pride, see your happiness, see your joy at following a big-ass dream; you are following through on a very difficult and often courageous decision and bringing it into fruition. Now watch what happens. Some people will absolutely get it. They'll share your joy, celebrate the process it took to get there and the process it will take to move forward and support you as you make that big leap in your life and begin again.

Then there is the other faction, the people who (maybe shockingly) will *not* get it.

They'll question you, tell you you're making a mistake, tell their friends that you're crazy for making such a huge decision or taking such a massive risk. They'll criticize you for making this massive change and may even express genuine anger, disappointment, or fall out of touch because of it.

Are you familiar with this feeling? If you are, I bet you've been tempted to take people's feedback, both positive and negative, ultra-personally. But here's the thing: it actually isn't about you.

Inner child recoils in horror. Wait, what? But it's my decision! My life! My risk! My choice! My fucking happiness on the line here! What do you mean, woman, that it's not about me?

That's right, lovely, it's not about you; it's about *them*. You are merely a mirror, reflecting qualities in someone else back *onto* that someone else. No matter which camp people fall into, trust me, the ones who are most vocal are the ones whose mirror is the most reflective. For better or for worse.

Let's start with Team A, the Get-Its.

Chances are when you make a life-altering decision or otherwise bold move in this game of life, the Get-Its get it for a reason. They see qualities of growth, bravery, willingness to try, willingness to fail, confidence, unbridled enthusiasm, and the desire to dare live a big life, dream deeply, and pursue happiness. Maybe they live a life along the same guidelines and share that tenaciously courageous spirit. Maybe those are qualities they aspire to have and you are a sign or marker on their own path that they need to make some changes, and they feel like your experience gives them permission.

They see qualities of themselves right inside you, and they love it, so they celebrate you for it.

Now let's talk about Team B, the Soooo-Don't-Get-Its. When they see you making progress in your life, they might see all the same qualities that the Get-Its do . . . but they don't like it.

Most often the So-Don't-Get-Its are living with safety, some denial, and a *lot* of fear. So when you have the audacity to want more, want less, do better, break status quo, or push the ejector button on a situation—like a lucrative but soul-sucking job—they do not compute. For them to understand why you would do such a thing, they have to confront their own narrative in a highly self-aware way.

"Well, I hate my job too, but I would never leave! How could I? That's so selfish. Irresponsible! This is just the way it's supposed to be; you don't have to feel happy every day—that's just a fairy tale. A job is just supposed to be a means to an end, and it's a complete joke to think that you can find something better or more fulfilling. How dare you threaten to uproot the safety and well-being of your family just because 'you're not happy.'"

They see qualities of themselves right inside you, and sugar? They hate it, so they criticize you for it. Forgive them (we're going to talk about this in Part 3. Even if this sounds offensive or impossible, know that it's 100 percent possible, and freeing, and I can show you how to do that. In the meantime though, while we're here, if you're having a painful reaction to the idea of forgiveness, what does that reflect back to *you* in this moment? Oh snap, right?). Whatever their criticism is of you (and the more emotionally charged, the more this is true), you can almost be sure that you have reflected back a true insecurity or vulnerability of yours.

As an example, when I announced the end of my marriage, the feedback I got from people was shocking. Truly shocking. Absolutely, some people were incredibly supportive. Their feedback ranged from messages of congratulations, how can I support you, this is so brave to honor what you know in your heart, I know this must have been really hard for you, and I will be here for whatever you need. Those were the people who felt secure in their healthy relationships (or self-partnerships) and knew that me getting a divorce affected them in no way.

And then there were "the others." Their messaging ranged from how dare you, this is the worst thing you can do for your kids, you're making a huge mistake, you can't handle life on your own, you're going to be poor for the rest of your life, *now* who are we going to go to the cottage with, I full out do not support you, he's going to kill you for leaving him, are you sure you aren't hormonal, you have no idea what you're doing, maybe this is perimenopause talking, and my all-time favorite: "When we get married, we sign an agreement, all of us do. And you broke that pact; you pushed the ejector button. You're supposed to stay in and suffer through like the rest of us, cut the cake on your sixtieth anniversary together, and look back at the photos and think about what a happy life you had."

Quote.

Un.

Quote.

Now? I can't tell this story without laughing.

At the time? Oy. It felt crippling.

Some of this "feedback" came from people whose opinions didn't really matter to me . . . but most of it—*most of it*—came from people I thought were *so close* to me. And it felt devastating.

Knowing what I know now about our human experience and about how we process events in our lives and environments, I can connect some common threads here, namely that each of those people simply voiced their fears back to me: the people who stayed with abusive partners, unfulfilling marriages, sexless partnerships, feared being alone, stayed together for the "financial benefits." It really and truly was not about me, it was about me holding up a mirror that reflected some truths about their own lives that they didn't necessarily want to, or feel ready to, face.

And, knowing what I know now, I can say very matter-of-factly that that's okay. Why?

Because it's not about me.

Knowing this little jewel of information (that I bet you're now kicking yourself for having kicked jerk-face back in the day when he basically spat the words out in your face), you can rest easy that you can go ahead and make any old decision you want provided it's the right one for you: the clothes you wear, the company you keep, the relationships you stay in versus the ones you don't, the food you eat, the lifestyle you live . . . everything.

Everything you do is for the betterment of *you* and doesn't need to be proven or justified to anyone (although it's *hella* satisfying when someone doubts or criticizes you and you succeed anyway, let's be honest). Provided that you are not victimizing anyone along the way, this life is yours. You need to become the best version of you, for you. Because when you do, you bring out the best in everyone around you.

Even the naysayers. You've got to understand that they're working through their own process, at their own rate, in their own way too, and that's okay. That's the way it's supposed to be. Just by honoring your truest self and your feelings and living your version of what the most satisfying life is, you are lifting up the people around you. Challenging them. Inviting them to go deeper, to look harder, to dream bigger and more authentically. Asking "why" when they revert to simply going through the motions of the status quo.

Focus on that. Let others be a mirror for you; observe what you feel and what those qualities are bouncing back. Are they inviting you to go deeper? Think differently? Challenge some old pattern of thought that you haven't been ready to challenge yet?

When you become hyperaware that this is basically a house of mirrors we're all walking through, almost instantly you learn that you don't have to hang on to things as tightly as you once did. The outrage over "can you believe she *said* that to me?!" dissipates because now you *can* believe it: you know too well that she, too, is human and figuring out her own truths along the way. This knowledge is a wildly powerful gift because it allows you to let things go so much more easily and lessens the weight of whatever you're carrying. When you appreciate that we are each responsible for our own actions and feelings, you don't have to put so much effort into seeking out validation and approval from others about what you're doing, and you become aware that if it's the right thing for you to do, it's the right thing to do. No matter what other people may think or say.

Consequently, you no longer need to feel burdened by the actions of others because you can now appreciate that they, too, need to do what's right for them—it's not at all about you. And again, this knowledge enables you to let things go so much more easily because your value is not dependent on the action of any other than yourself.

When someone reflects something back to you that makes you uncomfortable? Have the courage to observe those feelings and ask what is happening within you when what is happening externally so clearly has nothing to do with you. Meanwhile, keep your mirror clean and polished so that when someone tries to throw something at you it bounces right back and nearly blinds them with the light.

Can you love yourself to look at what is being reflected back to you?
Can you love yourself to accept that which is not about you?

Yes, you fucking can.

CHAPTER 17

Healing is not linear

Our healing is not linear: it's a winding, twisting spiral that invites healing of each little part of ourself along the way, one part at a time. Remember we talked about the Self being made of many other selves, all under one umbrella? We're coming back to that notion here. So often people think, "Haven't I healed this already?" But what we often don't see is that while we may have healed something (say a fear of rejection) for one self, when we feel triggered by something around us, it's simply feedback alerting us to the fact that there is another part of our Self that is still hurting by this vulnerability and it, too, is now calling out for attention.

This notion is always so interesting to me because "what's wrong" or "what's bothering us" is seldomly what's actually wrong or actually what's bothering us. More often than not, something happens to trigger an old and wounded part of us, thus inviting us to go deeper and heal it too. When something is bothering you and more than likely causing the icky feelings of anger/resentment/jealousy/anxiety/bitterness, you can be sure you've just hit a trigger of something old and otherwise unattended by you that is waving and calling out to go deeper with it.

So go deeper with it. Circle back to your Taco Tivities (that I know you definitely and diligently completed), and ask yourself:

"What is the story I'm telling myself? And is that story true?"

Again, *these are the magic words.*

We are inundated with and driven by old beliefs, old narratives, and old stories that we inherited or have otherwise been told / picked up along the way. Typically, we're not aware that we believe them or if we even WANT to believe them. So when we are unwittingly triggered by something and start to emotionally freak the hell out, a really simple grounding technique is to prompt yourself with these magic words: "The story I'm telling myself is . . ." and trace it back as far as you can go until you get to the root. And THEN ask, "Is that story true?"

So, for example:

"I'm so mad that she is doing better than I am. The story I'm telling myself is . . . that I am not successful. The story I'm telling myself is . . . that I will never be successful. And if I'm never successful, the story I'm telling myself is . . . that I don't have any real value. Wait. Is that true? NO! So . . . do I really care that she's doing better than I am? Or do I focus on what I'm doing now and what I'm doing next? How can I use her success as an example of an end point and reverse engineer to how I can go step by step and be the success that I want to be too?"

And honestly, most of the time, as if by magic, the anxiety, resentment, dread, jealousy, anger . . . it just melts away.

Our thoughts hold a lot of power and are driven by our subconscious beliefs. We must be brave enough to challenge ourselves with these tough emotions if we want to grow and feel/act differently because challenging them is the only way to figure out where the fear they are based in is coming from.

We learn what we repeat, and what we repeat, we learn. Want to get really good at something? Even my little girls will tell you that "practice makes perfect." We tend to get better at the stuff we do over and over again. What's so POWERFUL here is that if you are repeating good and healthy patterns, you're learning great stuff and probably moving forward with a joyful life. But what if what you're repeating over and over is toxic or unhealthy? You just keep confirming THAT to be true. Which isn't "great."

The good news is, to break those old, unhealthy, or unwanted patterns (including patterns of thought as well as behavior), you replace them with new, healthy, purposeful patterns and you do them over and over. Then you do them over and over again after that. And you keep doing them UNTIL you have adopted them AS your new pattern.

It is the same as flexing a muscle—working it out and building it up to the point where it's so damn strong that you don't even have to think about that heavy lifting anymore, you're just doing the lifting and it doesn't feel heavy.

And now that you know we heal different parts of our Self at different times, when we feel subconsciously and emotionally safe to do so, we can start practicing more self-compassion for where we've come from and where we are.

That's the thing about grief, and about healing—they aren't linear. It's easy to look at the Kubler Ross model of grief that suggests our grief (leading to our subsequent healing) unfolds along five stages:

denial, anger, depression, bargaining, acceptance

Bam. Checklist complete.
Wound = healed.

But it doesn't work that way.

Grief is cyclical, and our healing is not linear. We experience each of these stages in succession and then we experience them again. And again. And just when we think we've run the course of grief, we find ourselves parked at a red light, or shopping in the cereal aisle at Walmart, and blamo! Suddenly out of nowhere it hits you again for a victory lap.

The trick to understanding our grief is that each cycle is okay to feel, which is part of why it is so important to be aware of our emotional health and wellness. You have to learn that "feeling" is not a four-letter word; it's a natural part of our human experience to feel, heal, repeat.

There isn't one final or complete state (other than death, I suppose)—we keep cycling through. And it's up to each of us to really become versed in our emotional health so that we can clearly navigate our own behavior, actions, and responses in a healthy way rather than feel tanked or overwhelmed by them.

This awareness is also part of what it means to come home to yourself—to know that nothing in your experience is necessarily good or bad, it just *is*. It just is a part of your experience, and when you allow yourself to process your feelings about an event during this experience, you are able to move through it in a much more peaceful, almost neutral way.

It's a very Buddhist or Zen-like approach to learn to be comfortable with all experiences life has to offer. Nothing is good or bad, it just *is*. All things come to pass, and the more we learn to simply appreciate what they are and as they are in this moment, the easier, richer, and more abundant our life becomes.

Think of the image of a wave: even if it comes crashing over you, know that it will subside. And each subsequent wave that comes crashing in will get gentler, especially as you learn to accept those crashing feelings of grief. When you know that they, too, will pass, you know it's safe for you to feel and release.

And that's okay. It's totally "normal" to experience this yin-yang dance of healing and grief, grief and healing. It's our acceptance that the two go together and unfold in waves over time that moves us forward. Helps us find peace. Helps us accept the things we simply cannot control, choosing instead to feel the joy of the moment and being honest about feeling the loss when the time is right.

A very intimate and personal example is that I lost my younger sister when she was twenty-one. She had just finished her winter exams in her final year of university. It was two weeks before Christmas, and she went on vacation to Mexico. She was with friends by the pool when her heart stopped suddenly, and she died on the spot.

It was awful. Beyond awful. Every part of it.

Losing my sister was a profound loss. Sibling relationships can be complicated, and very sadly, ours was. The diametrically opposed ways in which we were raised all but necessitated this dynamic, compounded by a seven-and-a-half-year age gap between us.

I knew when she graduated that she would likely move in with her boyfriend (who lived just three blocks from my house), and I had a joyful, intuitive gut feeling that when that happened, we would finally get to connect as adults in a way we hadn't been able to connect when we were growing up.

And then four months before that was supposed to happen, she died without any warning. The suddenness of her passing felt like a double loss: I mourned the loss of the sister I knew and loved, and the sister I was yet to know and love even more. I mourned the loss of the woman I knew would teach my kids to ride horses and sneak them licorice when I wasn't looking. And I miss her every day.

Even more powerfully, I feel her love and presence every day. Sometimes it's a clear and energetic presence, and sometimes it's the ridiculously ironic timing of something that can only be interpreted as a cosmic joke, and I can't help but laugh out loud because I know she played a role in orchestrating it. I see her in my dreams from time to time, and every now and then, if I'm really lucky, she'll pop up during a meditation to weigh in with what I should do at the cusp of making a difficult decision. I tell my kids stories about her, and we imagine what it would be like to have her here with us.

She's gone but never forgotten, and it feels like that grief can be processed in a healthy way, even if it's a wound that may never fully heal (if that makes sense). It's a dance of healing and grieving and the relationship between the two that helps create an intentional, peaceful life.

Our healing is not linear, and that's okay. It gives us the opportunity to get real with the true dialogue happening in our heads and find freedom in what we feel deeply is our real truth. And when we get to that freeing place of authenticity, we can start to gain clarity in what we want, confidence in who we are, and courage to stay true to both.

Can you love yourself enough to appreciate that every day is healing you in new ways?

Yes, you fucking can.

CHAPTER 18

Gratitude

I f there were *one* shortcut to healing, it would be gratitude. Gratitude is the ultimate game changer in terms of your mindset, perspective, and how you internalize the external world around you; it is the one subtle shift that *will* change your life forever.

Because perspective is *everything*.

Why practice gratitude? In short, because it makes you happier. Period.

We have created a world for ourselves that is suffering a plague of loneliness. The human condition is often to feel lonely on its own, but by living in more densely packed but isolated communities and with more and more of our interactions coming from digital channels and less from in-person interactions, it feels like we're getting lonelier.

And when we feel lonely, we can get to a dark place that feels as if we live in chaos—as if we are the only ones who feel what we feel, and that we are less understood and less connected than we'd like to be. And when self-love is low or not fully cultivated/developed, it can feel even more isolating.

The daily moment-by-moment mindful practice of gratitude kick-starts the *undoing* process of those feelings and reestablishes a baseline feeling of calm and connectedness to ourselves and to others. It's a way of slowing us down so we can appreciate all of the simple joy and wonder that is present in our lives *every day* and pulls us back to a feeling of peace in recognizing that.

You know that feeling when you find the black sweater you forgot you had and suddenly you're filled with joy? Gratitude is like that feeling over and over again: it's a subtle and joyful celebration of something so simple that adds so much value to your life, making you feel at home from the inside out.

Gratitude is a daily practice; it's a lifestyle. It is the ability to mindfully look at your life through the lens of "life is always giving, and I am always receiving." Gratitude is the process of becoming aware of how truly blessed we are to be alive, finding an appreciation of that awareness, and thanking the awareness for everything it offers to you—right down to a cellular level.

Gratitude is an essential component to living an abundant life; it continuously draws your awareness to *how much you already have* instead of what you are lacking. The fact that you woke up this morning in a comfy bed in a safe and clean and warm home with a heart that is beating and lungs that are breathing and food in the kitchen that your able-bodied self was able to turn into something that you have the luxury to taste while checking for cool photos and inspiration on Instagram, that is a whole series of things to be extremely grateful for that happen every day, likely without you even noticing.

(And a perspective head's up? For every one of you who is blessed with these luxuries, how many others are there, across the globe and in your own community, who can't say the same?)

More and more research supports the positive effects gratitude has on your mental health by not only focusing more energy on positive emotions, but in doing so, increasing levels of serotonin and dopamine. A grateful brain is one that sleeps easier and makes for a more resilient person in how you react to and cope with adversity, reaffirming that perspective really is everything. It's not what happens to you, but how you handle it when it does.

Consider this poem by the one and only Rumi:

The Guest House

This being human is a guest house.
Every morning a new arrival.

A joy, a depression, a meanness,
some momentary awareness comes
as an unexpected visitor.

Welcome and entertain them all!
Even if they are a crowd of sorrows,
who violently sweep your house
empty of its furniture,
still, treat each guest honorably.
He may be clearing you out
for some new delight.

The dark thought, the shame, the malice.
meet them at the door laughing and invite them in.

Be grateful for whatever comes.
because each has been sent
as a guide from beyond.

***

Happiness is a series of grateful moments.

We spend so much of our lives in the pursuit of happiness: "I just want to be happy," "I just want my kids to be happy," "I just want to make my parents happy," "I just want to make YOU happy." We say it over and over again and often believe that happiness is this place you reach, a destination you arrive at, when in fact, happiness is nothing of the sort. Happiness is a series of grateful moments, back to back to back.

One of the amazing things about adopting the daily lifestyle of practicing gratitude is that more begets more, meaning that once you are living in that "high-vibe" state of looking for, experiencing, and then acknowledging gratitude, you naturally attract more things into your life for which to be grateful. Much like forgiveness, gratitude becomes this incredible drug that you can have whenever you want and as much as you like.

After reading this book, you will be well on your way to deepening your emotional awareness and cultivating your emotional intelligence; you have the ability to feel and heal each of your emotions in a healthy and forward-moving way, which allows you to shift into gratitude genuinely, almost effortlessly.

I like to use the analogy of a highway running through your brain with the cars on that highway representing little moments of happiness. You see one go by, you feel happy; you see another, you feel happy again. And when you are in the habit of practicing gratitude daily, more and more and more of these cars appear and you feel increasingly happier for longer as the cars start to jam together in one big pileup traffic jam of happiness. And YOU are the one who is in control of adding more little happiness cars to that highway.

This shift into gratitude is a simple mindset hack that is constantly available to you no matter what your circumstances. It just depends on how you choose to see things, which lens you choose to look through, and how you game the system of your mind.

So how do you game the system of your mind to see things differently, especially when everything just feels so tedious and hard and stuck?

Like this:

"Ugh, I have to go to the grocery store; what a pain in the ass."

Shifts to:

"I am so grateful that when my family and I need to eat, I walk into a room literally filled with food, choose whatever I want off the shelf, and take it home with me."

And then:

"My bills were $1,000 this month? What the hell?"

Shifts to:

"I am so grateful for the constant access I have to clean running water. How cool is it that I flip a switch and my house becomes bright and warm? I love that when I want to stay in touch with my friends and family, engage in culture, or learn any single thing in the world, all I have to do is pick up my phone or open my laptop; what a gift."

This:

"It took so long for my kids to go to bed tonight! I get so annoyed when they take up extra time in the evenings. I'm tired too!"

Shifts to:

"Wow, that was a challenging evening. I know not all nights will be like that, and I'm grateful that my kids are of an age in which they want to be with me and cuddle."

And this:

"I feel like crap; I can't believe how sick I am."

Shifts to:

"This cold does not feel great, but I appreciate the sign from my body that I need to slow down and rest. I'll take it. Hello, Netflix marathon."

Practicing gratitude was the beginning of a massive mental shift in my own life.

When I realized how much I had around and in my life without ever really appreciating it, it was pretty jarring. Someone suggested to me that I start practicing gratitude if I wanted to become truly aware of the richness in my life instead of focusing on the lack.

I was raised in such a way that I found a crumb of praise and a modicum of sense of belonging for judging others and being generally cynical about the world. It really felt that my parents were the only ones who knew how to do everything right, and it was the rest of the world that was wrong. And so I learned to participate in that, which, if you've ever experienced this environment, is incredibly toxic.

I spent twenty years comparing, criticizing, and cutting down just to seek approval, which ironically, I never got. The switch to feeling grateful and appreciating and accepting versus feeling resentful, jealous, and judgmental was huge. Having had twins and going through the awareness that no one is perfect and everyone is figuring it out had laid the base for this switch. I found a new compassion for people around me and in knowing how hard I was trying, and I eventually made peace with doing my best and having that be enough.

When I started practicing gratitude, I reverted a bit, which was uncomfortable. It started with really trivial and shallow things like: "So glad my hair doesn't look like that" and "Am I ever lucky my jeans look this good." It was far more judgmental than I'd been. But I forced myself to keep practicing; I knew enough about habits that maybe this was just a new one to form and would take some time.

I was consciously thankful for everything in my life, and it got easier. Four days later, I felt like a changed woman:

"Can you believe this sun? Wow, running water from a tap? How lucky are we? As if I can just walk over to the wall and flick on a switch and instantly have light and heat! Legs! How wonderful is it to have legs?!"

I felt like a stranger visiting for the first time and truly began to see everything in a new light.

Here are some gratitude-based Taco Tivities to help shift your mindset into a gratitude lifestyle.

Grateful heart meditation

Before you go to sleep, while you're lying in bed, slow down your breathing to make it steady and so that you feel relaxed. In that state, allow yourself to recap your day and highlight what you are grateful for. List at least five things (no matter how insignificantly small or unimportant they are) that you are grateful for today in this moment. Watch your life change. This is a daily practice.

Grateful for this moment, on repeat

Happiness really is found in the moments. So when you have a moment that feels great, capture it with your heart by saying "grateful for this moment." Think of it like a snapshot of happiness you're taking with your heart camera. Take it, feel it, hang on to it, and repeat it every single time it happens. Watch your life change. This is a daily practice.

TACO TIVITY 8

Perspective quick flip

When you hear or feel yourself getting negative about something, challenge yourself to find the gratitude in it because there is always something to be grateful for. Flip back through these last few pages for some simple and real-life examples and watch your life change. This is a daily practice.

What am I learning that I don't yet know? (part one)

Hard truth: There are going to be some challenging moments in your life, and those moments can easily lead you to despair. When that happens, have the courage to dig deep and be grateful for the lesson you are learning (that you don't yet know you're learning). Some things only start to make sense after (or even *way* after) the fact. There is peace in accepting that sometimes you just don't understand what or why but be open to the reality that you will take away something of value no matter how hard it is now. With that mindset, watch how your life changes. This is a daily practice.

***

And when there's nothing to be grateful for?

Ha, ha! Tricked you, sweet pea! There is *always* something to be grateful for. Always. Gratitude is a daily practice; gratitude is a lifestyle.

So even if everything feels completely out of whack, nothing is aligned, and it all just feels really hard?

You still have the air in your lungs. Close your eyes, breathe deeply in, and appreciate the quiet beauty in that.

Can you love yourself enough to shift into gratitude?
Can you love yourself enough to be grateful for the air
in your lungs?

Yes, you fucking can.

CHAPTER 19

Grit + Grace

In my mid to late twenties, my (then) partner and I bought a house in an up-and-coming neighborhood in the east end of Toronto. It was just on the cusp of being gentrified, which meant that when we first bought our house, people were doing crack deals in the alley behind it, and by the time we left a few years later, you could play a drinking game involving taking a shot every time you'd see a stroller . . . and you'd be hammered about five minutes in.

We lived there with our first baby (who was actually born in the guest bedroom of that house), some crack addicts in the alley, and a family of relentlessly pesky raccoons hell-bent on transitioning their tree house to inside our roofline.

If you've ever lived in an urban environment where raccoons cohabitate with you, you'll know they are like some kind of freak zombie hybrid animal: they aren't really wild, and they aren't really domesticated. Specifically,

+ They are unfazed by human interaction

+ They no longer have a reliable food source that comes from nature[3]

Also, they have surpassed the normal-size-range expectation of a raccoon in the wild, and to the untrained eye, they look a lot more like bear cubs than they do the wily, ringed-eye bandits from the cartoons of our youth.

At the risk of sounding like an eighty-two-year-old woman, they really are a nuisance. Even though they rely on humans to provide their food supply, they remain super fierce when under any signal of perceived threat to their safety. When you reach the point of having to strategically time your walk home or carry your garbage out to the curb so as to avoid a raccoon run-in, you know that there's been a tipping point.

So one night I decided to take back my humanness and no longer be subservient to these highly invasive creatures that were doing their best to burrow in the six-inch gap between my neighbor's semidetached house and mine.

It was dusk in the late spring, and my darling baby girl was tucked into her sling on my hip, hanging around our kitchen before I started her nightly bath and bed routine.

I looked out into our tiny backyard/patio and saw the familiar sight: a nursery of raccoons making their way down the neighbor's tree trunk, then up the fence and onto our patio. That was enough. I refused to let these vermin feel at home anymore. So with babe on hip, I went outside and waited. When the leader of the pack got closer, I waved my arms and made some (what I thought were) intimidating noises but soon realized my presence alone would not deter.

---

3 Unless you consider the neighborhood garbage and recycling night "a reliable food source that comes from nature."

It was mama a mama. *See what I did there?*

I picked up the garden hose and, with the nozzle on full-jet-stream mode, sprayed the raccoon mom square in the face between the eyes. And I swear, *I swear*, I watched as she took a breath, dug her claws into my patio, braced herself for what was to come, and looked me dead in the eye as if to say "bring it."

I was in complete disbelief.

She did not give a shit about me *or* my jet-stream hose. She knew she needed to feed her family, and she knew what it would take and what she would have to endure to make it happen. And that look in her eye of total and utter "I will do what it takes, and I will beat you" kinda startled me. So I gave up. I threw down the hose and ran inside, not too proud to concede my defeat. But even now, so many years later, I will never forget that look of sheer determination.

I will never forget it because I've lived it—the feelings that result in that same look. That same deep-breath moment of knowing a jet stream of unpleasantness and discomfort is headed my way, will hit me straight between the eyes, and that I will do what it takes to get through it in order to take care of myself and my family.

I think as women we each have at least one of those defining moments, the one that makes us feel like we have actually dug in our claws/heels and braced ourselves for what's to come, all the while remaining steadfast.

This is how we learn to handle our shit with grit and grace.

We dig in, buckle up, and brace ourselves for what we know is not the first of our challenges, and certainly not the last. And each time we do so, we come through it stronger, more confident, and even more ready for the next. Too often I think we are fed the notion that you can be either soft or fierce. Gentle or assertive. Peaceful or vocal.

And this notion is seriously misguided. Each of us possesses the necessary qualities and skills to exist in the space of both/and, not either/or. You can absolutely be both soft and fierce. You can 100 percent be both gentle and assertive. And by all means, you are certainly allowed to be both peaceful and vocal.

You don't have to choose; you can be both/and.

And as we get more confident in being both/and, and relentlessly doing what feels right and true and authentically us, we celebrate each win quietly *with* ourselves, knowing that once again we can do anything—whatever it takes to stand our ground—for as long as that feels right.

*Even if that celebration means pooping on the deck and eating through a bag of leftover Vietnamese take-out containers.

Glennon Doyle said, "We can do hard things," and when I first read that statement, it felt like uncovering a secret power: *we can do hard things* because we have done hard things before and have always made it through to the other side, alive and breathing, to tell the tale.

Grateful for the air in my lungs.

Remember, nothing is truly good or bad, it just *is*, and all things come to pass. And if it just *is*, and all things come to pass, then even if it's hard in the moment, this too shall come to pass, leaving (mostly) lessons in its wake.

After enough practice in doing hard things, you get that feeling of knowing exactly what has to be done, and exactly why you have to do it, and then the fear kinda melts away and is replaced by confidence and knowing.

So buckle up. Dig in. Know that whatever is coming your way—even if it's hitting you head on in a jet stream right between the eyes—you can do it. And when you do, you will emerge proud, strong, resilient, and still standing.

Change is not easy; still, it is required for this process of coming home to ourselves. Knowing that change is the only constant, because all things come to pass, we can shift into the mindset that really, change is predictable. And while we can't necessarily control the "hows," "whens," "whats," or "whys," we can absolutely control how we react and respond. And choosing to react to grit with grace is a powerful place from which to operate.

Can you love yourself enough to live your life with grit and grace?

Yes, you fucking can.

CHAPTER 20

Present-moment living

I was thinking of calling this chapter "A Brief Lesson in Quantum Physics" but didn't want to scare you off.

Wait! Don't leave! This chapter is really important, and I'm going to keep it as simple as possible. Because, quantum physics.

What you need to know for our specific purposes in expanding your emotional awareness, deepening your emotional intelligence, and truly learning how to come home to yourself, is this:

The present moment is the only thing that is real.

When you strip away drama (fear), worry (fear), anxiety (fear), and resentment (yep, also fear), it's actually pretty easy to see that:

+ The past is already over
+ The future is yet to come
+ The present moment is the only thing that is real

At a soul level, we know this to be true, unequivocally.

At a soul level, it is easy to live in the present moment and choose to be here now, trusting that every single thing that has happened is happening and will happen is already designed with perfect timing and execution for us.

At a soul level, all we need to do is show up and trust the flow.

The human design flaw here? Our mind doesn't really know the soul's plan and is our built-in security system (remember?); so while our soul is all chill and just taking things as they come, knowing that this is all working out exactly as it should (which is true), our mind is hard at work trying to protect us from perceived fears:

Yeah, but I'm single; what if I'm single *forever?*
Yeah, but I'm broke; what if I'm broke *forever?*
Yeah, but I really fucked up; what if I keep fucking up *forever?*
Yeah, but I'm hurting; what if I'm hurting *forever?*

Your mind is just doing its job by raising red flags every time it perceives something fearful to be true. And remember, it doesn't know the difference between "OMG, it's a bear!" and "OMG, I lost my job!" and "OMG, they were *judging* me!"

If you want to truly feel at peace, truly feel at home with yourself, you have to override that security system and sink deeper into trusting that your soul already has a plan for you, and it is perfect. EVEN when things are happening (or *not* happening) to your personal preference, you need to teach yourself to literally go with the flow and trust every lesson, every roadblock, every disappointment, every plot twist, and every failure as a perfectly designed stepping-stone on your life path to get you where you're going.

You have to trust that everything that has come before has brought you here, and here is exactly where you need to be in order to get to where you're going next to fulfill your soul-driven purpose.

You also have to trust that while you have a strong vision of where you're going and what that looks like, your soul will ultimately lead you to exactly where you need to be, when you need to be there, and doing what you need to be doing with whomever you need to be doing that with.

It's a mind bender, and it's also a profound truth: "Now" is the only thing that is real. Keep trusting in the perfection of this moment and truly just *being* in it without holding on too tightly to what happened in the past or worrying / fantasizing about what will or will not happen in the future.

The present moment is the only thing that is real, and all you have to do is trust the process.

Can you love yourself enough to trust the process?

Yes, you fucking can.

CHAPTER 21

The art of failure

F ear of failure is a real holdback.

So let's take a hot minute to dig into how to channel that fear of failing, and the act of failing itself, into something forward-moving.

If we let it, our crushing fear of failure will be the thing that holds us back from doing what we want, getting what we want, being who we want. You have already learned now that sometimes "what is wrong" isn't really what is wrong. You've also learned that our feelings are just feedback, inviting us to pay attention to what still needs to be tended to and healed.

Often, a "fear of failure" is the manifestation of a fear of being judged, followed closely by the fear of actually getting what you want.

One plays on our deep insecurities of never being good enough (confirming that "they were right all along"), and the other is very closely tied to the subconscious mind: when we start to succeed, we are also challenging the previous system and narrative of self-doubt and imposter syndrome and are replacing it with the hard-earned narrative that we are, in fact, worthy or capable of receiving what we've been asking for and working toward.

The trick is to appreciate these fears for what they are and keep forging ahead.

Personally speaking, I have "failed" *a lot* in my life, some fails being more spectacular than others.

(Of course, you just learned recently that when you have the courage to trust your soul, trust the process, trust the timing of your life, and just be here in the moment, you're never really failing but instead stepping along the path laid out for you. But stay with me here for bigger-picture context.)

One of the biggest, most spectacular fails happened just after my marriage ended. I was freshly minted as a single woman, hell-bent on rising from the ashes and reinventing myself with a new career—one with purpose and prestige, meaning and respect, overnight.

I met a dude with whom I fell in love (oomph, *fail*), and he hired me to initially work on one freelance project for his advertising agency consultancy. I was so keen to prove myself (in love and business) that I worked my ass off. Our relationship was very much like the one Molly Bloom has with that super skeezy, ultra-sleazy guy in the memoir/film *Molly's Game*, and my responsibilities were similar in nature, ranging from purchasing and delivering the underwear he liked (at my expense) to writing background "fact pack" briefs on potential clients and brands we were pursuing, on behalf of other clients and brands, which I'm pretty sure crossed the line on Internet stalking. The woman I am today looks back with great compassion for the woman I was then—just so desperate to be seen and heard and valued that she kept lapping up any crumbs of affection or attention—even from true-blue, pathologically lying, misogynists like "Christopher."

Fail.

He so liked my work ethic and complacency to do whatever the hell he asked (he often used the carrot and stick analogy for his leadership style) that he "hired" me full time. With no contract (*ugh, fail*). I shuttered the agency I ran with my partner and worked for him, often from 6:00 a.m. to 2:00 a.m., schlepping children around to full-day camp to accommodate my schedule. I based my separation agreement on the $100,000 salary he promised me, agreeing to far less in that separation plan than I was legally entitled to, to the extent my lawyer made me sign an affidavit that she had strongly recommended I not sign the agreement at all.

But here I was, so confident that I would be banking six figures within the next calendar year that I was reckless in the strategy of executing this binding legal agreement.

Dou.
Ble.
Fail.

Have you seen either of the Fyre Festival documentaries that came out? The dude I worked for (*fail*) was almost *identical* in his "operational sociopathic personality" to Billy McFarland. (Note: If you haven't watched these docs, *do*.) He had a silver tongue and a megalomaniac personality.

I thought it was odd that I hadn't been paid once in six months and that I had been asked to pay our interns $5,000 of my own money because "we were waiting for clients to pay us." But still, I knew we had clients—international clients!—who were legit and prestigious global ad agencies. I assumed it would just be a matter of time (*fail*) before he paid me.

And so I carried on working my ass off, which was not limited to planning strategy for Toronto and New York ad agencies, picking up the underwear I told you about, dropping off his dry cleaning, hiring a private investigator in New York to get dirt on the executive of a major sandwich chain we were targeting, and calling random girls in Christopher's cell phone who'd texted him but who he couldn't *quite* remember the names of after sleeping with them to find out who they were and what they looked like. Why? So he could figure out how he'd met them, when they'd slept together, and whether he'd like to sleep with them (or their friend) again.

FAIL. FAIL. FAIL. FAIL. FAIL.

I was blind.

I was hurting, I was desperate, I was willfully naïve . . . and I was still, somewhere in my gut, *certain* that this was the right place for me to be.[4] Eight months later, I realized there was no money, there was no prospect, and that I'd been had. Completely taken advantage of. He came up with excuse after excuse as to why he hadn't paid me yet and assured me over and over that it was coming. Then he had a $30,000 tax bill he hadn't paid; then his ex-wife was taking all his

---

4 I remain confident that the level of trust I had in the moment was a cosmic bread crumb, and I believe wholeheartedly that despite the many layers of shitstorm Christopher brought into my life, I absolutely would not be where I am today without that experience.

money. It went on and on. I quit, unable to cope with the demands of his borderline emotional abuse and total absence of paycheck, *still believing* that I would be paid in due time—at the bare minimum, what I had lent him.

Two years of correspondence and three bounced checks later, the heavy reality set in that he had been lying the entire time, had never had any intention of paying me, and that the last few months had been a colossal scam. Years later, I ran into his best friend and former roommate who, when I told him what had happened, informed me that he was in the middle of a legal battle with Christopher after learning he had stolen *and maxed out* his credit card during that same window.

I was out a shit ton of money and pride.

Fail.

However.

Among all that failure, and all the *shame* that went with it, I learned so much in the process of working together, not least of which was how smart, strategic, and capable my business acumen is, previous example of trust issues notwithstanding.

It was not uncommon for Christopher to delegate 90 percent of our work to me, prepping and planning for major meetings and presentations with the head honchos of global ad agencies whose bullshit meters are finely tuned to see through people who don't know what they're doing. I remember one particular phone call with Christopher in the middle of the night when I was self-sabotaging an epic presentation we had planned to deliver to New York City.

It was crazy. We were so close to sending this presentation off, I had worked so hard on it, and I literally could not finish it. I was exhausted, mid-divorce, and solo parenting, and just as I got close to the finish line on what felt like it would be a success, all my subconscious fears raged up and flooded my brain with messages of incompetence.

That night/morning (it was 2:00 a.m.), Christopher used a tone of voice no one had ever used before with me. He laid out that failing was not an option. I was one of the smartest people he'd ever worked with and that I had a responsibility to *myself* to follow through and get this presentation done—perfectly. I don't know if he was scared and blowing smoke up my ass, or if he found a moment to be genuine and sincere with what he really thought about me. What I do know is that it didn't matter. That state, that command tonality, that relentless end game that *this would be a success because of me* changed me. Permanently. That moment shifted something in my subconscious that released a previously pervasive narrative of self-doubt.

It was also not uncommon for Christopher to be too hungover to make it to meetings downtown, and I would often arrive only to find out it would be me, and only me, with the CFO and CEO of the agency. And in those conditions (when once again I was certain a team of secret agents in hazmat suits would descend from the ceiling to remove me for being the imposter I was) when I *over delivered* and impressed the C Suite with my smarts, authenticity, and uncommon sense approach to problem solving . . . I was healed.

Having to confront my own demons time after time like this taught me I knew more than I thought I did, I was capable of more than I thought I was, and that I truly had a knack for writing, so long as I wrote honestly and from my heart.

After I quit working for that total D bag (who yes, taught me some invaluable life lessons across the entire spectrum of life lessons to learn), I now had a ton of experience on my résumé. I had connected with an entire industry of contacts that, just one year prior, would have had zero interest in seeing my résumé as "former Montessori teacher, columnist, and stay-at-home mom."

Life is a funny beast. And through all those pivotal moments of the many mistakes I made, the many red flags I ignored, I am painfully aware that it was *that* experience that connected me to all the right people and all the right abilities I had buried within me for thirty years of my life.

This is the art of failure: to make a colossal mistake, or series thereof, and still have the ability to reframe each and every one to be purposeful in bringing you here, to this moment, so that you can be ready to move forward and onto the next.

Can you love yourself enough to reframe your own "failures" as stepping-stones to your success?

Yes, you fucking can.

CHAPTER 22

Confronting your fear of failure

"What would you attempt to do if you knew you could not fail?"

Someone gave me a pewter paperweight with this question engraved on it when I was seventeen, and it's never left my mind. While I used to use it as a hammer, before I owned a real hammer, its words continue to hold more meaning, as I have come to understand the power of what those words hold in store for me, and more importantly, for you.

If I can be very humbly honest with you? I am happy to say that I love my life, I love myself, and I am proud of each of the scary things I've tried and faced along the way that brought me here. In addition to everything I've told you about my own experiences so far, effectively using each event as an opportunity to teach myself to rewire virtually *all* my thinking patterns to believe in the good in me and others, I have also bought my own house, entered and came second in a karaoke competition, driven the Pacific Coast Highway solo in a convertible from L.A. to Seattle (in three days), told off an Italian sailboat captain—in French—when he was violating my safety on board, and lived to tell all of the tales as a stronger person than I was before.

I understand what it means to face adversity on an intimate level. And *still*, I sometimes feel the fear of failure.

No matter how many things I say yes to, no matter how many times I find myself on the other side of challenge, no matter how often I heave the sigh of "Oh my gosh, I DID it!" relief, I still have residual fears of failing.

And to be honest, I'm cool with it. Why? Because I am so aware of the purpose our fears serve.

Our fears *always* serve a purpose; they are designed to warn us of danger to our immediate environment and that's a really good thing. When we stop and listen to that fear and that fear alone, however, we are holding ourselves back from so many good things that we might not even know we are capable of having or experiencing. The truth is, yes, when you try something new, you might fail. Which sucks. Heck, when you try something old, you might fail. Which also sucks. The immediate feeling of failure just plain *sucks*.

But you know what? The flip side is that in trying something new, in repeating something old, *you just might succeed.*

Which feels amazing.

If you strip away the emotion, judgment, shame, and fear of being vulnerable, you are left with a literal 50/50 chance: you might fail and you might succeed. And when you have the courage and the self-love to go through the process of stripping away, you can see rationally that if it's a dead split between the two options that it makes sense to err on the side of possibility.

Allow yourself to get into a place of removing: "I can't. I might lose. I might get hurt." Thank those feelings for the purpose they served, then kick them to the curb.

Rephrase that thinking with: "This might just work" and "This might just be easy." Because it's true; you might not be able to. You might lose. And it might hurt, but you have an equal if not greater chance of this being the thing that totally works in your favor (and now, even if it isn't yet the right thing, you know how to reframe each failure as simply the next stepping-stone along your path to get to where you're going).

You are worth too much and have too much life in you to waste worrying about "what if." Come back to the present moment. This life is for the *living*, and truly *living* is about pursuing joy, chasing passion and pleasure, and trying and learning—over and over again.

The outcome never matters as much as the lesson you learn along the way.

Each person, each experience, each situation is an opportunity to give and receive, moving you one step further along on this winding road of life.

Failure is, at times, inevitable. For all of us. That relationship you launched into but just weren't ready for, the job you left that was not a good fit, the marriage you were (but are no longer) in, the great idea you had that fizzled out, the smart and savvy (at the time) investment you made that never paid out, the business you started and had to close, the karaoke song you tried but couldn't hit the high notes on—hell, the shade of paint you chose for your dining room that needed to be redone very soon after.

Sometimes we just don't get it right the first time around. So knowing that yes, this is a human truth, think about how you react when you *do* fail. How can we use failure as a means of getting closer to success?

Here are two of the most important things we need to know about failure:

1. Every time we fail, we learn.
2. The fear of failure is (usually) worse than failure itself.

We need to accept that we are all flawed. We are human and are in a constantly looped cycle of try, fail, learn, repeat. This is called evolution, yo. There is no such thing as perfection; perfection is a total illusion. Yes, we experience perfect moments, and sometimes those moments are blissfully longer than others, but there is no perfect state. We live our whole lives tangled up in these bodies on a journey of discovery. Cheesy, but true.

Our deeply rooted fear of failure is often disguising a fear of judgment. You know those nasty feelings: "What will people say when I tell them this relationship/business/marriage/ hair-brained scheme / terrible song choice / shade of white on my wall didn't work out? Oh my God, what will people think of ME when I tell them I flopped?! What a flake I am; I can't hold down a friendship let alone a romantic relationship. I can't follow through with my ideas. I can't even 'Robyn it up' on karaoke night OR pick a freaking dining room paint color properly. What the hell is wrong with me?"

Learning to let go of those judgments, both real and perceived, (and that nasty, crippling negative self-talk), is a good place to start in overcoming your fear of failure. It is safe to say that some of the most successful people you will ever know (or know of) have tried more new things, taken more risks, failed more than your average bear, and learned from each and every one of those experiences. (This would be your cue to Wikipedia Steve Jobs, Michael Jordan, and Einstein, for starters.)

These people are also the ones who give approximately zero fucks about what other people might think. They just live their life, commit to their purpose, make their mistakes, learn their lessons, try again, and eventually come to a place in which they have an eye-popping story to tell at dinner parties. (Or, you know, reinvent technology as we know it. Just saying.)

Fear holds us back from not only doing but trying. We're so terrified of getting it wrong that we forget we have an equally strong chance of getting it right. In order to start something, you just have to get started; it's that simple. And I *really* wish I could tell you not to worry, that the guy you've been seeing, the rotisserie chicken stand you've been wanting to open, the app you've decided to get in on the ground floor of, and the karaoke contest you've entered will all come up rosy and awesome. I also don't want to lie to you. And sometimes, shit just does not work out. Timing is off, something beyond your control is misaligned, the DJ isn't paying attention . . . sometimes, despite our best freaking intentions, things don't go as we planned.

And when we're right about being wrong, and actually do fail, how do we embrace that failure as a lesson we learn from so that we can move on? A lot of it comes from detaching our success from our value. Oh yeah, you knew self-love was going to be a part of this, didn't you? You need to detach what you do from who you are. Just because your action failed does not make you a failure. You need to dig down and find the resiliency to try again. And when it comes to relationships, and business, I get it: this is no easy feat.

You may have to force yourself to sort through the layers of twistiness that can happen in failure and learn the lesson. I bet if you practice, you'll learn a boatload of lessons. Grab a pen, or open up Notes on your phone, and think of a time in which you still feel some judgment or shame from feeling. Sounds like a real treat, I know. But trust me here. When (not *if*, but *when*) we mess something up, we can learn from it and then use that learning to push forward.

Boom. Success.

While it completely sucks that your biz didn't work out, how great is it that you learned a shit ton about your abilities to start, stop, and bounce back in the meantime? Maybe all that back and forth required in dealing with town officials will steer you toward a career more oriented in public service or local politics. Who knows?

When (not *if*, but *when*) we mess something up, we can learn from it and then use that learning to push us forward. Boom. Success. You have to keep that belief at the forefront of your mind and have the courage to try again, building on what you learned the last time around.

Full disclosure: You will very likely not get over your fear of failure in the above 1,500 words. But if you allow it, you will let in this seed of contrast to an old pattern of thinking that you'll probably mess it up anyway so what's the point in even trying, right?

Well, lovely, here's the point in trying:

My kids have this book about a girl who loves to invent wild and zany things. When her uncle laughs her off after a failed cheese-copter invention (hello, where have YOU been my whole life, cheese-copter?!), she is reluctant to build anything new ever again. After some gentle coaxing, she builds a plane that lifts up for a hot minute then crashes down. She can't even. She's just done—and dejected. But in the meantime, her great-great-aunt is at her side, celebrating. Why? Because just before it crashed . . . it flew. It fucking flew.

There is nothing more tragic in this life than playing it safe the whole damn time. So coming back to the beginning, what would you attempt to do if you knew you couldn't fail? Please. Do that.

And what if you fall? My lovely . . . what if you fly? You will never know until you try.

Leap. Risk. Fall. Try again.

Try it and be smart about it. Learn how to fail with grace and let that be your success.

So go ahead and love. Go ahead and be vulnerable. Go ahead and do the thing. Do it scared and do it anyway. It's the only way to give your fear of failure the finger, and come out better, and more you, on the other side.

Can you love yourself enough to face your fear of failure?

Yes, you fucking can.

CHAPTER 23

Facing the fear of getting what you want

Have you ever had the experience of wanting something, imagining something, craving to be a part of something and then work and work to get there—and when you do, you feel just a little let down or unsure that you even want it anymore? Imagine you're taking a trip to the Grand Canyon. You've thought about it, imagined it, Pinned all the images of all the views, saved your money, bought the ticket, and finally put it all into action only to show up and question "is this it?" and think "oh, here it is. Guess we can go for tacos now."

There is this natural and backward-feeling "phenomenon" that tends to happen to many of us when we finally get what we want and what we've been waiting for: we freak the fuck out. And it doesn't feel "great."

Our freak-out can come in many forms: self-doubt, boredom, imposter syndrome, and my personal favorite and longtime default reaction to good things happening, self-sabotage.

You see it in athletes who achieve Major League success then start to self-destruct with substance abuse, you see it in celebrities who burn too hot too fast and fall apart with doubt over their creative abilities, and I bet you see it a lot closer to home in your own life too.

You'll recognize it because the freak-out tends to show up *just* as something good—and likely something great—is happening in your life:

+ You struggle for years with infertility and the many layers that go with it, get approved in the adoption process or have success with IVF, then start to resent your baby
+ You work and work to build your brand and career, start to realize the strides you've made professionally, then find ways to push back deadlines, under deliver on projects, and ultimately tank the progress you've made so far
+ You battle weight gain and body image, find a fitness and nutrition plan that suits your lifestyle, start to see the results you've been waiting for, and promptly binge on a whole whack of foods that you know will undo your hard work

You hope and pray for the partner of your dreams, they finally show up and make you feel seen, heard, loved, appreciated, safe, and secure, so *naturally* you push them away and run screaming in the opposite direction while listing "all the reasons" the relationship won't work.

We are a strange breed, my lovely, a very strange breed. This kind of a reaction usually stems from a dark and shadowy place that many of us, even the most self-aware of us, aren't fully aware exists. And the painful part can be that this dark and shadowy place tricks us into believing something we can see with our own eyes isn't true but just can't seem to convince ourselves of otherwise.

You see, even if you've done "the work" and practice a deep love of self, there can be some icky and damn near painful subconscious beliefs that rear their ugly heads when things start to go well for you. That's the voice that pops up when you're *this* close to getting what you want and tells you on some visceral level "this is not for you" and makes it feel as if you are being forced into acting in a self-destructive way.

I dated a life-changingly *wonderful* man with a PhD in psychology who not only showed me what it felt like to be loved *as you are* but also told me that any time one of our internal systems changes we go through a massive transition, and as you likely know by now, transition is painful and hard because it's our evolution and transformation as we move from what *was true* in our lives to what *is true* in our lives.

It's uncomfortable AF.

When he gave me this explanation, I think I rolled my eyes and protested in doubt because how is it possible that we can react negatively to something so positive? Well, it turns out that it's very possible.

You've already read about establishing patterns of behavior in our earliest years; in those early years, we create attachments that are either secure or insecure and those inform the patterns of behavior we engage in for the rest of our lives until we consciously choose to do otherwise. And if you are someone who developed an insecure attachment as your baseline pattern, then what feels healthy, normal, and good to you is very likely unhealthy, dysfunctional, and bad for you.

No pressure, right?

The issue with having an insecure attachment is often that unless a person, environment, situation, or experience causes you to feel a little uneasy (like you might be rejected at any moment; that you're probably not good enough to have whatever it is you're having; and you sure as hell aren't worth the time, energy, or effort someone or something is awarding you), you will feel a little out of your element. Because in the presence of these *(hella dysfunctional)* feelings, you look for and complete your confirmation bias that yes, you are in fact unworthy of love and attention. And that (as fucked up as it sounds) is what keeps your subconscious brain feeling happy and satisfied.

That is the pattern of baseline security your brain has always known—even though it isn't healthy—and that is where it wants to stay.

So when you, my magical creature, have the *audacity* to dream, act courageously with intention and bravery, explore, create, inspire, love, be loved, and stand with confidence and pride in your truth, your subconscious brain engages you with the tantrum of a lifetime. This is your subconscious mind's way of desperately begging and pleading with you to stay in the space it knows intimately, even if that space is what keeps you underwhelmed and unhappy, feeling like you're constantly walking in circles, and unable to find the thing you've been searching for.

Told you—we're a very strange breed.

What's more, if you are even the least bit self-reflective about your thoughts and feelings (which clearly you are), on top of the tantrum your ego is having on the inside, you'll likely see how actually *crazy* it feels to freak out about something good happening. And when you are aware of the absurdity of freaking out over something good happening, you'll likely start to experience those big and powerful feelings of shame that go on top of it all: "Who am I to have these feelings? I'm upset about my success? I finally meet the man of my dreams, and now I'm not so sure I want this at all? I just invested two years of my life writing a book that I don't even want to publish anymore? What the fuck is wrong with me?"

So now, on top of battling the fear of being "found out" as afraid, and of rejection, and of loss of self and identity, you're dealing with shame—easily the most destructive feeling we can experience.

How do we move through it? How do we face the fear of getting what we want?

The good news is that you're already here and reading these words. The better news is that if they resonate with you in any way, you are already naming the thoughts, fears, and feelings you're having, and that, my darling, is a great thing. When I heard Brené Brown speak at a conference in L.A., she said "shame thrives in secrecy," so by naming your experience, and sharing it with your journal, a trusted friend, coach, or therapist, you are already attacking the negative patterns and behavior that are hell-bent on making you their plaything, and you are *taking back your own power.*

The challenging but critical thing to remember here is that those old patterns and beliefs *are not real.* Read that again, my lovely: those old patterns and beliefs are not real.

You are allowed to write your own story and create your own life and your own narrative. In fact, I would argue that to live a truly engaged and enlightened life, it's your *responsibility* to write your own story and stop letting your past control your future.

Talking to a professional, like a great coach or therapist, is an *excellent* means of support for facing these fears and coming to terms with your worth and magnitude of significance. Yet the only person who can convince you is you, and ultimately, it is you who needs to do the legwork and the undoing of the old patterns. But seeking out supports to help guide you while you do so will have you standing beside your own Grand Canyon, tacos in hand, taking in the resplendence and the wonder in which you alone are worthy.

*Can you love yourself enough to face your fear of getting
what you want?*
Can you allow yourself to feel worthy of receiving it?

Yes, you fucking can.

CHAPTER 24

Imposter syndrome (part two)

In the first six years of our life, our brain is like a freshly fallen sheet of snow. As I explained in Chapter 2, it's so easy to run around in that deep snowfall creating little trails and pathways with our feet. Around age six or seven, you can imagine a neurological deep freeze that casts a sheet of ice over that snow so any trails and patterns that are there freeze into place. For the rest of our lives, the easiest thing to do (and our brain LOVES "easy") is to follow those pathways and patterns. Of course, it is possible to create new ones, but it requires effort and work to crunch through that hard ice. So our default is to follow the same patterns over and over again, even if we don't like the places they take us.

The brain likes patterns so much that it will actually look for reasons to keep us on those pathways when we have the courage to take a new route: it tells us that the road less traveled is scary and unsafe, that we aren't brave or good enough to try something new, that if we venture out on our own we will piss people off and later be discovered as a fraud for trying something new when *everyone knows* who we really are.

Further, the brain will look for cues in our environment to prove to us why we need to stay where we are. It will steer us to choose the same people and behavior patterns over and over so that we get the same hurtful and disappointing result over and over, thus proving to us that this is all we get. We are destined to be like this forever.

It isn't true at all. It is just a built-in safety mechanism we are wired to follow. But you know what I'm going to say next, don't you? All you have to do is rewire that pattern, create a new pathway, and keep proving to yourself your new truth and new reality until you've taught your brain the new way it thinks—and then it keeps looking for THOSE healthy, beautiful patterns and behaviors to choose over and over again.

It's really a cool system, beautifully designed, and once you know how to work it, you can do anything, be anyone you want, and finally experience the love you've been looking for but have maybe felt was outside your reach for too long.

You know this.

And you know that behavior change is hard.

And, if I had to guess, I'd say you *also* know the way you think about yourself dictates the relationship you have with yourself, and THAT relationship is the one that will steer, shape, and guide every other relationship in your personal, professional, and family life.

Which is worth the hardship of behavior change.

Imposter syndrome, which so many of us suffer from (cough, indulge in), is basically the fear of being found out. We spoke in Part 1 that sometimes our emotional safety system has been *to* fake it for the sake of pleasing the greater good (especially when trauma is involved). We spoke about how in this case, you (even if well-intentioned) *have been* an imposter.

The fear comes from being afraid of being seen for who we really are, and for that not to be enough—to be rejected for the very thing we're trying to do, as people around us "catch on" and realize we're just a fake.

Sometimes, though, the perceived fear of "being found out" is a subconscious sabotage when you are in the midst of coming to terms with your success as a human in some way and are about to finally override those old icky patterns or footprints in the snow.

In this case, imposter syndrome is just a backlash of your old defense system doing its job to keep you safe even if "keeping you safe" means holding you back from blossoming into the badass you were born to be.

Any way you slice it, it's fear.

Every step to self-discovery will eventually be met (and often on repeat) with self-resistance and self-doubt. Going back to the footprint analogy, making change is hard work. Rewiring your brain takes effort and energy and, as you know, the subconscious mind doesn't like it, particularly when the new pathways and patterns are in opposition to what it's held as truth since our early years.

And this is why so many people are met with that overwhelming tidal wave of imposter syndrome and self-doubt, often just before they're about to create a massive and positive change for themselves. You have to learn to see that for what it is and to override that programming. It's like a system preservation error message:

"Are you sure you want to delete this?"

Imposter syndrome is what holds us back—especially women—from saying yes to things that we're not fully experts in. Because of the early gender messaging that many (not all, but many) of us get, we're preconditioned to wait our turn, let someone go ahead, and be humble about our abilities and achievements, which primes us to be inclined to assume someone else knows more than we do, and so we pull back for fear of being found out.

The wild truth about life is that we are all in the process of figuring things out. Essentially, we are *all* faking it to a certain degree, and when we do so with gusto, we call it "confidence" and "success," and when we do so with malice, we call it "faking."

Men absolutely experience imposter syndrome too, and in my experience, they just handle it differently. Let's say there is a position opening up that really catches your attention. In the requirements of the job posting, there is a list of ten skills each candidate must possess to be chosen for the hire. Chances are (again, this is *by no means an absolute* but is very often the case) that if you are a woman, you will read through that skills list and, unless you meet all ten, you'll think "Ah, crap. I guess I'm not qualified; I won't apply." Even if a solid seven or eight are masteries for you, it's likely you'll pass up the opportunity. And chances are (while this is no means a guarantee) that if you are a man skimming through that same skills list, even if you only meet three or four of the requirements *and not the other six or seven,* you'll think "Fuck it. Let's try it" and apply for the job.

This is the entire premise behind the television show *Suits*.

It's fascinating. Frustrating, but fascinating. Our fear can be so overwhelming that in working in conjunction with whatever messages we've been fed, whatever stories we've been told over the years, *and even if we would easily outshine other candidates*, we likely let our fears get the better of us.

So let's interrupt this pattern right here, right now.

More often than not we can truly do anything we put our minds to, we just need to overcome the self-defeating tendencies we have carried over from our past that are shutting it down. The best trick I can give you is to get crazy comfortable with asking, "The story I'm telling myself is . . . Hmm. Is that story true?"

I will say this over and over again because it's like an instant hack to get to the root cause of the fear that is holding you back.

I also have a few more Taco Tivities that will act as further disruptors to your old patterns, allowing you to make new footprints in your own snow to get you where you're going—starting now.

Choose to be confident

Love is a choice. Trust is a choice. Patience, compassion, and for-giveness are all choices. And confidence, too, is a choice. And really, confidence isn't that hard to cultivate if you know a few hacks to get out of your head/fear and into your body/soul: it just starts with your *decision* to be confident.

Decide that YOU are a confident person. Even if this idea makes you squirm, think about what you want, the choices you've made, the things that have worked / the things that didn't, and decide right now to show up for yourself and *choose* to be the kind of person that *is* confident.

If it's something that's calling you, there's a reason for that. Confi-dence in your work, in your art, in your relationships, in your singing, in your driving, in your whatever. Decide that *you* are a person here with a purpose (even if you don't yet know what that is) and *choose* to start making new decisions and engaging in new behavior rooted in your newfound confidence.

You are a person of value, and the first person who needs permission to see it and believe it is you. Take a breath and say out loud or in the mirror, "I am confident!" Say it again. And again and again until it starts to sit more easily in your body, mind, and spirit.

Confidence is a choice and there is no time like right now to start choosing it for you.

Love yourself enough to choose confidence.

TACO TIVITY 11

Act as if . . .

You know those people you really look up to? The ones you see living their lives and doing the things you WISH you could do? Do you know what one of the biggest differences between them and *you* is? They're just *doing* it.

That's it.

No one is any more special than you, more deserving, more entitled, more worthy, more capable—largely, they've just *decided* to do it.

Some people are born this way; they have that natural swagger and self-belief that they inherently belong here. They are allowed to speak up, take up space, make a mistake, try again. You know these people, and they are electric. They're like a magnet pulling you into their field, and you just want to BE in their presence.

Many of us learn and develop this confidence as we grow, if we *decide* to. Anyone can do it, you just have to decide to.

Picture the version of yourself you most aspire to be and make decisions from that place. Allow it to change your behavior now. Envision the most free and able version of yourself: In this vision, what are you doing? Who are you with? How does it FEEL?

With that future as your "foregone conclusion," capitalize on the feeling of being that person, this future iteration of yourself, and start making decisions FROM that point of view. Act as if you are *already that person* and *watch your behavior patterns change right now.*

Is that person an absolute boss? *What kind of decisions would they make to grow their business?*

Is that person in a fucking amazing and fulfilling relationship? *What does that say about the people they spend their intimate time with* (i.e., there ain't no time to dwell on the one you're chasing to text you back or rack up notches on your bedpost just to prove how not alone you are).

Is that person laughing around the table with family and friends? *Take a look around you and gauge if your "people" leave you feeling safe and warm or drained and judged* and cut the dead weight.

The vision you have of yourself is ALREADY you. Once you've decided to follow that little cosmic bread crumb laid out in a vision, all you have to do IS follow it and start acting as if that version of you is already here.

Can you love yourself enough to act as if you are already the person you aspire to be?

Yes, you fucking can.

TACO TIVITY 12

Love your body

I work with, and have worked with, *a lot* of women. And almost every time there has been a history of a skewed relationship with their bodies, at some point in their lives, to one degree or another.

Here's the mindset hack to cut to the chase of any body issues you have (or have had):

Is it my body that's holding me back from enjoying my life? Or is it my attitude toward my body that is holding me back from enjoying my life?

Remember, we don't want "the thing," we want the feeling we think the thing will give us. So if you are or have been fixed on "this will never be for me because of how I look" or "as soon as I look a certain way everything will be better and I will finally be happy," I need you to ask yourself incredibly honestly:

Is it my body that's holding me back from enjoying my life? Or is it my attitude toward my body that is holding me back from enjoying my life?

Subtle shift, huge difference.

Take a look today at how beauty has been defined through the ages: for many artistic periods, beauty *is* the softness, the folds, the curves, the cherubic flow of a woman's natural body.

Did this change and evolve into a LITERALLY IMPOSSIBLE STAN-DARD that is photoshopped and sold to us with a multibillion dollar ad spend behind it?

Oh hell yes it did. Unequivocally.

You have to remember that our perception of beauty is still intrinsically linked to our biology (ergo, which physical body traits will be best for either bearing children or for protecting the children from danger once they're born), and the rest is just a marketing campaign with endlessly deep pockets jamming "you will never be enough but [INSERT PRODUCT HERE] will help!"

I cannot tell you the number of women who tell me that "the media" makes them feel like they have to look a certain way. Yes, we have been largely programmed to see a distorted and absolutely fake image as "beauty." But, my darling, guess what?

We are the fucking media now. The way we consume content is so radically different than it has been in the past, and you have absolute choice in what you consume. So starting right bloody now, when you see a magazine that makes you feel less than beautiful, *stop reading it.* When you see a social media account that makes you doubt yourself, *stop following it.* When you're watching a movie that pushes you to feel something unhealthy about yourself, *stop watching it.*

Just like you would protect a young child from seeing something that would frighten/upset her or otherwise be considered inappropriate, so too must you protect yourself.

A woman's body is designed to evolve. To flow. To fold.

Go to a beach/gym/spa (any public place anywhere) and really *observe* the bodies that you see:

They. Are all. Different.

There is no metric. There is no standard. Your beauty comes from within and is wrapped in this uniquely wonderful package that *you* decide how to decorate and carry. Commit to only seeing the ones who are normalizing *this* message in our new media.

The sexiest outfit you can put on, especially if you want to "impress" someone, is your natural ability to shine. And that ability to shine *is* your confidence.

Can you love yourself enough to shine confidently?

Yes, you fucking can.

Stop apologizing for shit you didn't do

This is a major aspect of embodied confidence, and yes, it gets its own section in this book by design. Get it on your radar now, too, because sometimes it feels like its own emotional epidemic, especially for women and girls.

People-pleasers and anyone who has ever started a sentence with "I don't mean to be annoying, but . . ." need to pay particular attention here.

Listen, I'm *all about* accountability and personal responsibility. So when you mess up, or cause someone legit pain or inconvenience, please do apologize.

But the over apologizing and constant explanation of why you did what you did? Like having the *audacity* to speak up, stand out, or honor your own healthy, loving boundaries? Yeah. No apology necessary.

Here's a next-level glow-up to take it one step further: shift your apology into gratitude. "Thank you so much for waiting for me! Traffic was a little heavier than usual, and I so appreciate your effort and understanding." When you over apologize, you unwittingly create an imbalanced power dynamic in which you are indebted to another. It's up to them, even if unspoken, to forgive you, thus creating a condition of success.

Shifting to gratitude very subtly communicates your position, while praising the other person for being so awesome. It leaves them feeling like they're a compassionate and understanding person, and immediately, the psychological effects and dynamics are working more in your favor.

You are learning to take up space without condition, explanation, or apology.

Can you love yourself enough to take up space and use your voice without guilt or shame?

Yes, you fucking can.

TACO TIVITY 14

Trust your damn self

Yes. This.

What I know is this: When you get that little whisper that pulls you in the direction of what you need to do next, follow it—only *you* need to trust your intuition.

Now I know that is a big ask if you've never learned how to do it before. It's an even bigger ask if you have been taught (as I personally was) to explicitly doubt yourself and intentionally act in opposition to what you feel instinctively.

I share that detail of my own life with you to show you that if I can do this, you can do this. I was literally raised to do the exact opposite of what my intuition told me, and it messed me up for a long time. I had to unlearn that habit, unlearn the pleasing of people as a safety mechanism, and teach myself how to tap into what I knew to be true—and trust *the hell* out of it. This is for sure a practice, but here's how you can get going: just start asking and answering.

One weekend I was in New York City walking around on my own, with a flexible time frame and a list of a few key places I wanted to stop throughout the day. I let myself be led, not by a map, but by gut and chance. If the light was red, I stopped and turned, and if it was green, I took it as a sign to keep going. This super simple exercise to *just trust* gave my subconscious brain the *proof* it needed that I could, in fact, be trusted, and it was okay for me to trust myself.

If you need to start this simple way, do. Carve out some time for yourself to do something similar and watch how your day unfolds with grace. Ask yourself, "What do I need right now? What would I love?" and follow that, feeling the actual sense of magic and wonder that happens when you "indulge" your true needs in the moment.

Then you build from there. You do my fave Brené Brown exercise and take a one-inch-squared piece of paper and write down everyone whose opinion matters to you (!) and literally practice trusting yourself to do the right thing, over and over, without feeling the need to explain yourself.

To anyone.

Only *you* need to trust your intuition. And doing so is *the* compass that will continuously guide you to where your soul is showing you to go. All you have to do is allow it.

Can you love yourself enough to trust your damn self?

Yes, you fucking can.

CHAPTER 25

The myth of competition

Too often we are conditioned to feel the need to be in constant competition. There is a misguided perception that being who we are, as we are—in business, life, and love—won't be enough until we prove we are better than someone else . . . and maybe not even then. We didn't create that story on our own, and we do not have to live it either.

Where does this intense need for competition come from . . . and is it actually all bad?

Let's talk about that. Maybe competition isn't such a bad thing if we understand the "why" of where it comes from.

Remember, after you take away the clothes, the houses, the fancy job titles, the luxury cars, and the take-out pizza, we are, in our DNA, animals. Pack animals at that, which means that embedded into the very fiber of our genetic code, we are programmed to be a part of the group, and we depend on that group for our very survival.

When you think about competition from that perspective, you can see how (way down deep in the primordial programming of our actual species) we *need* to look to see what others around us are doing and make sure that what we are doing is in alignment so that we can continue to be accepted as a part of the group that keeps us safe and alive.

Further, when you look even closer at basic biology, you'll see that we are programmed (again, *way* down deep in our genetic code) to understand viscerally that only the fittest survive, while the other "less-than" members of the group are left behind to perish.

So I'll ask you again: Where does this intense need for competition come from . . . and is it actually all that bad?

The drive to compete, compare, and contrast is a part of us, and realistically? I think it's naïve to believe we can gloss over the biological roots of this compulsion.

However.

While we are at our core social animals who depend on a sense of belonging to maintain our very survival, we have also evolved as a species beyond those primitive needs. So while the compulsion may still exist within us, there are some checks and balances we can put into place to help us manage it in a healthy way.

One of these ways is to be very clear about where the origin of this drive is coming from—and letting yourself off the hook a little. The next way to manage this internal drive to compete, compare, and contrast is to make peace with the other very real truth that someone will *always* be better than you. That's not a dis, that's a fact. Even if you are at the pinnacle of your game and your experience is at its apex, we know that change is the only constant, and eventually, someone else will come up behind you and surpass your ability.

Likewise, you will *always* be better than someone else. That is also a fact. So you can see that "being the best" is a moving target, a finite moment in time, and is also completely relative to each individual's experience. So you can let yourself off the hook a little here too.

The reason this is so fundamental to understanding and expanding our emotional awareness and intelligence is that truly, there is no one ultimate achievement except for what the ultimate achievement is defined by *you*. If you're always going to be better than someone else, and someone else is always going to be better than you, then, baby, there is no "best." There's only momentary success.

This understanding is so freeing because it creates the new head-space to always be as good as you can be, right here in this moment. I *love* the iconic quote from Maya Angelou that says:

Do the best you can until you know better. Then when you know better, do better.

Do the best you can with what you have right here in this moment and then, when you know better, *do* better. Doesn't that just bring you an instant sense of relief? Of peace? It takes the pressure to be *the best* away because the only thing you really ever have to be is *your* best in this moment. The next moment might look different than this one, and in that moment you might do better or you might do worse. It kind of doesn't matter because we're only ever living right here in this moment, and this moment is the only thing that is real.

So if you are continuously doing your best in this moment? Then you're already the best.

Boom. No more competition.

And how does comparison factor into this? I am sure you have seen on the Internet, at least a thousand times, the saying from former U.S. President Roosevelt that "comparison is the thief of joy." And why, exactly, is that?

Because you can only ever do your best, right here in this moment. That's it. Right here in this moment, doing your best and giving it your all is all you can give. And that's enough for you.

But if you allow yourself to drop out of living in this moment, and instead allow yourself to drop in on someone else's moment, you are no longer paying attention to what your best is in this moment because you've chosen to see what somebody else's best is in that moment. And if their best in this moment is better than your best in this moment, then you suddenly get the feeling that your best in this moment isn't actually good enough at all because someone else's best in this moment is already better than yours.

What you are not seeing, if you choose to remove yourself from your own present moment and instead engage in this kind of voyeurism that allows you to spy on someone else's present moment, are the many other moments when their best in the moment was nowhere near as good as your best in the moment. It's only just a moment, so how on earth would it be possible for you to bear witness to each and every one of their moments and also still appreciate your own?

When you break it down like this, even when you appreciate where the tendency comes from to pay attention to what someone else is doing, and even when you appreciate why you are inclined—at a biological level—to pay attention to what someone else is doing, it seems, from where I stand, pretty fucking stupid to pay attention to what anyone else is doing if what you're actually paying attention to is whether they're doing better or worse than you in this moment.

Are you with me? Cool.

So, living in the cultural context in which we live, I'm going to next level this for you: social media and social sharing platforms have, without question, infinitely expanded our opportunities for connection. What they have also and unwittingly done is set up a twenty-four-hour window of opportunity to take yourself out of your own best and present moment and drop into not *one* other person's best moment but *millions* of other people's best moments.

And depending on the subconscious filter and lens you are inclined to use to look at the world, depending on the stories and narratives you personally choose to believe in this very moment, you will—if you spend your time looking at what those other millions of people are doing—*always* be better than they are or *always be worse*.

Either way, this is a superlatively unhealthy way to live and spend your energy. Because as you already know from reading this book, the present moment, *your* present moment, is the only thing that is actually real. Everything else has already happened and is no longer real or hasn't yet happened and still isn't real.

This is where things really start to get interesting.

Something else you've likely seen on the Internet, almost ad nauseam, is the platitude promoting "collaboration over competition." This phrase, based on everything else you now know, in this moment, which is the only thing that is real, is *literally the dumbest fucking thing I have ever heard.*

One, it is incredibly condescending. To me, when I hear those gross three words, what I really hear is "play nice, girls." Show me a room of men—*show me* any example of any group of men anywhere, in business or otherwise—who are being told to champion "collaboration over competition."

Nope, it does not exist; it does not happen. Why? Because it is assumed that "men can handle it" and can handle being in competition with one another without anyone getting hurt. The implication is that women, therefore, cannot, and in an effort to ensure no one's feelings get hurt, they have to park their competitive nature and do all things together. Seriously, this is one of the most officious, misogynist platitudes of our generation. Please memory charm it out of your brain, *Harry Potter*-style.

Two, collaboration and competition are in no way mutually exclusive. If it makes sense for you to work together with someone on a project, on a deal, on a strategic partnership, by all means collaborate with them! Healthy, intentional collaborations are not only good for your business, they're good for your soul. But do not think for one second that you have to choose either collaboration or competition because it doesn't work that way.

To assume you have to pick either collaboration (read: we will play nice and work together) or competition (read: we will seek to destroy each other) harkens back to that old, patriarchal and further misogynistic narrative that women have to be either/or, not both/and.

You are allowed to do well in your business, in your life, in your love. Why? Because it's *your* fucking business, life, and love. When you live your life and conduct your affairs in an intention-centered way that operates with the understanding you live with integrity and do the right thing, while remaining true to yourself and not hurting others, you're doing it right.

Can you love yourself enough to see your best as your only competition?

Yes, you fucking can.

CHAPTER 26

Love + Fear

L ove and fear are our two most primal emotions from which all others stem; they are two sides of the same coin, have a huge influence on how we make decisions, and it's up to you to decide which one will guide you.

Like so many things in our life, love and fear exist in intimate opposition to one another. It is one of life's great paradoxes: what we love most is what we're most afraid of losing, and what we fear most is the opposite of what we most strongly desire.

When we experience the juxtaposition of love and fear, and especially when we start to feel fear take the lead in how we see the world and make our decisions, it's as if we're preparing ourselves for what can go wrong. For example, how many times have you gotten in a car or on a plane and thought that it could crash at any moment?

It's a real thing. When we hold something so dear to us, in this case our lives, our brain starts to protect our hearts and minds by bracing for worst-case scenarios. I call these "disaster fantasies," and as I say, our brain prepares us for how awful something could be.

We seldomly prepare for how *wildly amazing and perfectly* something could go, even though statistically, and soulfully, there is a greater chance of something amazing and even miraculous happening than something going terribly awry.

Fear does serve a purpose and has done so throughout our history and evolution of Self; we have talked a lot about this fact already. The problem is that when we let fear lead us, we let it color the way in which we see the world and see it through a very distorted lens: the lens of "what could go wrong?"

Often, that fear is based on something we've already experienced (typically at a young and formative age, but not always) that distorts our reality. Maybe it's a past trauma, a negative relationship, an insecure attachment, or an outlier experience that was super rare and a statistical anomaly but happened anyway, and it shook up what we knew to be true.

That's a big deal; when something does go wrong, or even if we're in the company of people who assure us that something will go wrong, it really messes with our mindset and perception.

And when our perception is off, we look for more evidence in our environment to confirm it. Confirmation bias is the looking for things to confirm what we think to be true, to be true: you know one person who's suffered a heart attack and suddenly all you see and read about is others who've suffered the same. Our brains look for more examples of what we fear to be true, to be true, and that further confirms the fear is real. You see this a lot with "crime waves": when a particular crime has been reported, the news picks up—with a meticulous comb—other similar crimes and reports on those too, and before you know it, there's an "epidemic" of that particular crime being reported. But in reality? It's just that the attention and awareness *to* that particular type of crime has seen an increase, not the act of the crime itself, and therefore, the bias we confirm to be true becomes "true."

But the great thing is that it isn't true, it is simply a misconception. And when you are aware of the misconceptions in your own life, and how you see the world, you can very easily change them and *disprove* what your brain is desperately trying to convince you of in order to hold you back from breaking outside your comfort zone.

Fear *has* served a purpose throughout our evolution and will *continue* to serve a function as we evolve further. It's fear that tells us intuitively when danger is near, and when our (or our dear ones') safety is being threatened. It's fear that tells us to hold off from eating that unknown mushroom, from jumping from that rock, from going into unchartered areas, from running away from a bobcat . . . and that fear is a really good thing.

Our natural response to fear, as you already know from your own daily life, is that of fight, flight, or freeze—we either run toward that fear and tackle the danger head on, we run the hell away from it, or we stay frozen, paralytically unable to respond in either of the other ways.

You can see how, when it comes to our physical survival, these response mechanics make sense.

But what about our emotional safety? Fear has a role in our emotional health when it makes us take heed and proceed with caution: when fear warns us to be aware, to be wary, to proceed with caution, it's doing its job to protect and keep us safe. However, there is a tipping point when our fear oversteps its boundaries and pollutes our mindset with a distorted reality, thus preventing us from moving forward or experiencing the world in a healthy way.

Consider, for example, buying a house; that's a scary thing. It's a huge financial undertaking, it demands a new level of responsibility in the maintaining of the house, and it declares commitment to a particular location for at least some intention of living in one place for a decent length of time. Healthy fear tells us to evaluate the market, to assess the neighborhood, and to evaluate our long-term personal, financial, and relationship/family goals. It tells us to be mindful and careful as we make our decision.

When fear starts to overstep, it tells us buying the house is too risky, we could never afford it, something will go wrong, and we will fail. It creates an identity for us that is out of whack with who we already think we are, causes too much dissonance in our minds, and prevents us from getting to where we consciously know we want to be. You can think of especially powerful examples in relationships and business decisions too: yes, we can exercise caution, with a healthy dose of respect and concern for ourselves, but if we consistently listen to our fears, we won't get anywhere—we will exist in an anxious, nervous, almost paralytic state of not being able to make a conclusive decision or making a grossly uninformed decision by choosing to listen only to fear and not to our natural state of love.

Love is our natural state, meaning we are born into the feeling of love. We are programmed to trust from day one that our parents will care for us, meet our needs for safety, security, and comfort, and keep us alive. The very act of being born vaginally and then nursing upon birth creates a flood of oxytocin—the same chemical responsible for many addictions—for both mom and baby. We are programmed to be literally addicted to one another.

If you haven't had your own child, go and watch a group of young children playing: They are joyful, love-filled, play-based beings. They become playmates with someone over one tiny shared moment or connection, and they see no other way. They are eager to hug and express affection for any and all around them.

You were born into that state as well. It's your environment (and your role in that environment) that has shaped your perspective of and relationship to that state of love over time. And love, if you let it, can come back into your life in that same baseline, in that same powerful and natural state.

Love in its purest form is unconditional: It accepts people and situations for who and what they are, exactly as they are. Love is moment by moment, appreciative and tender, and has little attachment to an outcome. Love is encouragement, joy, respect, independence, and acceptance; it is truthful, honest, vulnerable, without shame, and present. Love is a state, a mindset, a choice, and a practice.

At first it can seem difficult to realize and accept the gravity of the above: If someone is treating you unkindly and without love, you might want to respond in the same way. Short term, that feels better, less risky, more appropriate. But every decision you make is *yours* to make. When you take responsibility and ownership over how you act, how you show up, how you choose to exist and with what language, pattern, and tone, YOU can respond with love to anything.

That practice takes time and begins with the understanding that no emotion is bad, even fear. Again, it's the balance of fear in relation to everything else that matters most.

I want you to imagine again (like I explained in Chapter 12) that your brain has a family table set up in it; decorate that space however you wish and however feels right to you. All your feelings are welcome to the table because they are a part of you. But now, as head of this family, you have a new awareness and responsibility, and that is to ensure that everyone at that table gets a chance to speak, but that their opinions are held in balance. Fear is welcome to speak up and make her concerns known, and it's your job to thank her for bringing fear to your attention, appreciate every single thing she has done for you so far, and then to move on.

Fear, no matter how present she has been previously in your life, needs to be taught that while she is valued and appreciated, it is love that now holds powerful court over your decision-making process.

We know that love and fear are each so powerful that they are truly our only emotions: every other emotion we feel is an offspring of one or the other. When we have secure attachments, and when we've had positive, loving, healthy experiences, it's as if our brains are programmed to look for and see the good, to anticipate a positive outcome, to believe in ourselves and our abilities, and to know unequivocally that we deserve good things to happen.

Conversely, when we have developed insecure attachments, or when we've had negative, threatening, traumatic, or otherwise unhealthy experiences, it's as if our brains are programmed to look for and see the bad and to anticipate a negative outcome, doubt ourselves and our abilities, and question our self-worth and our entitlement to live a happy and fulfilling life.

Wow, right? Big difference, especially when you consider that that state of mind is the platform from which we make our decisions.

Where and how self-love plays into this programming is exactly what you're doing: teaching yourself to unlearn the old patterns, removing your old lens, and teaching yourself a new way of seeing the world—this time with a renewed perspective that tells you anything is possible because you deserve happiness, pleasure, joy, love, and success. It is making peace with where you are, in this moment.

When you teach yourself to meet each of those needs for yourself, without relying or depending on anyone else to do it for you, you are learning to see everything all over again for the first time through the lens of endless possibility, goodness, faith, trust, and unconditional love.

Now that you have the awareness about where your decision-making lens comes from and where those thinking patterns are rooted, you can start to challenge your first fear-based reaction to something when it comes up. Remember we talked about confirmation bias?

You know now that when you expect something, you unconsciously look for examples in your environment that support that expectation. So moving forward, if you have a fear of something that is holding you back or holding you hostage from doing what you *know* to be right and true for you, you can challenge it and *consciously* seek out examples of what will support you to make the right, healthy, loving, even-if-it-feels-hard decision.

A huge point of arrival is to have the courage to self-reflect enough to listen to your true/gut/intuitive feelings versus the old pattern that has taught you how or what to feel. It is a genuine, true-blue expansion of your emotional awareness and deeper cultivation of your emotional intelligence to choose to adopt love-based practices in place of fear-based ones.

Doesn't this sound like a great opportunity for some Taco Tivities? Ah yes, I thought so too.

Here's what I'm afraid of . . .

It might sound simple, but sometimes we are *so afraid* of what we are afraid of that we don't even know what that fear is. So get out your pen and notebook and write down what it is that you are *really* afraid of. Be fucking honest.

Once you've figured it out, see if you can go a little deeper and identify where that fear came from and where it originated. This activity takes you way back to Chapter 1 when we talked about tracing the tendril of each emotional vine back to its root and killing it dead.

Now—and this instruction is the big boy—write out *AT LEAST ten examples of how you can disprove this fear*, with tangible examples in your real life. If that makes you feel angry, or like you want to puke and cry, congratulations! You are about to heal some serious shit from your past.

When you make yourself see how this fear is absolutely not legit, you can train yourself to *shift* your mindset to be far more open to possibility than to fear.

TACO TIVITY 16

Do something that scares you, then do it again

If we have low self-esteem or high self-doubt, we tend to lack confidence in our abilities, and we let fear get in the way of us even trying. So think of something that scares you (making the phone call, singing in public, sharing your art, dating online, having the conversation, etc.), feel the fear, and *do it anyway*.

Challenge yourself to do something scary, write it down in your journal, and come back to it to debrief after the fact.

Experiencing success in confronting and overcoming even the *tiniest* fear or discomfort will develop better patterns to saying yes and doing hard things. Over and over. Get into the habit of doing uncomfortable things to teach your brain that you are still safe. This is healthy mental rehearsal.

Speaking of mental rehearsal . . .

This request is a big one: I want you to walk yourself through the exercise of what you fear coming true. Like your worst-case scenario.

What would that be, how would it feel, what would you do? Sometimes we are so scared of something that it prevents us from thinking about it, so we keep repressing it. It's okay, and actually super healthy, to acknowledge your fears; and, in fact, the only way out is through. So walk yourself through the feeling of not getting what you want, or getting what you least want, and experience what that would feel like. Chances are that when you start to work through it, it's not so bad and doesn't seem so heavy or threatening. Working through it is how you begin the practice of letting go of worry and anxiety while creating a healthy detachment from outcome.

Whenever I feel afraid, I whistle a happy tune

Remember that song from *Snow White*? To update it for you, whenever you DO feel afraid, instead of slipping into anxiety mode, say out loud: "Grateful for this moment." Whenever you feel it, say it. That one exercise will powerfully let love creep in and power over any fear you have.

When you strip away all the noise and all the drama, you are essentially left with two human emotions: love and fear. Every other emotional vine we hack away at arrives at one of these core roots.

It's up to us to choose from which place we will act: out of fear or out of love. I spent a lifetime acting out of fear: fear of getting caught, fear of failure, fear of rejection, fear of abandonment, fear of disappointment, fear of judgment, fear of being alone.

After getting tired of my own BS and toxic patterns that came up over and over again, I made the conscious choice to ask what the story was that I was telling myself—every time I felt afraid or threatened,

I coached myself back to a place of being able to make a good and healthy decision based in love. This, too, was a lengthy but valuable process.

I know firsthand that this process was possible for me. Which means, lovely, that *I am your subconscious proof that this process is possible for you to do too.*

It is this simple, it is this complicated. And this is big work. Like *big* work. Listen to your body—what do you need now? A rest? Fresh air? A hug or maybe a glass of water? Allow yourself to do what feels good for you.

Can you love yourself enough to keep choosing love over fear?

Yes, you fucking can.

CHAPTER 27

Epic love

The first love of your life must be yourself, period.

No matter what movie, song, or story tries to convince you otherwise, the first, best, and longest relationship we'll ever have is the one we have with ourselves. And it is worth investing in, both your time and energy.

Much of our lives are centered around human connection. We experience love for a parent, love for a sibling, love for our extended family, our friends, our lovers, our partners, our children, our pets. We feel love for another when we feel connected, and when that connection feels weak or less healthy and satisfying, we feel that love subside. That connection is relatively easy to measure and feel, because if it's one that makes us feel good, we want and invest more in it, and if it's one that makes us feel diminished or less than (and if we have a healthy attachment system in place), we withdraw from that relationship.

In that way, we tend to feel a continuous ebb and flow for how we feel toward or about other people, and often in relation to how other people feel about and treat us. But there's one key relationship left out of that equation, and it's the one relationship—above all others and above all circumstances—that we are absolutely guaranteed to be in for the rest of our lives. And that is the relationship we have with *ourselves*.

Ironically, the relationship we have with ourselves—yes, the ONLY one we are 100 percent committed to from birth to death—is the one that tends to be the most underserviced, the most tortured, and the least understood. We toss out cutting words like "selfish" and "narcissistic" to describe people who seem to be focusing time and energy on getting to know and spend time with themselves, and we do it from a place of judgment and misunderstanding.

It's a pretty commonly accepted phenomenon that we are a sum of the five people we spend the most time with, and when we hear figures like that, we instinctively do a scan of whom we hung out with the most that week. And again, very few of us write "myself" on the list of people we spend the most time with, because that sounds kind of weird, but it's true! It's like that age-old saying that wherever you go, there you are.

True self-love is the ability to look in the mirror, meet the person you are going to spend the rest of your life with, and feel total appreciation for that person looking back at you. Want to know the amazing news? Even if this is a brand new concept to you, you are here, right now and in this moment, taking the incredible action of pulling up a chair, pouring the coffee (or the wine), and cozying up next to the person who's been waiting for you to show up all along. Nayyirah Waheed wrote:

"'I love myself' [is] the quietest, simplest, most powerful revolution. Ever."

And it's true. This, my lovely, is a beautiful bell you cannot unring.

The way we feel about ourselves will set the boundaries and standards for every other relationship we're in. Period.

Personally speaking, every bad decision I ever made was made from a place of fear and low self-worth.

After I quit my job with Christopher the Megalomaniac, he said to me, "You know, Leisse, I thought you were worth it at the time, but now I'm not so sure." I was gutted. I had literally bled, sweat, and cried for this man, and after having "the audacity" to quit after almost a year of no pay—as a single mom of three—he just discarded me without a second thought. Because I "wasn't worth it."

And I realized that I had heard these words before, almost verbatim, over the course of my life.

I heard them when I asked for a raise when teaching, and my boss—clad entirely in Michael Kors while living in one of Toronto's most affluent neighborhoods and driving a Mercedes truck—said no. It's not that she couldn't afford it: *I just wasn't worth it.*

I heard them when my parents withdrew me for a year from the little private Mennonite school where I was thriving socially and academically because they just couldn't afford the $3,000 tuition. (At the time, my dad was an internist who had been chief of staff for a number of years. My sisters, who owned and rode about five horses and would later be gifted cars to get to the barn to ride said horses, were enrolled for their *entire* education at private schools.) It's not that they couldn't afford it, it's that *I just wasn't worth it.*

I heard them when my stepmom found out my ex and I were moving in together and told me outright, "You're his problem now."

I heard them during divorce across many examples and in the many years that followed.[5]

5 Which, out of respect for my family, I've chosen not to include in print.

And I heard them in a Chicago art gallery when my best friend told me she had "stood aside to let me shine for long enough, and now it was her turn."

What I kept hearing over and over, what I enabled some of the closest people in my life to say to me over and over, was *"Leisse, you're just not worth it."*

And for so long, too long, I believed them.

I always thought someone was coming to save me: my stepmom "saved me" from my absent mother, my husband "saved me" from an abusive family, Christopher "saved me" from a directionless career, my best friend "saved me" from loneliness.

And each time I perpetuated this narrative, that I was damaged and waiting to be rescued, I single-handedly created that toxic narrative of codependency and a power dynamic that put me at a dramatic weakness and deficiency.

Eventually enough was enough. After I heard the pattern repeating over and over, I decided to interrupt it once and for all. I furthered my self-discovery to come to love and appreciate me for me, whole on my own, exactly as I am. I taught myself to show up as and for myself, and to meet my own needs instead of waiting for someone else to do it for me. This transformation changed how I dated, worked, parented, and lived—all for the better.

We often attribute how we show up, how we attract others, or whom we are attracted to, to our first relationship with our parents; yes, we get a lot of our "wiring" from those earliest days, months, and years with our primary caregivers, no question. Someone pointed out to me that our childhood is actually a quite short period of our lives.

And while it has a super high impact on our thoughts, beliefs, and behaviors, there is a lot of life that comes after childhood, which is ours to live how we want to live.

As we mature, we need to appreciate or accept that we are the only ones *at cause* and responsible for our lives and the happiness therein and that it's up to us to care about ourselves in the way we want to, not necessarily the way we were taught to.

This reality can be a tough pill to swallow at first, but it is also home to much freedom. We are responsible for our own lives and our own happiness. When we accept that fact, we can accept that whatever the standard is for how we expect to be treated and loved and cared for starts with how we treat ourselves in each of those same ways. How can we expect someone else to show up, care for, protect, nurture, spoil, entertain, nourish, appreciate, and love us if we can't (or are unwilling to) do that for ourselves first?

Self-love sets the tone for every other relationship we choose in our lives. It's what helps us be paid fairly and well for the work that we do, ensures we are in friendships that make us feel light and loved, allows us to choose partners who truly see and value us for who we are, and lets us raise children who respect our need for independence in an interdependent family unit.

When our love of self is healthy and deep, we set clear boundaries for others that show them how to love and treat us; when our love of self is unhealthy and weak, we tend to oscillate between letting others walk all over us and leaving us feeling unseen and used or pushing them away so that no one can ever truly get close to us with any degree of intimacy.

If we consider that our life's happiness is informed and supported (at least in part by) those we have in our lives personally, professionally, and intimately, suddenly the need to connect with ourselves in an authentic, loving, and genuine way is paramount to our success in welcoming the other relationships that will deepen and "next-level" our experience with the world around us.

This reason is why self-love is so important: when we show up for and choose ourselves, we are letting it be known, without ever speaking the words, that this is how we will be treated by every other person that crosses our path. So yes, it's kind of a big deal.

I bet if you stop and listen, you can hear that little voice inside your head. You know the one: the one that is either encouraging you to move forward or to pull back; the one that tells you that you're doing a great job or the one that tells you that you will never succeed, and if you do, it's only temporary until you inevitably fail again.

I bet if you listen really carefully, you can identify where that voice came from or who it is. So how did it get there? It's usually a little voice that is more accurately a pattern, and one that you probably picked up or even absorbed in your earliest years. It's a pattern of thinking that someone else gave to you in childhood (or in another formative relationship like an intimate partner) that taught you that you are capable or not, accepted or not, loved or not, worthy or not, safe and secure or not. It's a pretty powerful voice because it's the one we relied on to protect us as a kid and learned to see as healthy and normal (even if it wasn't) because we relied on it to make sense of our world.

The bad news is that often other people are instrumental in writing that narrated script for us, and we assume we just have to follow it well into our adult years. The great, fantastic, jump-for-joy, kablamo, awesome news is that just by being right here right now, you have made the decision to call BS on that old pattern of thinking. You have taken it on to write your OWN story by taking what you need from that voice that shaped you and then getting into the empowering place of telling yourself what YOU know to be true about you while letting go of whatever else someone told you to be true about you. And that, my lovely, is the beginning of true freedom.

Much of the actionable "Taco Tivities" are practices centered around pressing pause when you have a thought, then challenging where it came from and why; these practices require a degree of detachment from yourself, which might feel a little weird at first but is totally necessary. That detachment is an invitation from me to you to listen to the words in your head and really hear what they're saying.

When you pause and really HEAR them, I want you to think the following: "How would I react if I heard someone saying this to my child? How would I react if I heard someone say that to my best friend? What would I do if I heard my partner saying that about themselves?" I'm not a betting woman, but I'd be willing to place a hefty bet that the chances are if you heard someone using that language to or about someone you love deeply, you'd lose your mind with rage and step in to protect them from that unkindness.

My darling? Self-love is stepping in to protect YOURSELF from that unkindness, even if, *especially* if, it's coming from you.

Have you ever heard an expression to the effect that our thoughts become things? That what we think, we become? That we have the ability to speak things into existence? It's a pretty powerful realization to take ownership over your own life and take accountability for not only your own actions but your own thoughts. Your thoughts give language to your beliefs, thus guiding your physical actions.

For example, when you really believe that you can do something, you tend to be able to do it. Conversely, when you believe that you can't have something or that you will fail or that you will never be loved or appreciated (yuck), you tend to make that happen too.

Again, powerful.

And what that means for you, right here, right now, is that you change what you are thinking about yourself if it is anything less than "you are a beautiful, capable human who deserves to give and receive all of the love and all of the joy." THIS mantra is the inner dialogue you deserve to have because THIS is the life you deserve to create for yourself. And I have to tell you that if you are reading these words and thinking "this lady is nuts; I will never think that," I want to gingerly hold you by the shoulders, look into your eyes and tell you that "yes, you can. Yes, you can have this, and yes you can believe this. Even if it seems impossible right now, I PROMISE you that you are on the right path to shifting your old patterns of thinking to a place in which you recognize, accept, and love the hell out of your badass self."

So if you are sitting there thinking "I could never; I'm an idiot; I made ANOTHER mistake; I always fuck things up; It's really hard for me to; I'm not the kind of person that . . ." then THAT is the first place to start. Because whatever you are thinking and then saying (even in a "funny," joking way), THAT is the reality you are creating for yourself. And it simply isn't true. Your story has no room for negative self-talk. It has no space for you to speak to or think about yourself in any way other than what you are doing well, what you learned, and how you would use that learning to move forward in a healthier way the next time.

There are no mistakes, just opportunities for reflection and growth. You are stronger, more capable, more beautiful and deserving than you know, and literally anything is possible for you—no matter how young or how old you are—because this is your story and YOUR life. And chances are the only person we have to convince that of, is you.

Can you love yourself enough to be loving with yourself?
Can you love yourself enough to write your own story?
Can you love yourself enough to come home to yourself?

Yes, you fucking can.

Part 3

Healing forward

"You have breast cancer, Leisse, and it's aggressive."

I will always remember that color-draining moment, sitting up on the examining table at my surgeon's consult office. I had juicy, luscious, double-D breasts, and I loved them *so much* that I would often walk around holding them, just living my life.

I had felt a lump in my left breast four months prior to my diagnosis when I was staying overnight at an off-grid cabin in Gananoque, Ontario. That night at the cabin, my left thumb happened upon a pea-sized, kinda rubbery lump, just southeast of my left nipple. I felt the color drain out of me then too, knowing deep down what was happening but refusing consciously to believe that this would be my story.

I prayed and tried to negotiate with God that if he could just make it so that it was not cancer after all, I would herein never complain about my body again. There is nothing like a health scare to put all the things into perspective.

I prayed, put it out of my mind, and first thing Monday morning (I found the lump on a Friday. Why does it all explode on Fridays? Ever notice that?) I drove to my doctor's office to be the first one in line, hoping to get a last-minute appointment with her. I went up to the wicket, but when I opened my mouth, no voice came out. I literally could not speak the truth I was feeling. I was thirty-six, healthy, single, self-employed, and an almost full-time parent to three kids. "Finding a lump" could not be my reality.

I leaned closer and whispered to the gal at the desk, "I found a lump." Her entire body energy and facial expression dropped. She very gracefully and tactfully said, "Come with me, we'll get you right in."

She brought me to my doctor's examining room, who, upon her arrival and her own manual exam, found a second lump deeper down than the first. To my surprise and delight, my doctor was able to book me into the breast clinic at our local hospital *within the hour*, where I had a mammogram, ultrasound, and second physical exam by the radiologist on call.

The radiologist confirmed the presence of a second lump, praised my family MD for finding it in such an awkward place, and told me that because of all the factors above, I didn't have to worry. "This doesn't present as cancer, especially considering your age, family history, and the fact that there are two."

He told me to go to California and have fun—I was booked to leave the next morning to attend a conference in Pasadena (at which Brené Brown was speaking), and had planned on renting a convertible to drive the Pacific Coast Highway all the way up from L.A. to Seattle.

And so I did. I skipped out of there thinking, "Thank you for the wake-up call. I will never complain about my body again," and I felt free. I continued to have that feeling of freedom in my 2018 Mustang, roof down, music up . . . eating all the tacos up the California coast, embarking on the epic road trip I'd envisioned for years.

I was living my best life.

Three months later, per the radiologist's instructions, I went back for my follow-up, and he observed that each of the two lumps had basically quadrupled in size. We did another ultrasound and mammogram and added a needle biopsy (ouch) to get some tissue samples, just in case.

His words? "I am 99 percent sure you have nothing to worry about; we just want to be cautious." The tech turned to me after the doc had left the room and said, "If he says 99, he means 100." So off I skipped again, grateful to be alive and well.

The following week, my kids and I were visiting our family at a cottage when I got a phone call midday. My family doctor was away on holiday, so it was the physician covering for her who said, "We have your biopsy results. Don't worry, it's not cancer, but it *is* precancerous, so we'll need to do a lumpectomy to remove it. Just to be sure."

I was shocked.

I thought I was free and clear, so the news that I would have to remove at least a third of my left breast was really hard to accept. But hey, it wasn't cancer, and that was something to be grateful for. I talked it through with my aunts, and we knew that it would be just a simple day surgery, and it would all be okay.

Plus, I had *just* found out from my children that their dad was getting remarried—in like, two weeks—and the only reason *they* knew was because one of them had read the RSVP card at their dad's friend's house. My own kids hadn't been invited to, included in, or even *told about* the marriage, and this knowledge was a massive emotional challenge for me. Not only was it less than two years since we'd divorced, after fourteen years of being together, but the idea they hadn't even been *told*, let alone included, was incredibly painful to witness as their mother.

This scenario triggered the almost identical moment when my dad had done almost exactly the same thing, which was the beginning of my highly emotionally abusive upbringing. The one repeating pattern triggered a flash-forward thought that my kids were possibly about to endure the same experience I had worked so hard to overcome was unbearable. (And as you've learned in Part 1, it doesn't even matter if something is true—if the subconscious *perceives* it to be true, it feels like it's real . . . and that you're experiencing it all over again.)

So when it was time for my surgical consult, I was much more distracted by the fact that my appointment was the same day my ex was getting remarried. It's moments like these that have often left me wondering if I am a part of some *Truman Show*-style experimental video, with Woody fucking Allen directing it.

Nonetheless, I went to my appointment a little distracted by the remarriage but grateful that I didn't have cancer. When my very handsome, very kind, very tall surgeon came into the room with me, I also stopped a minute to think that all wasn't so bad.

He said, "So. How are you *doing*?" in a really attentive, empathetic way he has. I said, "I'm great! I am just so grateful to know I don't have cancer." And then I watched as his face fell, realizing what was about to happen.

And then it happened.

"You have breast cancer, Leisse, and it's aggressive. We have to get the lumps out *right away*, and biopsy your lymph nodes to see how far it has already spread, and you will likely require chemo, radiation, and possibly a full mastectomy to fully treat this."

I fell apart. I remember the feeling of leaving my body, just feeling like not only had the color drained out of me, but so had my spirit and hope. It felt like I was stuck in a Kafka novel, and that no matter what I did, or how much I healed, it would never be enough; something would always happen to derail my life.

I thought I was going to die. I thought I was going to leave my children motherless (trigger) with a father who didn't seem aware of or interested in their emotional needs (trigger).

I felt, in that moment, like I wanted to just give up.

I looked up at my surgeon and said, "My ex is getting married today. I can't do this. I can't have cancer. I'm single. I have three kids. I'm self-employed. I can't. This can't be happening. What the fuck am I going to do?"

He sat down across from me, held my hands, and fought back his own tears. He said, "You will not believe how strong you are. You can do this, and you will be amazed by how many people will help you."

I refused to believe him, telling him I had no one, *no one* to help me, that I was completely alone, and that I would not have the resources to make this work. I was terrified.

I shared that terror with my aunt. Every part. I told her I was certain I was going to die, and that I wasn't going to tell anyone. I would just slowly check out, knowing I did the best I could for my kids, even if I didn't manage to find an amazing stepdad for them. She very calmly held space for me and talked me down in her own calm, grounded, and rational way. I spoke to her every day, sometimes twice, and before and after every appointment (which, at the beginning of a cancer diagnosis that is rapidly growing, is a lot of appointments). Every time she was able to hear me out and emotionally course-correct what I was feeling to make it slower and less intense.

I remember going to each appointment, waiting at the hospital registration desk and feeling as if I had completely surrendered my identity when I traded them my health card for my ID bracelet. I would sit in the waiting room before the real waiting room—where time and schedules do not exist—often in some kind of genderless and backless blue gown, waiting for another confirmation of my address and date of birth, another needle, another weird test with a scary name.

And I hated it. I was scared, I was angry, and I felt like all the momentum I had built up in the past couple years from leaving my marriage, starting my business, completely investing in myself, and handling layer after layer after layer of crap was coming to a complete stop. And it did not feel fair.

Like, at all.

I knew that chemo was on the table as a suggested course of action, I knew I was going to lose my hair, and I kept imagining the image of "cancer patient" we've all seen shared by well-intentioned friends and family members on social: you know, the one with the bald, emaciated patient in a gown on a gurney giving a thumbs-up with a caption that goes into great detail. And that made me even more mad.

I kept thinking that after all these years, all this bravery, all this *strength* that I was going to be reduced to an image of "ooooh, just not strong *enough*."

This image, on top of *"my ex got married, and I got cancer."*

I guess he wins.

I was not in a good place.

I felt very supported by my aunts, uncles, and close friends, but I still felt pretty alone. I remember coming home from the hospital one day after forgoing work for another round of tests and knowing that I still had about an hour before I needed to pick up the kids from school. I vividly remember lying on my living room floor and rage screaming. There were just primal screaming sounds pouring out of me at the injustice of it all.

Anger, anger, anger.
Fear, fear, fear.

Lying there, I *screamed* out "HOW THE FUCK AM I GOING TO DO THIS?" and hand to God, without a word of a lie, I swear I heard, or felt, a response from way down deep within me:

You are going to make this beautiful.
My breath caught. What?
You are going to make this beautiful.
And that was it; *that* was the turning point.

I realized that while I didn't have control over what was happening, I absolutely had control over how I reacted. I decided to accept what was happening in my life at that moment and to make every single part of the experience absolutely *beautiful*.

I softened my attitude at the hospital. I was nicer to and more patient with everyone around me. I decided then and there to trust my team, even if what they said scared me, and to get to know them more openly . . .

without the intense defense mechanism of judgment.

I wore my leopard print Jimmy Choo's to my appointments and would text friends pictures of my latte, blue gown, and Choo's Instagram-style—from the waiting room.

I took my girlies to Winners to choose a large makeup bag that would house all the chemo pre- and post-meds.

We created a schedule and chart for those meds (each of which has a terrifying name) and coded each vial lid with a rainbow, heart, unicorn, or star sticker, which corresponded *to* the chart we made. So now I knew instead of taking two beta-mexa-hexa-tri-opoly-ethyl-waxadone (or something like that) at 8:30 a.m., I just needed to pop two "shooting stars" at 8:30 a.m. with a light snack. And similarly, if I was starting to feel icky after treatment, I just needed a couple of "rainbow" pills and I'd feel better instantly. This schedule involved my kids in a super accessible way, and *it brought us all joy.*

Beautiful.

I carried all my medical papers and files (of which there were many) in a beautiful watercolor bifold folder with me, and my eldest daughter knit me a coffee cozy I'd use for my paper cup in the waiting room.

We hosted a head-shaving party at home and invited people close not only to me, but to my kids (including their teachers). We made amazing snacks, like our family's famous party popcorn, so that *even if* my shaved head proved to be traumatic, my kids would have friends and snacks as the bulk of their memory to look back on. My *boss* of a friend just tackled the shaving head on, stopping only to give me a mullet (and mullet photo shoot) along the way.

Turns out I look fresh as hell with a shaved head.

Beautiful.

I dug deep and found the bravery to share what was happening on Instagram, and I was met with overwhelming community, support, and love. When I was feeling my most scared and most vulnerable, my most unsure and most insecure, my aunts and uncles were there *without condition*, offering me emotional, medical, family/childcare, and financial support. One of my uncles, a doctor, sat with me and reviewed all the numbers, stats, facts, and figures my oncologist had given me, and he helped me face my fear of doing chemo. He told me it was a no-brainer. He said that without question, it was the right thing to do (not only was the hair loss scary, but because I was so young and healthy, they recommended a very aggressive dose). He told me, through all my tears, that *thousands* of other women had done chemo before me, that I absolutely was capable of doing it, and that it would change me—and make me even stronger.

When I phoned him later to weigh in on radiation versus a double mastectomy (between which I had to choose to endure with my four-month chemo regimen) and confessed in a moment of extreme vulnerability that I was afraid that since I couldn't find a man when I had long blonde waves and double-D boobs, how the hell would I find a man when I was bald and flat? He told me that *any man who would overlook every other awesome thing about me because I was going flat wasn't really a man.*

Beautiful.

When I made the epic decision to go flat, I reached out to the Toronto-based lingerie brand Mary Young and pitched them to be featured, topless, in a photoshoot for their muse series. They said yes.

I reached out to a gal (and now friend) I knew who runs her own personal stylist business and asked her if she'd teach me to dress my new body. She said yes.

Only after that did I book my surgery, and subsequently booked a trip to Austin, so I could take my tits on a taco tour of Texas before I removed them. It was a truly beautiful celebration and great way to mark the end of an era, complete with bumping into Brené Brown (again) and seeing Chris Stapleton live at the perfectly small Austin City Limits, playing a charity event hosted by Matthew McConaughey.

Less than eight months later, I was featured on the cover of NOW magazine in their annual Love Your Body issue.

Fucking *beautiful*.

I had decided that since I was going to have extra time on my hands and wouldn't be able to go out very often because of the weakened immune system chemo provides that I would take the four months of treatment and start a podcast (now top 100 in five countries and five-star rated) and write my book proposal. I pressed Send on that final 102-page document to the literary agent I was pitching at the time from the hospital waiting room moments before my last treatment.

And I think we know how that story ends, and it's *beautiful*.

At the time, and even more so in hindsight, I am profoundly aware of the many miracles I was blessed with along the way immediately after I made a shift in my thinking:

My cancer had not spread to any other part of me.

Miracle.

I tolerated chemo so well that I was able to do each session on track and on time without ever getting sick.

Miracle.

People at every checkpoint in the medical system pulled strings to make my experience more enjoyable, easier, and way more affordable.

Miracle.

My nurses knew me from Instagram before I was a patient and saved the best corner seat in the best light for me so I could write peacefully each session.

Miracle.

For each of my surgeries I was assigned my incredibly handsome and charming surgeon as well as the sexiest, *funniest* anesthetist, and I felt so comfortable in their care I fell asleep not from laughing gas but from the jokes we were cracking in the OR.

Miracle.

Blessed, blessed, blessed.
Love, love, love.
And my family. I still can't share this part without welling up. This experience brought my family closer in ways I had no idea possible.

My aunts formed a dream team: taking care of me, cooking, cleaning, organizing my basement, and driving me to pick up my kids from school (I refused to change any part of their routine because I am stubborn as hell).

My kids were absolute angels. I told them information in a super age-appropriate way, as it affected their lives and when they needed to know it, and encouraged them to share any and all feelings along the way:

Things like "I'm afraid you'll look bad with a shaved head" turned out to be false.

"You look like a giant baby now that you're bald" turned out to be true.

Drawings of family photos now included me with no hair, but happy and smiling was also true. Laying low in the evening after treatment with my aunt, pizza, popcorn, and a movie became a tradition. My kids went to their dad's for the weekend after we dropped them off at school in the morning, so things stayed pretty normal.

Postmastectomy, I had "drains" coming out of my sides. The idea of these drains had caused me so much anxiety because of how gross they sounded. They were tubes, literally embedded into the sides of my body. The tubes drained liquid from the surgery sites and gathered it into little bulbs attached to the ends of the tubes. Which *was* as gross as it sounded.

For two weeks, every day, twice a day, the color and volume of the fluid in the bulbs had to be measured, recorded on a chart, and emptied out. I was horrified by it. But my girlies thought it was kind of science-project-creepy-cool. So we made this procedure beautiful too.

My kids were responsible for charting the content results, meaning they each took turns describing the color, and measured then recorded the volume of each bulb as I emptied the contents into the little beaker. "Vampire red," "candy apple," and "dark cherry" were my favorites, and before I knew it, even this super weird, very gross post-care procedure became . . . *fun* and something to look forward to. It brought joy to something that I never anticipated would *be* joyful.

My girls were respectful of my energy levels and my need to lay low, and they gingerly snuggled me on the couch. It was so *easy* and peaceful with them, and while we were very close before, this experience, too, deepened our love and connection because of how open and bonded we were throughout the whole thing. They were eight, six, and six, by the way, so this was ultra-impressive to me.

My friends showed up so powerfully. They did research for me when I couldn't bear to look up "going flat" and "risks of chemo," then vetted the info back to me. They drove me to appointments and stopped for breakfast sandwiches along the way. They made cookies and snacks and mac 'n cheese in small, freezable portions, which made our home life so easy. They came to the great "ringing of the bell" ceremony when chemo was done.

Parents from our school community organized a little fund and asked me what I needed most. And sure enough, the first snowfall arrived, and so did the driveway guy they hired to take care of snow removal when I literally could not.

I was honestly overwhelmed with the kindness, love, and support unlike any I had ever felt before.

Cancer, for me, was a Trojan horse for deep healing. It forced me to confront deep and old fears of being unlovable and then face them head on to finally, finally disprove them and move on. It taught me to lead with my light and to appreciate that beauty genuinely does come from within, as does confidence. It led me down paths of forgiveness, by necessity, for even the ones who have never—and will never—apologize. It forced me to let go of my own agenda and trust the flow of my life, for real this time. And it taught me that when you do have the courage to let go and trust that everything is unfolding in perfect order, in perfect timing, you appreciate that things do, in fact, work out.

Cancer gave me some of my greatest lessons. It brought me closer to my connection to the divine and unseen, while giving me the ultimate perspective that everything has a season, each of which really does come to pass. It taught me to shed layer after layer and remove mask after mask to arrive, finally, at the me-est version of me, and it better informed each area of my business to help other people shed these layers for themselves. And finally, it let me feel free to show up and just BE.

It was cancer that was the ultimate culmination of life experiences that allowed me to live fully in my true calling because it was the final push for me to not only love but *accept* myself exactly as I am.

This was the birth of Emotional Alchemy.

Cancer was a wild card. I had dealt with my shit. I was living the life I wanted. I'd had the wake-up call already and made the changes I needed to make. Getting breast cancer, out of nowhere, took me deeper into my self-discovery and self-creation than I'd known to be possible.

I never anticipated illness as a part of my life or as a part of my story; while my ex was getting married, traveling the globe, building his dream house, I was getting cancer and losing my hair.

It was tough to come to terms with it all. And I firmly believe that had all that had come before not come before, I would not have handled this time period well.

Having cancer was a massive flag that there was some deep work to be done, and it guided me to do it. I remember reflecting during treatment and watching how my professional momentum had actually grown during what I thought would be a massive setback, and I realized that I had played an active role in that: I chose to make having cancer a meaningful, purposeful experience. I refused to feel victimized, and I refused to use language like "fuck cancer, kick it's ass, cancer is a bitch." It actually makes me wince to hear those words. I am confident that my decision, ability, and commitment to surrender, trust, and flow with the diagnosis and treatment had a huge impact on my mental and emotional health.

I reflected on every part of my life. No matter what level of adversity I faced, I had always chosen to repurpose the pain and make it my own—make it into something beautiful. Just like the alchemist turns lead into gold, I was turning trauma into beauty, and I knew it needed to be shared with more people who could use the support.

And voilà . . . you're reading it.

Shadow work—confronting the darkest parts that you don't even want to know about, let alone feel—is fundamental to being able to fully heal and next-level the love you have for yourself . . . exactly as you are.

Can you love yourself enough to go to your shadow parts
and bravely turn on the light?
Can you love yourself enough to love and accept yourself
exactly as you are?

Yes, you fucking can.

CHAPTER 28

Emotional Alchemy

"Take your broken heart, make it into art."

~Carrie Fisher

It's time to stop letting your past dictate your future. The only way to move forward is to let go of what has been holding you back.

Emotional Alchemy is the term I use to label your ability to take every single thing that has happened in your life and make it make sense. Take the dark, heavy, ugly pieces and transform them into something light, beautiful, and uniquely your own, and allow your experience to be shaped or informed by them, not defined by them.

This next section is action oriented. Inspired action.

I've broken down the process I used (and still use in times of perceived chaos and stress) into an emotional tool kit to process the dark stuff into the good stuff. Alchemy itself is an ancient art: "The teacher appears when the student is ready." If you are here right now, it's by design—let me be your teacher who guides you through the outline of what the process looks like, then find a way to perfect it for yourself and make it your own.

Healing isn't linear, so use this process in the way that feels right for you in this moment. We are effectively talking about choosing love over fear, and you know that while some fear is very purposeful, some is limiting and self-sabotaging. Keep that in mind as you proceed because some of this work will feel like a big ask of yourself. That's very good feedback that it's *exactly* what you need to do to heal and make your own experiences make sense in order to move forward from them in a healthy way.

Self-love is at the root of this process, and the cool thing is that as you get further along in the process, your self-love, confidence, and self-acceptance will grow. The reality is that yes, behavior change is hard but also that nothing changes if nothing changes. *To get to the next phase of your life you have to GO DEEP.* It is all about finding clarity in what you want and finding confidence in who you are.

Can you love yourself enough to find the courage to stay true to both?

Yes, you fucking can.

CHAPTER 29

The how-to of emotional alchemy

This chapter is effectively "how to deal with your shit in a low-key and lifestyle-friendly way to make the changes you've been avoiding making while feeling the things you've been avoiding feeling."

Big breath.

Emotional Alchemy is the bridge I took from how I felt to how I *feel,* making radical internal shifts to do so. I had to learn to get very clear on where the source of all my emotions was coming from, what was triggering them, then learn to persevere and push through (as illustrated in "The Vine Story"). Frustratingly, the only way out is through, so I had to learn effective coping mechanisms to manage my thoughts, emotions, actions, and behaviors so I could navigate the most challenging periods of my life, while remaining the woman I wanted to be.

Here's what I did, and what I genuinely believe anyone can do, to heal from just about anything.[6]

---

6 To help make sense of my past and get clear on the depths of abuse that I personally had experienced, I chose EMDR therapy, which dramatically helped my C-PTSD.

The following is what I pieced together as I moved on to where I wanted to be and ultimately to where I am now.

These ten NLP and mindset practices are what made up the tool kit that helped me do just that; borrowing from Buddhist principles and all of the various therapies, energy works, and courses I had taken, I was able to carve out a highly effective skill set to coach myself through anything. It worked for divorce, became central to my own coaching practice, would prove to be fundamental in navigating cancer as well as I did, and ultimately is THE guidebook on how I completely transformed my life. I call this process Emotional Alchemy.

THE TEN EASY[7] *(ha ha ha ha ha ha)* STEPS OF EMOTIONAL ALCHEMY

1. INTENTIONS

Every morning when you wake up, take a moment to set your intention for the day. Write it down as soon as you wake up, even if it's in the Notes app on your phone (or here in the margins).

You can use an intention deck (I love anything Buddhist inspired, especially Thich Nat San who I use as a resource) or come up with something on your own that feels good and resonates deep within your body.

---

7 There is nothing easy or overnight about this process. It's deep and layered and cyclical and often is made easier when someone is helping facilitate your healing. And you know what? It's worth every second. When we are talking about success, we are really talking about inner peace; my inner peace is the most valuable thing I own, and yours will become your greatest asset.

Prompt:

"Today I am guided by . . ."

"Today I choose to . . ."

Whenever you start to feel challenged in the day (by yourself or those around you), I want you to come back to yourself and your intention. Only you control how you act, and a daily intention will shape that level of calm. Your ex sends a nasty text? Shit hits the fan at work? You find out something on social media that makes you feel left out or unseen?

"Today I am guided by patience / kindness / finding the good in everyone / keeping my cool . . ."

Over and over.

Setting and living with daily intentions is a huge part of how you teach your brain to see things differently; you already know that if we want to see things differently we have to change the lens we look through, and daily intentions will absolutely get you there. It's like setting a boundary for your own reaction so that you can start to control what you allow to get to you and what you allow to melt away. It is highly powerful and effective, particularly in times of stress and chaos. When you need an easy way to ground yourself, come back to center and regulate your own emotional response. Intentions are your best friend.

Can you love yourself enough to live with intention?

Yes, you fucking can.

2. MIRROR TALK

Imagine you had a friend who told you that you were fat every time you went out; that you deserve to be in a shitty relationship because you'll never find anyone better (and God knows you can't do this alone); that you'll never succeed because everyone else has better ideas and is smarter than you, and frankly, they're prettier too, so you may as well give up now and quit dreaming about anything other than what you have already.

It wouldn't take long to block this friend's calls and spend time with someone just a little bit nicer.

So what the heck are you doing talking to yourself like that? The longest and best relationship we'll ever have is the one we have with ourselves; yes, we are taught to focus on the relationships outside ourselves first, and that is a wildly misinformed fallacy. Sure, we are social beings who need connection, but we also share literally every breath of this life with ourselves, so shouldn't we take some time to know us? Like us? Appreciate us? Admire us? LOVE us?

If you want another "easy" mindset hack, you must change your inner dialogue. For me, doing this was not easy at first. I had learned and internalized so many toxic messages from other people in my life that I had adopted them as my own. So telling myself "hey, I believe in you and your abilities to start this business" was the equivalent of me saying, "Oh look, the sky is actually green."

At first I'd think: "Yeah . . . no. You can say that, but I don't believe it. Basically everyone is more qualified and more liked than I am," just like I would have thought: "Yeah . . . no. The sky is always, and has always been, blue." For me, the biggest shift in my inner dialogue was talking to myself in the mirror in the same way I talk to my kids:

"Hi, sunshine! Did you sleep well? Hey, we've got a big day today! We're going to write that pitch together, and I am here to support you the whole time." Likewise, at the end of the day, it might sound something like: "My darling, I know today did not go as you planned. And I know that's frustrating. Let's focus on everything that went right and what we learned for next time. No matter what, I am so proud of you for trying."

If you wouldn't say something to a young child, friend, or family member you love and respect, you will no longer say it to yourself, period. No more "I'm so bad at . . ." or "I could never . . ." or "There's no way I can . . ." No more sarcasm or self-deprecating humor either because it's actually incredibly spiteful language fueled by self-rejection. From now on, put yourself on a steady diet of positivity, hope, light-hearted humor, encouragement, and support.

Even now I coach myself in the mirror when I'm going through hard times and lift myself up with pep talks throughout the day. Do you feel a little nuts at first? Totally. But then you become aware of this really lovely relationship you've been building with yourself, and even in the loneliest or most challenging times of your life you realize and appreciate that you are never alone.

The more "enough" you become, the more satisfying this relationship gets.

Can you love yourself enough to speak kindly to yourself?

Yes, you fucking can.

3. AFFIRMATIONS

I read the book *You Can Heal Your Life* by Louise Hay at exactly the right time in my life and continue to use the practice of *repeating what you want to be true* over and over in my current life. We have talked about the power of our thoughts and beliefs and changing the lens on what we thought to be true versus what we want to be true, and affirmations are a great tool to use. I started speaking about myself and my life as if what I wanted was already here and happening—until it was—and practiced gratitude for it as if it were already mine. For example:

"I am so grateful for my loving, healthy, happy family."

"Let abundance flow through me so that I may serve others."

"I choose to let love in."

"Thank you for the freedom and wealth I have created in my business."

"I love myself enough to trust the process; I know that things always work out for me."

During my cancer experience, I would go down to the lake and scream out *"I am healed and whole"* until I believed it and could teach myself to expect it to be true.

Cultivating a relationship with affirmations is a significant part of creating new "footprints" in your snow and building new neural pathways. You basically flood your brain with the story you want to be true until it feels effortless to believe it.

Can you love yourself enough to trust your ability to affirm what you want in your life?

Yes, you fucking can.

4. GRATITUDE + JOY

You'd never know it now, but many years ago I was *the most judgmental person*. I came by it honestly: I grew up loathing myself and judging with great criticism everything I did, and it felt natural to judge *literally everyone* around me. At home it felt like we earned street cred if we could really cut someone up and point out all their flaws, and this practice became my pattern of relatability.

I remember someone saying to me in my twenties, "Why don't you take a look around you and think of everything you have to be grateful for? That might help you feel better off." I also remember feeling exceptionally confused when I heard it. I had no idea what they meant. But it was getting close to the moment I was "waking up," and I was ready to start making small changes.

When I first started my gratitude practice, it was just more judgment: "Thank goodness I don't look like that" and "I'm so happy I'm smarter than he is." It did not feel good.

But then, after literally four days of consciously looking for things to be grateful for, my world changed. It's hard for me to look back and imagine my life without gratitude because it's just my natural baseline now, but at the time it did take work.

It started with: "I am grateful for this green light. And this parking spot. And this beautiful home. And my children. And my hot tub. And my car, and and and and . . ." I went from judgment to material things. Until I really got going.

"I am so grateful for this sunshine. And this breeze. And to live in a safe and peaceful country. And for this healthy body. And my legs. And my family. And my EQ. And my sense of humor. And this food on my plate. And and and and . . ."

And then I learned to shift even the stuff I hated into gratitude: "How lucky am I to have electricity? It's so amazing that I just flick a switch and the light or heat comes on. Man, I love running water. I can't believe I get to turn on my tap and out comes fresh, clean, cold water for me, anytime I want! Oh, how I love my phone! I have built an entire business using this little iPhone, and it only costs me $80 a month to do so! *The Office* is my favorite show, and I get to watch it over and over just by paying this bill. Wow, wow, wow, I am so fortunate to live in a place where, when I am hungry, I can walk into *an entire room of food*, bring it home, and make something awesome to keep my family healthy and full. I love taxes! Paying a lot of tax means I am doing really well in my business, *and* it buys me the opportunity to live in a clean, safe place where my healthcare is paid for in advance. AND I get to help support other people who aren't quite there yet. And and and and and."

It's remarkable.

When you deliberately take stock of what it is you *actually have* right here, right now in this moment, it's *beyond* abundant. And for the times when it all feels like it's falling apart and we have nothing?

"I am grateful for the air in my lungs."
"I am grateful for the lessons I am learning through this time of unknown."

It's such a humbling exercise and is probably the fastest way to shift your entire outlook on life: just shift into what you are grateful for and immediately you feel better off, wealthier, and more supported than you knew possible. One of the coolest things about gratitude, from a mindset perspective, is that it allows you to *amp up the joy* in virtually any situation.

Repeat: Gratitude amps up your joy in any situation, and because more always begets more, once you have a little bit of joy, you'll start to find more of it. And because practicing gratitude becomes basically an addictive lifestyle, you just keep amping up the joy and magnifying it until it takes over. And because joy is such a powerful feeling, it calms your parasympathetic nervous system, allowing you to stay less anxious about and more aware of the reality of your life.

> *Can you love yourself enough to choose gratitude?*
> *Can you love yourself enough to find the joy?*

Yes, you fucking can.

5. EMOTIONAL AWARENESS

I had always felt sad in my life and had always treated "sadness." But sometimes our feelings present as one thing and are actually the combination of two other things. When we see purple, we experience purple, not the combination of red and blue. I started to be more aware of my true feelings, many of which I had been terrified of having (hello, decades worth of anger) and ashamed of (talking to you, resentment), and in giving myself permission to feel them, I was able to process them, reconcile them, and let them go.

The more you listen to your own needs and limits, the more you honor, respect, and love yourself. And the more you honor, respect, and love yourself, the better you get at listening to your own needs and limits; either way, you're winning. All you really have to do is listen, even if you don't like the message you're hearing.

You always have the answers inside of you, and chances are if you're having a hard time hearing them, it's because you've become very good at tuning them out. Let yourself get quiet while you sit in the stillness and hear what it is your gut, your heart, and your intuition have to say. They're not wrong and will always guide you to the right decision in the right way at the right time—you just might not like the action that requires you to take.

As with any inner growth work, this period of transition (you know, the one in which you stop listening to and meeting the needs of others before your own) can feel messy and complicated, especially if you're used to listening to other people's versions of what is best for you and how other people expect you should live your life. But that, too, is now an old pattern, an old behavior that you're allowed to get rid of. This next chapter of your life is focused on how YOU take care of you and meet and care for your own needs. So know your limits and act accordingly in a way that makes you feel safe, supported, cared for, and loved.

Declare that you will honor your own needs for emotional health and wellness before you honor those of anyone else. This declaration doesn't mean you're going to be a jerk to people, it means you're going to take a good long listen to what you need before you agree to being a part of what someone else needs; if that doesn't align with what you know your limits are, you have permission to say no.

Can you love yourself enough to honor your own feelings?

Yes, you fucking can.

6. ACCOUNTABILITY + ACCEPTANCE

You are *at cause* for your life.
And the sooner you realize it, the easier everything will be.

Nobody is coming to save you.
Nobody is to blame.
Nobody has *made* you feel a particular way.
Nobody has done anything *to* you.
Nobody is holding you back.

You are here to live your life.
You are here to take responsibility for that life.
You are the gatekeeper of your own emotions.
You are able to choose to see all of the events in your life as that which has happened *for* you.
You are your own best advocate, champion, and hype squad.

We are all born into our own unique circumstance; there is a deeper spiritual perspective that suggests we make a soul contract or agreement, before we even enter into this lifetime, that lays out all the lessons we need to learn while we're here. And from there, across our whole lifetime, we simply follow the cosmic bread crumbs our soul and intuition hint at for us to pay attention to and participate in, in the unfolding of our lives. And in that way, we know that every single person we meet, song we hear, and experience we have is by divine orchestration.

That *we* agreed to.

I find this notion exceptionally comforting, and here's why: In nature, there are no mistakes. There is order and perfection, with an absolute balance in its orchestration. In times of great challenge or strife, when everything feels chaotic, unknown, or out of control, I like to zoom out the focus on my life, and instead of seeing the split second of history that we're in right now, to see my life as the sum of its parts.

What is so comforting to me is that this means anything that happens, good or bad, isn't really good or bad—it just *is*. And when I can ease myself back to that place of neutrality and acceptance, I can get curious about *why it is happening*. I'm not angry or sad, but curious.

And when I can come at my life through that lens, knowing it is all unfolding exactly as my highest self has already planned out, then I am able to be exceptionally honest with myself.

"Yes, I did overspend, which is why this month feels so scary. I chose to be unprepared."

"Yes, I did play an active role in that relationship, and it was I who settled for 'less than' for too long."

"Yes, I understand this opportunity didn't work out, even when I thought it should. I trust that something better is already on the way."

Shifting into a lens of accountability shifts you *out* of victim mentality.

"Why does this always happen to me?"

"How come nothing good ever comes my way? Nothing ever works out the way I want it to."

"I always get hurt in relationships; it's like I am a jackass magnet."

When you let yourself sit in victim mentality, you are assigning all the power and all the control to something external to you. If you want to *take that power back*, you have no choice other than to shift into a state of accountability and accept that you play an active, cocreative role in your life. You have a say. You can take action. You can change the circumstances of your life.

This is one of the most empowering tools I can share with you: You are not the product of your story, you are the *author*. So write it accordingly.

> *Can you love yourself enough to take accountability for your life?*
> *Can you love yourself enough to choose acceptance?*

Yes, you fucking can.

7. FORGIVENESS

Forgiveness is the art of letting go. I love how John Steinbeck worded it: "Time works like a damp brush on watercolor. The sharp edges blur, the ache goes out of it . . . and from the many separated lines a solid gray emerges."

This is the Mack Daddy of the tool kit, and possibly the most challenging. It is also essential as part of your growth and healing to master this skill; go gently as you do so.

In order to truly feel free from your past you need to find a way to forgive the ones who have hurt you, including *yourself*.

Ooooh, baby. Get the tissues.

This is a big ask in itself. What's even bigger? The people you most likely need to forgive are the ones who will *never ask for your forgiveness*. They are the ones who will probably never apologize, at least not on your timeline, because it's more than likely that if they were able to hurt you as badly as they did, they don't even believe that what they did was wrong.

This knowledge is a painful realization because it punctures the illusion that things are always fair. They are not. And when someone, especially someone close to you, hurts you like this, it simply isn't fair. And it isn't fair that they won't say sorry, and it isn't fair that they don't feel remorse.

None of that is fair. And still, it is what it is.

If this understanding is making you queasy, let me put it this way: It is your choice to sit around feeling the unfairness of it all and waiting for an apology that is likely never going to come. Or you can take back control, find a way to make peace with it on your own, and finally move on.

There is really only one choice here.

Trust me, I know intimately that having to take on the responsibility of forgiving the person (or people) that hurt you *is not fair*.

But you know what is most unfair of all? Living the best of your life with anger, resentment, and bitterness and with the story of how someone hurt you and just won't apologize.

Again, *we don't want the thing, we want the feeling we think the thing will give us.*

In this case, it's not necessarily the apology we want, it's the feeling of validation, being seen, being worthy, being acknowledged in your pain, and wanting to move on. So, entertaining the very likely possibility that the person who really hurt you won't apologize to you on your timeline, cut to "the how" of how you create this feeling:

Really see your experience for what it was.

Validate your feelings.

Acknowledge the realness of your pain.

Know you are worthy of feeling good and letting it go. Be free to move on.

Forgiveness is a release process. It's the process of releasing old shit you've been hanging on to for a long time and releasing the feeling of being angry or resentful toward someone. And that's a big ask. When you feel that you've been wronged or hurt by someone, the tendency is to hang on to that hurt and stay in a victim state: "This happened to me." When you are in that state, it becomes a part of your narrative and starts to define the story of who you are, which you know you don't want. So you need to find the resolve to forgive, and as Gandhi himself said, "The weak can never forgive; forgiveness is an attribute of the strong."

When we allow ourselves to hang on to the pain of the past, and the people who caused it, we are actively holding space for them in our being. We are actively nourishing them and their damage as a part of our narrative, and it's really unhealthy. It's really unhealthy because we let that pain and those people define who we are through their actions and because holding that space for them takes up valuable space that we could be using to house new, beautiful, loving people and actions. It really is like a closet that you need to purge: even if you've had that sweater forever, and even if it has sentimental value, if it ain't serving you, get it out of there and bring in something that makes you feel as beautiful as you truly are.

Start by forgiving yourself.

Forgiving yourself goes hand in hand with letting things go. Personally speaking, I was very angry and resentful for a very long time about the fact that no one had been there protecting me from my parents, and no one had been there protecting me through my divorce. It burned; it felt like no one was there and that no one cared.

But then I had an "aha moment" one day when I realized there actually *was* one person there all along who had witnessed all the bad behavior and abuse and enabled it all without speaking up or taking action.

And that person was *me*. Ouch.

That was an even more painful realization—that I had never spoken up on my own behalf.

I had to learn to forgive myself for standing by and accepting all of it and allowing it to happen. When I became comfortable forgiving myself, I began to forgive others too.

Learn to forgive yourself for being there or not, for making the decision or not, and for anything else you have been punishing yourself about for too long. Yes, this is a process.

Then forgive someone for doing something petty that annoyed you or inconvenienced your day. This forgiveness is like a trial run. Use the guy who was kind of a dick at the coffee shop this morning or the gal who was super dismissive on the phone. Allow yourself to feel and release the anger, then forgive them.

When you get good at that kind of forgiveness, and it starts to feel easy to forgive, start to map out how you can forgive "the big one." *(Big note to underline here: Depending on your own unique context, you may feel comfortable doing this on your own or you may choose to work with a psychologist who can safely guide you through working through physical or sexual trauma of the past. Again, our subconscious cannot differentiate between real and perceived danger, so if you are getting triggered in a real way, this might be something you need to work through with a trained therapist.)*

You might find it helpful to write out:
1. Who has wronged you
2. Why it hurt
3. What you learned
4. Why you are *grateful* for it

The above is a shockingly freeing exercise because it allows you to get to the root of your emotional vine as well as illustrate the clarity that *there is always something to take away from every experience.* In reconciling those feelings of resentment, turning them into forgiveness, and shifting into gratitude, it's as if you let go of all the baggage and make room for so much more *good stuff.*

You may need to confront those who've trespassed against your boundaries and heart. You'll know it if it feels right, often because you'll want to throw up. Sometimes, because of context or circumstance, confronting someone head on isn't the best plan, and if there is past violent or sexual trauma, this is a guided or facilitated process you will want to work on with a psychologist to keep you physically and emotionally safe. There is power and strength in that too.

Know your limits; this kind of work is massively evolved, and many (yikes, most?) people choose not to do it. So the fact that you are strong enough to not only recognize but confront and deal with your demons speaks volumes of your character, your heart, and your passion for a life worth living. Truly.

Integrating past pain is essential to feeling like a whole person, and self-love is, at its core, about accepting and loving each of those parts. So this deep and sometimes painful work is paramount to getting to that blissful "other side."

Know too, however, that it's okay to go *slowly*. It's okay to move through the work in a way that protects and honors you. Sometimes protecting and honoring yourself will mean limiting your interactions with certain people and environments or interacting with them from a safe distance until you feel comfortable and ready to face them head on. And sometimes it may mean cutting off contact entirely, even if temporarily, if that is what serves your emotional health and wellness most authentically.

You're basically a certified doctor of love now.

Can you love yourself enough to forgive yourself?
Can you love yourself enough to forgive others?
Can you love yourself enough to let go of the past and move on?

Yes, you fucking can.

8. COMPASSION

Once you've found the ability and desire to forgive, you are able to have so much compassion for the ones you are forgiving. Let's circle back to appreciating that we—all of us—are just children of children. And let's circle back to the perfection of the beautiful Maya Angelou-ism that tells us we are all doing the best we can with what we have, and when we know better, we do better.

That is a straight-up life truth.

We are all perfectly flawed. It is conceivable that each of our "short-comings" is also designed to help someone else learn vicariously through us, and that in the realness of each of us figuring it out, we are also teaching one another.

Some of that teaching and figuring out *is* making mistakes. People can cause us a lot of hurt, and sometimes it's because they don't know any better in that moment. Listen, I am not saying by any means that we have to tolerate, condone, allow, enable, or approve of that behavior, nor am I advocating that we need to have a relationship with the person who has hurt us before. Boundaries are essential to our well-being and foundational in our own unconditional love of self.

I am saying that we can all choose to dig way down deep and find compassion for where someone was at a particular time in their life, making the mistake they were making at the time. This, too, is a process. This is a huge ask and is next-level maturity to be able to engage in this epic mindset shift; love rewards the brave and mastering the art of compassion is an ultimate harbinger of inner peace. When you can teach yourself to let go of the anger and welcome compassion in its place, you will find you are more and more at home within yourself.

Can you love yourself enough to find compassion for others?

Yes, you fucking can.

9. SURRENDER + FAITH

Personally speaking, through the process of learning to forgive, have compassion, take accountability, set intentions, have gratitude, find joy, speak to myself lovingly, and affirm what I want to be true to *be* true, I found myself calling to some kind of spirit for help and comfort and guidance.

I had been raised a staunch atheist for decades, so the thought of saying "God," let alone *believing* in God, used to make me feel very nervous. I don't know what you call your spiritual entity or connection; people seem to be very comfortable saying the Universe or Source, but for me it's G-O-D. I don't think it matters what you call it, but I do think it matters that you name it for you and cultivate a relationship with it, even if it's just dipping a toe in the water to get started.

Because here's the thing: we are not alone.

We are never alone. We are always divinely protected and guided, often in ways we simply cannot, or choose not to, understand at the time. Amid all the emotional upheaval in this life, it can feel isolating if you think you're doing it alone. It is often in our darkest times—when we feel the most alone—that we start reaching for a power bigger than ourselves.

That's when even the nonbelievers start praying for things to turn around, and it's amazing: no matter what brings you to this spiritual place, this place of surrendering to the wisdom of the unseen, it's like God is always there waiting for you, welcoming you home. I think we are born into this state of grace and that we feel the unseen very naturally in our early years, and I think it's the adults around us who tell us we're wrong, that our imaginary friends aren't real, that our dreams don't count, and that a lot of things just aren't possible.

I think we suppress, in many cases, our connection to the divine (not to an institution of organized religion, but to *the* divine), and it's in those dark and shadowed moments of our lives that we tend to *start* that journey home.

Personally, as someone who had been trained to not feel her feelings and to never trust her intuition, when I flipped that script and started leaning into not only how I felt but also following something I felt to be true—with no physical "proof" other than what I felt was right—I was looking for guidance and anchors to let me know I was doing the right thing as it happened.

I turned to tarot and oracle decks, found myself drawn to more spiritual people and practices, and eventually found the humility to understand that *I was talking to God.*

And God was listening.

I found after all this time feeling lonely and alone that I really had never been alone at all—I just hadn't realized the power that was there with me and within me. Because that's exactly what it felt like: I didn't have to go anywhere or do anything to talk to God, I just had to feel into it. And it hit me again that God dwells within me and is always guiding me.

Truthfully, I believe God resides within each of us and that is what, foundationally, connects us all. I don't fully understand it, but to me it feels like God is an energy, God is love, and we are all tapped into this loving energy as if we're cut from the same cloth, sharing the same thread. It's so peaceful. It also means that by honoring what is best for me, I am honoring what is best for the greater good. And by honoring what is best for the greater good, I am always honoring what is best for me because we are all connected.

And if we're all connected, if we're all sharing the same source of loving energy, then not only are we never alone, we are always loved and are always walking some wild ride of a path that is unfolding for the greatest good in all of us.

It is that simple, and it is that complicated. What it really is, is magic.

Once I appreciated the interconnectivity of it all, the perfection of it all, the divine orchestration of it all, I learned that I could allow myself to *let go,* little by little, and trust the process.

When I really thought about it, I had always been physically safe and cared for; I had made bad decisions but never the kind that put me in danger of devastating addiction or violation, for example. I let myself surrender and trust that everything would not only work out just fine but that it already was, that whatever I wanted to create, I could, and I began to let go of the control of the "how" and the "when" and focused more on how I wanted to feel.

You can do it too; it might be as simple as asking a question and listening for the answer. Or have your natal chart read. Or study human design. Or find a great tarot reader. Or sit in meditation and ask your guides to reveal some clues to you. Or look back on things you *wished* would work out, and perhaps forgot to notice when they did. Or have amazing sex with someone you love and trust, looking into their eyes the whole time and feeling the insane energy of sacred connectivity.

Or or or or or.

There are so many ways to get in touch with your divine. It's fascinating because while a lot of what we want to have or feel doesn't necessarily fall into place on our preferred timeline, it tends to always fall into place on the right timeline. And when we are only looking for things to work out in the way we want them to, when we want them to, we forget to pay attention to the beautiful mandala of a cosmic dance happening around us at any given moment.

Look up.

> *Can you love yourself enough to look up?*
> *Can you love yourself enough to have faith?*

Yes, you fucking can.

10. OPTIMISM, PATIENCE + HOPE

If forgiveness is the most empowering gift I can share with you, then optimism is the greatest gift you can share with yourself.

Learn to err on the side of possibility. Sure, things might not work out (cough, the way you expected), but they have an equal (if not higher) chance of working out even *better* than you expected. And because we cannot say for sure which is which until it's happened, then our choice becomes to sit around and worry or sit around and have hope.

Generally, what you think, becomes. Especially if what you think is what you believe. Then it *really* becomes.

But also? Having hope, being optimistic, and being patient throughout the process is a little more relaxing and a lot more fun.

To keep a positive outlook, to create joy in your life and for yourself, and to keep on keeping on, you have to appreciate that sometimes good things take time. When you teach yourself to live in that place, everything changes. You assume the best, you enjoy things for what they are, and your anxiety plummets as you begin to appreciate that there really isn't a one-size-fits-all timeline: the key to inner peace is trusting that it's all happening and unfolding as it should and that you are being guided along a path that is yours alone to explore and create.

Getting comfortable with that mindset is its own point of arrival; having that conversation with other people in your life is a whole other beast. You might find, through each of the tools in this Emotional Alchemy tool kit (and throughout your life as a whole), that there are some people who just won't get there with you.

Many, actually.

And while that may hurt in the short term, it's important to honor your own boundaries that protect the path you're on . . . because it's leading you to where it's going. And the others? Now that you are a master of forgiveness and compassion, you can accept that you are still connected to them and they are still connected to you, even if it's not in the way that you thought. What did you learn? What did you teach? Were those lessons aligned? Did they cause friction?

This questioning is all powerful for your own emotional awareness and deepens your understanding that they, too, are on their own path home to themselves, learning the lessons that they, too, divinely orchestrated for what they needed to learn in this life. Whoa, right? They, too, are figuring it out; they, too, are making mistakes; they, too, are setting loving healthy boundaries—and their own current moment may not include or align with your present moment.

And that's all okay.

You can keep moving forward knowing that you are more and more ready, every single day, to call in and attract the ones with whom you *are* aligned with in this moment. You're ready for the next opportunity that *is* for you and *is* supportive of your ultimate path of exploration.

Because we never know (until after the fact) what's going to happen or when, you have to have enough faith in yourself to believe that you are a tiny part of the bigger whole, all designed to live harmoniously.

Can you love yourself enough to choose an optimistic
outlook?
Can you love yourself enough to have hope?
Can you love yourself enough to be patient?

Yes, you fucking can.

***

So there you have it. Ten foundational elements that make up my brand of Emotional Alchemy, all working in their own harmony to heal from just about anything. Use the chapters on fear, love, and your subconscious mind to really drive home that not only is there a *how* to heal but that you are *allowed* to heal. You are *safe* to let this go.

Too often we hang onto things for the express purpose that we've always hung onto them. They've become our story, and who on earth will we be without that story?

You are more than the sum of your parts; you are a dynamic, living, breathing child of the universe, and you are not here by accident. Everything that has ever happened has happened for a reason, even if we don't know that reason or don't particularly like it. Understanding Emotional Alchemy will help you let go of that old story and allow you to become the person you were meant to be—the one you already are.

You are not defined by any one event or trait in your life; you can use them to inform your experience by hanging onto the embedded lessons with emotional neutrality, then let the rest go.

Can you love yourself enough to practice Emotional Alchemy in your own life?

Yes, you fucking can.

CHAPTER 30

How to set healthy, loving boundaries

The most valuable thing I own? My peace. Hands down. And man, I have paid a high price for it, both literally and figuratively.

Although I had very much hoped to Amazon Prime my peace (like I do with most of the other things I want in my life), I instead had to learn how to set very clear, very healthy, very loving boundaries. "Boundaries" is a fancy way of saying "self-protection."

Setting boundaries is a highly valuable concept to you if you:
+ relate to being a people-pleaser
+ do or act for others because you feel like you have to and fear what would happen if you didn't
+ feel like your energy is drained a lot of the time from listening to other people's problems (because hey, you're supportive)
+ do things and go places out of a feeling of obligation rather than of intention

+ have ever snapped at someone out of the blue for invading your personal or energetic space

+ feel like you are constantly giving and giving but with very little reciprocity

+ are constantly being sought out for your advice and expert opinion on something you do professionally or as a "hobby" but are never paid for your time or expertise

Establishing healthy, loving boundaries is a way of protecting ourselves from being constantly at someone else's beck and call, particularly emotionally. If you have set boundaries in your life and in your relationships, you are sending an effective and comfortable message that you value and respect your time.

We've all had the experience of being taken advantage of, of leaving a conversation feeling drained, or of having the anxious pit of dread kick in before a family function that we REALLY don't want to go to but feel as if we have to. These experiences stem directly from having little to no boundaries, and there's only one person who can control or change that:

You.

You are running your own show, calling your own shots, and directing the nature of your relationships, and although it might be a bitter pill to swallow (because it's way easier to blame someone else), *you are enabling* these nasty and borderline soul-crushing behaviors.

The good news?

You can absolutely change that.

Here's why boundaries matter and how you can set (and honor) them in a healthy, loving way.

The phrase "not everyone has to like you" is a pretty basic platitude and life lesson that has taken some of us a long time to learn. It's easy enough to say these words. But what are these words really saying?

Well, what they're actually *saying* is, "Hey, guess what? There's going to be a whole bunch of people in your life that just don't like you," and for all of us recovering people-pleasers out there (I see you), this kind of sucks.

It kind of sucks to think that no matter how well-intentioned you are, how genuinely you show up, and how accommodating of other people's needs you are, it just won't be enough for some.

In fact, for a few, it will *never* be enough. (You should go ahead and see above note re sucking, especially when your defense mechanism is just to do whatever it takes to keep the peace.)

Circle back to what you already know now: this isn't good or bad, it just *is*.

When you strip away fear and judgment, it's actually very *freeing* to know that for some, you will just remain a constant source of disdain and stress, and yes, they might reject you, even when you are your most authentic self.

Hard truth? For some, it's likely *because* you are your most authentic self.

And still, this is absolutely fine. Because by standing in your truth and living your own life, you're going to piss some people off, and you are going to frighten others who choose not to find the courage to just be themselves, and you will disappoint a handful of others when you draw that line in the sand that says, "Dude, enough. I am not okay with this anymore." Mirror, mirror, remember?

Having healthy, loving boundaries is a *beautiful* thing and establishing them is a really good thing to do. You have to know that in learning to do so, you will also have to learn how to feel comfortable with feeling uncomfortable and then do it anyway. You have to do what feels right for you. You have to live the life that feels like your own, and you have to make choices that honor that path, but you have to be very aware that you might lose some of the people you thought were going with you on that path.

Honor yourself, have compassion for where you're going and where others are at, and then keep going.

Now it's very easy for me to sit here and just say that now that my own healthy, loving boundaries are in place. It was not necessarily so easy to implement these boundaries, and it still requires discipline to maintain them from time to time. And at the same time, it's been such a valuable lesson to learn.

You are probably familiar with the fact that we keep learning a lesson until we've learned it. And sometimes we keep learning it after that, just to ensure that we really learned it—like for real this time. And for me, this has been just like a staggeringly painful lesson that I keep learning over and over again. I used to joke that I had Biff Loman syndrome in that I just wanted to be liked.

I'm a nice person.
I'm a good person.
I'm a good human.
I live with intention.
I do what feels good for me and for the greater good.
I do what feels right and true for me and always in a way in which
I am conscientious of respecting the needs of the greater good.

So it can feel relentlessly painful when I reach that moment of realization that there are some people for whom *this will never be enough.*

I will admit I am a recovering people-pleaser; I thought I was a recovered people-pleaser. And every now and then one of those "opportunities" comes along. (Pssst, "opportunities" is another word for "challenge" in the personal-development world.)

One of those fantastic opportunities will come along and kind of smack me in the face that *I am still not finished learning this lesson.* So on the one hand, that sucks. On the other hand, it makes me shift into gratitude, thankful once again for an incredible opportunity to learn and to grow and ultimately to heal deeper parts of myself that will make me stronger and more engaged in my life, which I think is a huge trifecta of why we are here on this planet at this very moment in time.

So yes, it's very easy for me to say that it has not always been easy for me to do, but I will always stand behind the importance of learning to do it.

I have three little girls, and this is advice that I give to them probably once a week, if not more:

One of them will come to me and say:

"So-and-so says I am _____."

So I'll say to them: "Are you _____?"

And they'll say: "Well, noooo, but..."

Then I will say: "Then it doesn't matter what someone else says or thinks because you already know the truth."

It really doesn't matter what other people think about you. This might be a hard pill to swallow, but swallowing it brings you home to yourself, which *does* matter.

If you are living in alignment with your truth and doing what you feel is right, it really doesn't matter what other people think. The tricky part is to get really comfortable with embracing and embodying every part of that truth. What this means is that *you have to be so comfortable in living your truth that you do not need to seek validation and approval from other people.* And you must accept, on a very deep and loving level, that the only approval and validation you ever need comes from one person. Go and look in a mirror right now if you want to meet that person.

Here's the paradox: While you have to learn how to set healthy, loving boundaries and know deeply that validation and approval has to come from you, you also know you have to honor your genetic nature of being a social being. You still need to coexist in an interdependent society. So, while it might be very tempting to just pack up and move to the middle of the woods and live off-grid, never having to speak to another human again, for most of the population that is neither an option nor a healthy choice.

We instead really have to learn how to set these healthy, loving boundaries that protect our emotional freedom, that protect our mindset, that protect our heart, and that protect our values—all the things that protect ourselves, while being able to show up in our relationships. And the reality is that there are going to be a few people in your life with whom you have to have a relationship, even if you don't like each other.

Adulting.
Am I right?

This is a truth, and it is what it is. While I am a huge fan of intentionally and mindfully surrounding yourself with people who inspire you, make you feel great, make you feel seen and appreciated and valued, I am also profoundly aware that *there are going to be people in your life who play a role in it that you are not going to get along with.*

And that's where the concept of boundaries becomes particularly important.

Anytime you're meeting a new person, having healthy, loving boundaries in place is an amazing skill to have because it acts as a natural filter for allowing in only the people who really deserve to be there. But as I said, there are going to be other people in your life who maybe you only see, for example, at Thanksgiving or at work. Or maybe you share kids with an ex-partner.

There are all kinds of examples of people who are going to be in your life who you cannot run away from and who you need to learn to deal with in a way that doesn't feel like it's killing you and eating you alive from the inside out. So once again, we circle back to boundaries—how to set them and how to keep them.

One of the earliest points I mentioned was (and this is especially true for people-pleasers) that we use our people-pleasing abilities as a defense mechanism. That tendency to keep everybody else happy often stems from a place in which we are protecting ourselves. Does this sound familiar at all? We sometimes learn in our early lives / in our childhood that if we want to keep the peace, if we want to protect our own self, and if we want to minimize the damage happening around us, we have to do "whatever it takes" to keep other people happy.

If you are somebody with a highly sensitive personality, who is empathic, who has a very high emotional intelligence, I'm speaking your language right now. When you are naturally and physiologically tuned in to the emotional frequency of other people, it is excruciating (like nails on a chalkboard) when someone is upset. It feels *awful* to see other people upset or not having their needs met.

And so we learn to accommodate. And now, as a highly emotional or sensitive person, not only do we feel someone else's distress, but we feel our own distress on top of that. And so we learn from a very early and genuine place that building up a safety mechanism of accommodation moves us away from feeling that pain: "In order to feel better, and feel the way I want to feel, I'll just do what it takes to make you happy. You want me to creep around the house in silence as if I don't exist? Perfect. You want me to pretend that I actually love chemistry class so that I don't have to deal with how much I really love writing? Easy. You don't want to have to deal with the fact that I hate soccer and I never want to play it again and what I really want to do is pursue piano? I've got this."

And as we grow up and attract more people into our lives and get into more adult relationships, that safety mechanism is no longer a safety mechanism—*it's just the way we behave.*

I know men have this experience, but if I were to guess honestly? I'd say that more women experience it because we are also taught from the very beginning as girls that "boys will be boys; boys are supposed to be loud, boys are not supposed to be able to listen, boys developmentally require movement so they don't really have to sit still and behave."

Conversely, girls are told that "it's developmental for girls to easily sit and listen better and be more polite. Play nicely, share, wait your turn, finish your turn early, give it away, prioritize others, and be nice."

We already get sorted by gender early on, and girls are told to sit and wait their turn. "It's not your turn to speak. You have to be quiet right now." Usually, the impact of these messages becomes baseline behavior.

For example, it's not uncommon for boys to wrestle outside in the backyard because we expect them to play like that. If girls are wrestling in the backyard, unless you are an evolved person, it tends to be something that is frowned upon or something viewed as almost deviant behavior because girls "don't do that."

Girls are taught from early on to sit quietly and listen and not to speak up. Girls shouldn't say something because it might hurt somebody else's feelings. And a girl's job is basically just to keep the emotional peace around her. I suggest for the next twenty-four hours that you go and observe some children and adult relationships you have in your life. Sit and listen to the messages that are given to girls and the messages that are given to boys, unwittingly.

One year a boy in my daughter's lower-elementary class brought bullets to school.

Bullets.

His punishment? He got sent to the office.

That same year, my daughter said to another kid in the class, "Wow, your lunch bag smells," and another girl nearby laughed.

My daughter's punishment? She got sent to the office. I had seven texts from the parents, one conversation with the teacher, two conversations with the vice principal, and one email thread looping the VP and teacher in together.

What the actual fuck.

My long-winded point is that from a very early place, girls—on top of everything else—are very much instructed to not say what they mean for risk of hurting somebody else's feelings. So we are literally taught from almost day one to ignore how we feel because we might offend somebody else. So we'll just keep that thought to ourselves.

We are effectively taught to ignore our own needs so that we can meet the needs of others. If you are a mom, you'll know this training comes back to bite you later on, as you are basically expected to attend to everybody else's needs without expecting someone else to meet yours (cue the "mom guilt" if you dare to ask for help. And also, where is dad guilt? Nope, not a thing because boys are taught to get what they want).

When it feels like your needs keep getting pushed to the back burner, that, too, becomes another safety mechanism where boundaries come into play.

So yes, we women have this learned behavior where we suppress our own needs and suppress asking for what we want and are instead encouraged to do what is easiest and best for everybody else. So, with that baseline and now defense mechanism in place and accepted as fact, those beliefs become ingrained in you as you get older.

Here's the rub: you always have a choice.

You may not always like the choice that you have, but you always have one. You can consciously choose to undo that behavior and establish new behavior, with new action. And all of that comes from changing your belief system.

You have to consciously decide that you don't want to feel like that anymore, so you're going to choose to not *act* like that anymore. And you have to consciously implement a new way of acting by going up into your brain, rewiring the existing belief and reprogramming it to believe something new. So if the existing subconscious belief is "I am happy when everyone else is happy," you are immediately making your happiness and basically your sense of self-worth, your sense of feeling connected, and your sense of feeling like you belong *conditional* on something external to you.

"If somebody else is happy, then I feel happy" also means "I can't feel happy or loved until somebody else does ____."

And that's not healthy.

I understand that it comes from a genuine place, a genuinely protective place. But at a certain point, if you don't like the way that you feel, it's up to you and *you alone* to change that.

When you're going through the process of changing, it feels gross at first because behavior change is hard, and as you know, your subconscious mind doesn't want to let go of that because the subconscious belief is that "if I get rid of that way of acting, I will become so vulnerable. I am so exposed to being rejected. I am so exposed to not belonging." So our ego will do whatever it takes to keep us swamped in that protective blanket. But having courage is to remove that blanket, to go through the process of removing that mask to reveal who we truly are and to ask for what we truly want.

Additionally, as we dare to show up as we are and as we dare to ask for what we want, it becomes clear that we can no longer please everyone. And when we are learning that lesson of what it means to not please everyone, we are very much going to displease some people.

That's really, really hard. As I said, we are social creatures, social beings who value—at a primal and genetic level—being together. We *need* to be a part of the group because being a part of a group is what is crucial to our success. So when we open ourselves up to that kind of vulnerability in which we say "hey, the way that you're acting, you over there, it's not okay with me anymore," and when we dare to change that pattern of behavior and no longer do whatever it takes to please other people, we are met with the stark reality that we are going to make some people mad, thus opening ourselves to rejection. And rejection, at a genetic level, tells us "now you're dead."

So how do we overcome that?
How do we do it . . . and is it worth it?

I say it is always worth it. Even if it isn't always easy.

When your love of self runs deep, so too do your feelings of self-respect and self-worth. It is a pretty powerful and awesome power trio to draw from. When you love, respect, and see your own worth, you begin to value your own time, energy, and space. When you value your own time, energy, and space (both physical and energetic), you are free to lay down the law of what is acceptable behavior from others and what most certainly is not.

The amazing thing is that change is never too late, and I really mean that: it's NEVER too late. If you are someone who has had little to no boundaries, then you have established a pattern of behavior that shows other people how to treat you. So when you decide that that is no longer how you wish to be treated, *all you have to do* is break the pattern.

For some people, your change will be easy, and they will completely understand and adapt; for others, the establishment of your boundaries will come as a shock, and they will be angry that you've changed the rules and the dynamic. Let those people go.

You are the only one who knows what feels right and true for you, and you are the only one who knows how to loosen or tighten the reins on your own space to the point that it feels comfortable and healthy. And because you are the only one who can honor your needs, setting (and sticking to) your boundaries is the ultimate act of self-love.

Those who appreciate your boundaries will love and respect you more because they, too, understand and value your time, energy, and worth; those who don't will no longer fit into your life the same way as they did before. That's okay.

Loving yourself means respecting yourself enough to have a small and mighty circle of people who connect with you, unconditionally, for who you really are.

So rather than letting people walk all over you, take advantage of you, and then snapping one day for how much you feel they've taken from you, start to change the dynamic.

Here's how to start:

1. CHANGE THE DYNAMIC

You know that friend who's always coming to you and using you as an emotional dumping ground? Be very clear that while you value your friendship (if you do), you feel like the dynamic has become negative. Offer to support them in finding a good coach or counselor who can guide them through the process, and offer to do something physical or outdoorsy together that changes the mood and the conversation (while still showing that you can be together and have fun, not just complain about an ex).

2. COMMUNICATE YOUR INTENTION

If there's someone in your life who keeps demanding things from you that you don't want to give so you've been avoiding that relationship, consider being honest. Have a conversation that opens with: "My intention for this conversation is to ensure we are both on the same page; I'd like to have the chance to start and then give you the chance to respond."

3. LET GO OF THE IDEA THAT EVERYONE WILL LIKE YOU

Ouch, right? But true. Sometimes we hang on to behaviors and patterns that do not serve us, and do not make us feel good, just to appease the ones around us. Well, guess what, lovely? If you have to work to set up conditions JUST so that someone will like you (or not judge you), you are working hard to honor their needs and not your own. You are not for everyone, and everyone is not for you. When you have the courage to be aware of your own needs and how you seek to meet them, you can reflect on how others in your life do or do not meet your needs too. Letting go of some of the people you've been desperately clinging on to is hard, and sometimes lonely, but you need to do what is right for you and not what you think is right for someone else.

These are the messy parts of growth and of getting real on your love of self.

It cost a lot to invest in myself—in the person I wanted to be—and it cost a lot to walk away from the person I no longer was. I value peace so much, and I paid dearly for it, and it was so worth it. It was worth every penny, every dollar, every hard decision, every word of every uncomfortably necessary conversation, and every moment I thought I was going to throw up, pass out, or not ever be able to figure out what to do next.

It was worth the expense.

That arrival is worth the price of admission and every toll paid along the way. And it starts with getting very clear about what YOUR values are, then drawing your own line in the sand to live in alignment WITH those values.

Can you love yourself enough to set healthy, loving boundaries?

Yes, you fucking can.

CHAPTER 31

How to have a bad day

No matter how healthy and loving your boundaries are, no matter how much you've healed from your past, no matter how disciplined your mindset is, there is a certain reality when dealing with humans that shit is going to go wrong. Kids will wake you up in the middle of the night, coffee will spill on your laptop, the car door will be left ajar all night leaving you with stolen change and a dead battery, an ex-flame will pop out of the woodwork when you least need it, a colleague will do or say something triggering or disappointing . . . there is a laundry list of teeny tiny little things that can go wrong in our lives, because *that's life.*

It would be naïve to think that once we've done the work—like really done the work—that every single thing is going to go smoothly. Most of it could go smoothly, but as the Buddhists say, it's not the climb to the top of the mountain that kills you, it's the pebble in your shoe along the way.

Life is full of pebbles, and when you're as committed as *you* are to your own divine purpose of learning and growing, at a certain point it can feel like "are we there yet? What is this feeling I *still* haven't healed?"

There is a great cosmos joke that because we are always learning and growing, we always need those "opportunities" to learn and grow from. Sometimes we're just going to have a bad day.

And that is not a bad thing.

I am all about the bright side. Why? Because in every interaction, every exchange, and every relationship there is a lesson to be learned that makes you grow and evolve. Sometimes that lesson is a little more hidden than we'd like and can be harder to find. The grittier reality is that shit happens, and when it does, we need to know how to cope and bounce back. Despite our best efforts and intentions, sometimes things don't work out, and that, too, is always for a reason. But even if you have that faith running strong in your core, the short-term acceptance of things going south can be challenging, scary, or downright deflating. In those times, it's crucial to know how to react with resiliency and not get tanked by adversity.

Some will tell you that the key to overcoming adversity is to stay positive, and they're not entirely wrong—but they're not entirely right either. In the long term, and as a general state of mind, yes, positivity is essential; hope is essential. In the short term, however, constantly and immediately reaching for the positive can be detrimental to your well-being because it can act as a mask that prevents you from truly feeling your feelings. Sometimes things just suck; they feel unfair, unjust, out of control, beyond your scope, and entirely unexpected. When those things happen, they trigger feelings of sadness, fear, anger, rejection, loneliness, jealousy, rage, depression, isolation . . .

And those feelings deserve a seat at the table; they don't need to stay long, but they need enough time to speak to you and be heard. When you ignore them, you are ignoring your true self and the true impact from events and moments in your life. Ignoring pain doesn't make it go away, it just suppresses it until it gets bigger and stronger and comes back later to haunt you in a more noticeable way. So when you have those icky feelings, welcome them. Identify them, listen to what they are telling you, and start to trace back where they are coming from. And once they've made their presence known and you've acknowledged that presence, you are free to move through them and move on.

Happiness is found in moments; the feeling of a state of happiness is a series of moments that we notice and appreciate, and we learn to stack those moments back to back to feel prolonged joy.

Sadness, anger, frustration, fear . . . all those icky feelings that come up are *also* moments, but the weight of them feels like they take up more space. When we get hung up on the weight of those feelings, one moment can sour our experience to the point that any other moment of joy is overshadowed by our attachment to the feeling of sorrow.

One time someone told me they'd had a *terrible* day because they hit the dreaded Reply All to an instant messaging app during a work meeting, and the words they'd sent were definitely not intended for all to read. Fortunately, a colleague flagged it, signaled back privately, and the comment was deleted without anyone else reading it.

Phew, right?

Wrong. For this person, their day was "ruined" because they had *almost* made a huge mistake.

My response? "But you didn't make it . . . you just *almost* made it." Even without any repercussions or drama of any kind, this person chose to let the feeling of guilt, shame, embarrassment, and fear override their day because of what "almost" happened.

The mind is a funny thing.

We all have bad moments; it's natural, and it's okay. What is *not* okay is to let those moments color your day and pollute it with feelings of discomfort.

Allowing those icky feelings to overstay their welcome not only brings you down after the bad moment but also prevents you from finding the many more moments of happiness, joy, and levity. When something goes wrong, let yourself feel that gut reaction and honor that place of emotion, then wipe your own emotional slate clean; bring yourself back to a healthy baseline so you aren't weighed down by a negative experience and are still able to openly receive the good moments that the day's course and interactions will bring.

Sometimes there are periods of time when the bad moments do seem to happen in rapid succession. In times of significant loss or shock, for example, it's as if our brains are flooded with the reaction to trauma, our systems are being reset from whatever loss has occurred, and one bad moment really does breed many more that stem from it. This, too, is a natural part of our lives.

Wiping our emotional slate clean can feel like far more of a challenge in cases like these because we don't have the physical, mental, or emotional reserves to pull ourselves out. It's in these times that we need to be clear on the value of staying connected, both to ourselves and to others.

I'm sure you've had the experience of something catastrophic happening in your life. We all have, and it's always hard to accept it when it does. And when we go into the mode we need to in order to settle the details of that loss (I'm talking major life events like death, divorce, moving, employment, betrayal, and others), we can get into a dark place in which we don't have the energy or even desire to connect.

These are the times we stay closer to home or to our bed, stop returning texts or phone calls, start eating salty and fatty foods, begin to shower less—we start slipping on the slope toward a dangerous mental and emotional state. These are the times we have to be self-aware enough to override the sinking feeling of despair and make a conscious effort to stay connected. Yes, it is important to honor, respect, and even embrace your own need for quiet solitude, and yes, that can be a very important and healing place to be. The caution comes in when you know you're at risk of "hiding out" on your own and not only disconnecting with yourself and others but actively avoiding connection, and for too long.

Be aware of what you need to help you feel like yourself again, what will help you feel that connection to the world beyond your trauma, loss, or otherwise emotional funk, and be diligent about making that a reality for yourself. Spend time with someone, even if your "date" isn't 100 percent talk-based: see a movie or go to a concert. You might find you can recharge just from that human connection.

Above anything else, after a bad day or a bad moment (or something more significantly bad), it is imperative that you take care of yourself. Self-care is self-love and is a very tangible practice in loving yourself. And sometimes, to make self-care feel like more of a priority and therefore more of a reality, you need to treat yourself as you would treat a child. This treatment is the beginning of inner-child work.

We each have our childhood selves inside us all the time. Some of us have learned how to integrate her into our adult selves, and some of us have ignored her, her presence, and her needs for too long.

When you are practicing active self-care, you are effectively mothering your own self, which becomes a deep and beautiful relationship. It is the part of you that steps up and asks what YOU would really like to have for dinner and then makes the judgment call whether

Pop Tarts are what you need to feel attended to or if you need to be the heavy and insist on eating something far healthier to nourish you from the inside out. Parenting your own inner child means stepping in and ensuring all the daily acts of self-care are happening, like having clean clothes, a tidy room and made bed, enough time outside, or stimulation away from your screens.

You may have never had someone care for you in this way; that's a sad reality that many of us experienced in childhood. But it doesn't mean you can't care for yourself in this way. Rather, caring for yourself in the way you always wanted and needed but didn't have, or didn't consistently have, can be incredibly therapeutic to your own self-love and growth. It might mean feeling like you are detaching from your adult self and really speaking to yourself in the third-person. You check in and pay attention to the little one inside of you in the same way you would check in and attend to the favorite little one in your own life. When you externalize that process, you are internalizing next-level care and love that will prove to be an anchor and safe harbor for yourself during even the hardest of days. I pinky swear.

More often than not, and unless there is an exception like a major life-disrupting event, *bad days are just moments.* And yes, sometimes those moments feel like they happen in rapid succession, and they can feel overwhelming. When you reach that place of overwhelm, there is one surefire solution I know that will save you, even if you are hell-bent on staying down and don't want to be lifted up—and that is gratitude.

When you can't find anything good in your life and can't see anything but strife and hardship, go outside and take a walk. Look at a garden, watch the water, hike in the woods, touch snow or earth at your fingertips, stay up until sunset or get up early for sunrise. Tapping into nature will remind you that this is all so much bigger than we are;

we are playing a role in it all unfolding, and everything that happens is a part of the unfolding and unveiling of us.

Change your entire attitude from "now I have to get up, go to work, make dinner, pay bills" to "now I get to get up and start a new day. I get to go to a job where they give me money for being there! I get to prepare a meal that will sustain my body with the food I bought from a room abundant in nutrition. And I get to enjoy the luxury of having instant access to the Internet and clean water every day, for which I am happy to pay a user fee."

You have so much. Even when you think and feel like you have nothing, and even when you are determined by your ego to stay and wallow in that place of stagnant sorrow, you have so much. Gratitude will be the practice that lifts the veil and reveals that to you; it will pull you back to your true and experiential reality. Your energy is your own; with every unique situation you encounter, you will always have the choice to determine how you let it affect you. Gratitude will be the conduit to extend enough love to yourself to get back to feeling how YOU want to feel instead of feeling as if it's being dictated to you.

Here are some super easy, lifestyle-friendly mindset hacks you can use to shift back from a bad moment into feeling like yourself again:

1. SOUNDTRACK OF YOUR LIFE

Change your mindset by changing your mood. When you are feeling melancholy and down, it's easy to stay melancholy and down by listening to music that supports that state of mind. We all have days when we just want to reach for *The National*. Change that state of mind almost instantly just by playing music that raises you and your vibration and makes you move and toss your hair. It's even better if you can add movement—joy will always lift you up. I recommend The Fitness Marshall. You can also keep a playlist of your favorite high-vibe songs as your go-to for when you need it.

2. BRUTAL SELF-HONESTY

When you come home and feel like you had a terrible, horrible, no-good, very bad day, ask yourself in reflection whether it was a bad day or a bad moment. What is the story you're telling yourself? Are you acting from love or fear? What is one "rose" that came up in all the "thorns" today? Be honest with yourself. Feel your feelings and don't let yourself slip into the ease of being upset. It takes a lot of energy to hold onto the heavy stuff so be honest about the reality of what's bothering you and use the tools in this book to ride out the answer.

3. CONNECT

Sometimes we just need the company of other people to help us feel connected and a part of the bigger picture. Who can you reach out to? Do you need time of solitude on your own, or do you need to be held? If you do seek out the company of others, beware the story on repeat. Share your pain and grief, but do not allow yourself to dwell on it over and over with many people. While the initial purge helps relieve the burden from you, rehashing the pain consistently will hold you back more than it will move you forward, or worse, create a bond in a relationship that is founded in toxicity and negativity.

4. SPOIL THE HELL OUT OF YOUR INNER CHILD

This is next-level self-care and all you have to do is listen. Ask yourself, "What do I need in this moment?" and then deliver. Let yourself be honest; the answer you need is already in you waiting to be heard.

5. NATURAL THERAPY

Get outside, even if you have to force yourself. Take a shower and feel the water. Go to the lake and listen to the waves. Watch birds in flight, observe the growth patterns on plants, feel earth in your hands and wind on your face. Go for a walk. Breathe. We are meant to be this connected, and nature will grant this connection to you in a sensory way every time. Experiencing nature is the quickest (and probably healthiest) way to come back to center.

6. UNDERSTAND YOUR TRIGGERS

You can be the most evolved, the best intentioned, and the most self-aware person, and I all but guarantee that you will still experience "triggers" from time to time. Even when you get clear on and heal the core wound, and even when you learn to see the lesson and let go of the BS, you are still left with being human. And part of being human is to experience situations and people that will scratch your surface, trigger that old pain from way down deep and cause you to react in a certain way.

That's okay. Part of "the work" of being emotionally aware is accepting that you are always a beautiful work in progress. You are always learning, always evolving, always experiencing something in the present and integrating that into the future. Knowing this fact, you know that it's okay to feel whatever you feel, you just need to be aware of how you feel, where the feeling came from, and how the feeling informs your behavior in the now.

Now the six magic words come back to us: "The story I'm telling myself is . . ." The thing about triggers is that you can be in the most stable place, with the most confident vibe, in the most self-assured way, being so proud of who you are and who you've become, and blamo, it hits you, just like that. Something comes at you out of nowhere that causes all that old panic, anxiety, self-doubt, and fear to bubble up and get you all worked up in a tailspin. When you feel that tremor-style trigger, especially when you're in a good place and it comes at you, it's almost harder to process because it feels so out of context.

In any case, when you are comfortable in knowing what your trigger is / triggers are, you can head them off at the pass through your thoughts and ease through them as you feel them.

7. PRACTICE THE ART OF FORGIVENESS AND GRATITUDE

If you do feel triggered, and you are clear on what the story is that you're telling yourself, come back to these epic mindset shifts: forgiveness and gratitude—they are the key to your freedom.

So. My questions for you:

Can you love yourself enough to have a bad day and carry on?
Can you love yourself enough to appreciate that adversity brings you strength?

Yes, you fucking can.

CHAPTER 32

Surrender, trust, flow

My eldest daughter was born peacefully at home after a beautiful full-term pregnancy and an easy six-hour labor. It was amazing. She was such a calm baby—it was like she worked for a baby PR agency . . . and so I got pregnant a year later, with twins.

On the day my beautiful twins were born, my then-husband, eldest daughter, and I were standing on our front lawn under the shade of a huge sugar maple. It was, ironically, Labor Day weekend, in the hottest summer we'd seen in years. I was uncomfortable, out of sorts, and grumpy.

We stood under the tree, looking up, transfixed by the branches covered in monarch butterflies. There must have been hundreds (if not thousands) of them, turning the branches from brown to orange. It was astounding.

I remember just standing there in total awe, having never seen something so magnificent. To this day it baffles me, and I haven't seen anything like it again. I remember thinking, "I'm going into labor soon."

The twins were born *four hours later*, four minutes apart, about seven pounds each, at a hospital that we had to drive more than an hour to, with our toddler in tow. I had cramps in the car, but nothing too bad, and despite it being Friday evening of LABOR DAY weekend, there wasn't any traffic to contend with. Their birth was smooth; they were born *naturally* without meds, a day before full term. Each of these little tick boxes is almost unheard of in twin births and labor, and I still kind of shake my head at the many miracles that transpired back to back to back.

Having three kids in two years was challenging. I was home on my own with them most of the time, with help from my mother-in-law. There was just so much learning involved, so much adapting, so much acceptance and surrender about what life looked like now. What my body looked like now. What sleep looked like now.

While I had been afraid that having twins would make me a "bad mom," having twins made me an even better mom because of how much I had to let go with respect to perfection and judgment; I had to learn instead to start appreciating everything around me. Amid all the learning and adapting and letting go and *loving*, I was very busy. So the tree full of monarchs slipped my mind until about two years later.

When I did have some time to think back to that day of their birth and all those butterflies, I researched the symbolism of the monarch butterfly, and beautifully, what I found online was that butterflies herald a massive change in your life, signifying a total transformation. I think because of the thousands of monarchs in the maple, this heralding was even more pronounced.

I immediately felt a wave come over me as I started to process this information; I genuinely believe this heralding of butterflies was a beautiful and dramatically orchestrated gift from God that everything

I knew to be true was about to change. The old ways were not going to work anymore. The old stories were not going to be true anymore. The old patterns of behavior were not going to feel good anymore.

The entire process of how this transformation unfolded was the beginning of my spiritual connection—the birth of my twins marked the beginning of a new life, new mindset, and new acceptance of identity, without me even knowing it yet. It started with learning to let go and trust the flow of life.

I know, beyond a shadow of a doubt, that it was this spiritual connection, which continues to get deeper and more beautiful and enriches each day, that is the foundation of my own ability to trust every single aspect of my life. Period.

Without that spiritual connection I would not have come through the pain of my divorce the way I did. I would not have navigated cancer and the treatment thereof the way I did.[8] And I wouldn't have trusted myself enough to create the business and platform I have without that courage to look up.

I learned to trust the unseen.

I learned to trust my intuition.

I learned to get quiet and ask for help—and listen to the answer from within when it came.

I learned to pray.

I learned to let go of attachments.

I learned to appreciate things as is, without the need to label them as good or bad.

I learned to embody that everything has a purpose, even if we don't know what that purpose is.

---

8 I would not have stayed as calm through the COVID-19 pandemic as I did.

I learned that we are all connected to each other, and we are all here to be of service.

I learned that things always work out in the end, and that if it hasn't worked out, it isn't the end.

I learned I had everything I needed inside of me.

I learned the only approval and forgiveness I needed was from me.

I learned that I am my one true home and the one responsible for meeting my own needs of safety and love.

I learned that seeing the big picture connects you to yourself.

I learned that when you're connected to yourself, you are never, *ever* alone.

It was that last one that really got me; I'd spent so much time in my life looking out, seeking out, worrying out that I had neglected to go in. And when I learned to go in and start trusting the experiences I had in doing so, I let go, gradually, of the need I had had to control everything. Life started to feel more like a game that I could approach with less fear and more curiosity, keen to know what was going to happen next, and what on earth this event or that one would lead to later. It began to feel more like I was watching my life as a movie.

And for someone who had struggled for *so long* to love herself, it was a revelation to realize that no matter what, I would always be there to protect myself, encourage myself, support myself, and love myself. I also learned five foundational insights on what we tend to feel about that relationship we have with ourselves and why it is essential for us to "look up" when we want to come home to ourselves.

1. THE COLLECTIVE CRISIS OF LONELINESS

We are facing a widespread, collective crisis today, and that is loneliness.

There is a melancholic, lonely pain that is, I believe, a natural part of the human condition—that longing for connection and to be with an "other." As social beings, this longing makes sense, and it holds us together like social glue; we feel that pang and feel fueled to connect with people around us.

But we kind of messed it up. We live in increasingly fragmented worlds, often separated from our parents and family by many miles, living on our own or with our immediate family but separate from anyone else. We rely less on interpersonal connection and more on social and digital interactions, and we stopped, in many cases, finding community through the weekly ritual of going to church or other organized worship.

Many of those actions started as blessings. We have the reach to explore and live anywhere, we have the tech to stay connected, we have the freedom to think and value our own thoughts from within and not spit out what someone else told us was true about what we believe, where we came from, or where we're going.

But the pendulum went too far and the world we have created—unless we are consciously acting against it—is lonely. In some cases, cripplingly so. As we tune into the idea that, as Maya Angelou so aptly said, "[we] belong every place [and] no place at all," it is increasingly important to be able to find home within ourselves, independent of the people or environment around us. It is also crucial that we honor our natural tendency and burning need to communicate and gather in the presence of other people.

And much of that connection to feeling home within ourselves is the ability to feel connected to something bigger and beyond ourselves, feeling comforted and held that no matter what our current reality is, we are *never* alone.

2. CONSTANTLY SEEKING OTHER

I am a hopeful romantic and believe deeply in true partnership and connection; I also believe that we have been fed and have adopted many untruths about what a soul mate or a twin flame connection is and what its purpose is in our lives.

We have attached so much value to that kind of connection that it feels like the ultimate reward to find it and the ultimate failure if we don't. It's the kind of pressure that keeps us in excruciatingly lonely marriages and keeps us feeling like we are incomplete until we find true loving union with another. But love isn't something that happens to us, it's something we are.

It's a confusion that permeates our pop culture and continues to muddy and equate the waters of "loneliness" versus "being alone," which are 100 percent not the same thing. When we are constantly looking outward to find the ONE person who completes us, the ONE person who is our other half, the ONE connection that makes us feel seen and heard, we are doing exactly what we've been taught to do, going down exactly the path we are supposed to pursue. But in doing so, we are shifting our focus to constantly finding love from outside ourselves.

The problem is that when we're always looking for love outside of ourselves, we're not finding it within ourselves. And when we're not finding it within ourselves, AND we are experiencing the absence of the love that we have either felt and lost (or never felt at all), we operate at a deficit of love, which perpetuates and then AMPLIFIES those feelings of loneliness.

Pretty messed up, right? Further, when we get caught up in the pursuit of love (not just romantic love, by the way, but the kind of love that makes us feel like we belong), we keep ourselves in that state of pursuit and lack, which makes it further challenging for us to operate at the level that will actually call in the kind of connection that loves us unconditionally for being unapologetically us.

3. REACHING IN, REACHING UP

When you have that "aha!" moment and realize that the love you are looking for can, and does, come from within, AND you start to give yourself permission to love yourself like that, your world will change. And a part of that world changing is realizing that you truly are a divine being. A work of art. Created with purpose for a purpose. Not random. With intention. Put here to love and be loved, to experience joy and laughter and pleasure and learn lessons, do hard things, be grace and beauty with a path that is yours to follow, all the while constantly guided.

It's through reaching in that we start to reach up. Have a look at your physical self: the curve of your ear, the structure of your feet, all your intricate inner workings that create babies and heartbeats and breath. This design is not by accident; this design is purposeful creation. And when we accept and embrace (or even entertain) the notion of purposeful creation, it changes our perspective about why we're here and how we show up. When we allow ourselves to hold onto that concept of being in this life with a divine intention, and when we have the wisdom to get very quiet and listen to the messages and winks and nods and coincidences we receive, we start to feel that divine comfort—the love we feel comes from within and from beyond.

That comfort will wrap you like a blanket if you let it; it will wrap you in the safety of "whatever you are feeling or experiencing now will serve you if you let it. Let this teach you what it is you can learn." That lesson, that experience, and particularly that pain might not make sense immediately, or even for some time after, but when you are ready, you can let yourself be held by the idea that this is not random. This is not a mistake. This is moving you forward in some way that you just don't yet fully understand.

And when you let go of the need to control the understanding, you can welcome that presence to your life, knowing that wherever you go, whatever you do, someone / something / a divine and loving intelligence is looking out for you.

4. HOW TO RELEASE THE SELF-PRESSURE

When you indulge yourself in the deep feeling and belief that you are not alone, that there is a plan, and that every lesson leads you to where you are supposed to be, the pressure you've been putting on yourself will lift.

The pressure to get it right the first time, to not make a mistake, to take responsibility for it all . . . it lifts. It lifts because you start to appreciate that you aren't doing it alone; that the same kind of person and situation you attract into your life over and over again is just a lesson that keeps getting louder—all you have to do is identify it, trace it back to where the pattern comes from, and rewire your own thinking and habits.

Everything you have done so far has led you here. When you accept the fact that nothing you have done so far has been a mistake but rather has led you through a series of experiences to exactly where you are right now, you can accept that you're doing it—you're living this life, and you're exactly where you are supposed to be. And if you are less content with where you are, that, too, becomes a point of awareness because you have now taught yourself the skills you need to start making the right changes in the right way.

And you can make those changes and set those intentions, feeling pressure- and guilt-free, because you have the internal care and love of self—with the awareness that something bigger than you is overseeing it all and keeping you aligned on the right path. It's a pretty beautiful design when you think about it.

Take responsibility for your actions and do so with love. Integrate decisions that you've made in the past (for better or for worse) and allow them to be a chapter in your story without defining your whole book. Let go of the guilt surrounding those decisions and find peace with the fact that we are all doing the best we can with what we have at any given moment, and when we know better, we do better. Allow that freedom to bathe you and draw out your breath from what you've been holding on to; you're doing great.

5. YOU GOTTA HAVE FAITH, A FAITH, A FAITH-AHH

You are exactly where you are supposed to be; this is a fact that I know to be true. And still, when you are in a crisis, it is almost unbearable to see or accept or respect that fact. And it's in those times of crisis (when everything feels upside down and inside out) that you need to have even more faith in yourself and your connection to the bigger picture.

It's in the times when you feel most isolated, most disconnected, most panicky or anxious or grief-stricken that you need to bear down and believe that this, too, will not only pass but will become a functional part of your story. This reality is difficult to accept because it's in those times of crisis when you want to break down, surrender, wallow, and agonize the most.

So let yourself. Let yourself do all of that, and feel everything, for the time in which you need to do so. Then have the self-love and self-compassion to care for yourself as you would a child, being guided by a loving intelligence bigger than yourself. Have the strength to get out of bed, wash your face, moisturize, make some tea, have a snack and a nap when you need it, go outside and look at the stars before bed.

Know in those times of panic that resting is part of rebuilding, and know that even when you feel the angriest, the most alone, you aren't. You haven't been abandoned, you haven't been overlooked, you are being given something else that you need on your journey in some way, as hard as it may seem. Lean into the lesson that you didn't know you needed being taught.

Believing the lesson in your core, with your rational mind, will prove to be a great comfort to you, especially when you find it the hardest. The beauty is that you don't have to go anywhere to find this level of peace or relief; you can look inside yourself, sitting in stillness to feel that loving presence that assures you that you will be okay, you have always been okay, and that you are already okay. It is a demanding, but ultimately freeing surrender to a loving faith.

To help kick-start or deepen your own spiritual connection, here are—you guessed it—a few Taco Tivities to really sink into the juiciness and unconditional love of the unseen. And for what it's worth? As I said earlier, I was raised a *staunch* atheist. I was taught I had to see it to believe it. My own experience taught me how wrong that approach is, and when I let myself become a student of my own life and a keen observer of my own environment, inside and out, I learned quickly that in reality . . .

You have to believe it to see it.

So here you go. These five thought starters can get you to believe what you know in your heart to be true and will help convince your head to listen.

TACO TIVITY 19

What is my connection to something bigger than myself?

This is an *excellent* thought starter for your journal. Dig into it: Where do you stand? Is there a past history there that you're connected to, or has it been abandoned? Were you taught one thing but feel differently? Explore every feeling and connection that comes up for you: anger, fear, resentment, joy, reverence, curiosity, love, love, love.

TACO TIVITY 20

Challenge it

Whatever comes up, make a point of challenging why you feel that way and where it came from. Really examine the roots of those feelings, how they served you in the past, and how they are serving you now.

When in doubt . . . look up

Any time you feel doubt or insecurity, go outside. Sit by the lake, the ocean, go into the woods, look up at the sky and marvel at the stars, get up early, chase that sunset. The natural world is *spectacular,* and when you let yourself be a part of nature, and let nature be a part of you, I would argue it is impossible to feel alone or disconnected. Get back to your human roots and feel the elements in, on, and around you.

TACO TIVITY 22

What am I learning that I don't yet know? (part two)

This daily practice is designed to spark your curiosity and reframe your perspective and is essential to cultivating your faith in the bigger picture. There is always a lesson, and it's your job to learn it. Use that lens on everything you encounter, especially the stuff that seems to come out of left field to catch you completely off guard.

Explore your "woo"

Oh yes, yes, yes. Get a tarot reading. Get your own deck, in fact, and use it for divine guidance. Look into moon rituals and start following the lunar calendar with a keen eye. Attend a women's circle or follow some new and spiritual social media channels. Book an appointment with an energy healer, a Reiki master, an astrologer. Get your natal chart done, your human design decoded, your palm read. Allow yourself to explore this more ethereal side of you that has maybe lived in hiding but is itching to come out and play. It is so empowering to appreciate that you are not alone in this life and never have been—you're simply following the little cosmic bread crumbs your soul left out for you to follow along the way as you come home to yourself.

Can you love yourself enough to look up?
Can you love yourself enough to believe it and then see it?

Yes, you fucking can.

CHAPTER 33

Happiness

There is a wild misconception that happiness is a state of being, a point of arrival.

In reality? Happiness is a moment. And when someone is a "happy person," usually it's because they are a person who has learned to find the joy in *many* moments stacked back to back, and they have also learned that more of those joyful moments are in the process of unfolding right now.

It is that simple; it is that complicated.

Hard truth: The people running billion-dollar empires don't want you to know how simple it is to be happy. When you realize, alongside seven billion other people, that happiness comes from within and is something you essentially choose to create, suddenly they don't have a billion-dollar empire anymore.

So instead, they sell you a bill of goods. They tell you that for only $29.99 you can have longer, thicker lashes. And they show you, through bazillions of images and messages you receive subconsciously, that people with longer, thicker lashes have more fun, more sex, more money, more opportunity, more sipping champagne on yachts. They show you a particular definition of what "happy" looks like.

Your brain, being the shortcut taker it is, does two things in response:

1. Associates longer, thicker lashes WITH that definition of happy and assumes that if you have longer, thicker lashes, *you, too, will* "be happy."

2. Ignores the root cause of why you might not feel happy and encourages you to shell out the $29.99 "fix" because that is so much easier than doing the emotional work.

Now multiply that example by the insane volume of inundations of what else we need to buy/spend in order to be happy and notice the insane disconnected reality that *none of those things* actually creates *happiness*. None of them.

But nobody wants to talk about that.

And so we keep buying, we keep spending, we keep reaching, and we keep looking to something outside of ourselves to create the feeling we want within. Here's an interesting fact: There is a number associated with a "happiness quotient," which means that after that number, happiness does not measurably go up. In Canada and the United States, that number is about $75,000. Again, that means that when you hit that target, your basic foundational needs for safety and security are met—you can afford to live without fear of where your food or shelter or heat or cleanliness are coming from.

After that, it's all gravy. Just because you're making $750,000 does not mean you are ten times happier. It's a myth that happiness increases in direct proportion to our income increasing.

This, my lovely, is one of the greatest scams of all time. This myth is designed to keep you in a constant state of lack and feeling like you'll never have or be enough so that you keep reaching for the next thing that will make you feel how you want to feel.

We do not want the thing.

We want the feeling we think the thing is going to give us.

So instead of reaching out (for the mascara, booze, validation sex, skimpy lingerie, nice car, cigarettes, luxury vacation, exclusive opportunity, the latest trend), we have to learn to reach in.

Think about the feeling you want to create:

Joy

Love

Freedom

Appreciation

Validation

Nourishment

Community

Sense of belonging

And here's the magic: you just start creating and cultivating those feelings now.

It is that simple.

It is that complicated.

You have everything you need inside you. And if you can't feel that, it's just feedback that you need to go deeper. Get quieter. Listen more attentively to what your intuition and inner guide or Source (you know, God) is telling you.

There are no conditions, which means that you don't need anything to create these feelings, you just have to choose to create them. Put yourself back in the driver's seat of your life because you are at cause. You have control over how you respond to literally anything that happens. Your reaction is always your own.

The above is such a powerful realization because it shifts your entire physiology into having agency and accountability for where you're at. If you don't like how you feel, change it. If you want to feel happier, choose to be happier.

Your feelings are, shockingly, unconditional on anything external to you; they are yours, they come from within, and they can change according to how you want them to change.

The tendency is to have us all stuck in a state of the pursuit of happiness; it's a fallacy. Happiness is ours right now. You've already found it—as soon as you choose to find it.

Sometimes people get stuck in the "happiness of pursuit" because they can't come to terms with the fact that they are enough. That they have everything they need. That their happiness belongs to them already. Instead, they keep chasing and wanting for more, which actually perpetuates a state of lack and feeling never enough.

By all means, dream. Have a grand vision of your life, whatever that means to you.

You are worthy of feeling good.

Create a vision that supports the highest vision of yourself feeling that good.

And start in this moment, creating the feeling of what that feels like.

Can you love yourself enough to choose happy?
Can you love yourself enough to find the joy?
Can you love yourself enough to celebrate the little things?

Yes, you fucking can.

CHAPTER 34

We are all healing

We are all healing—some of us with scars on the surface, and some of us with scars buried way deep down. We are healing in our present, from our past, and preparing for our future.

Your pain is your pain, and it's relative to you and your experience.

And just like your pain is your pain, your healing is your healing, and it unfolds along its own course, following its own trajectory, in its own measure of time.

"Our lives aren't supposed to be perfect." Our lives are supposed to offer us constant opportunities to learn and grow. Learning and growing keeps our lives spicy, brings us deeper, shows us who we really are and who we can really become. It isn't easy; the easy part is when you master how to let go of the edge of the riverbank you've been clinging to for dear life and let the water guide you down its path. You're going to hit some bumps and rocks and it's going to hurt. But it's going to show you that even when you're hurting that you're okay and capable of moving on.

Any great artist—hell, any great HUMAN—will tell you that their life's adversity shaped and informed who they are today and how they got there. Those are the stories that sell books, tickets, fill dinner tables and podcasts.

Shit fucking happens, love.

The work is to stay the course, choosing to respond and react with naïve optimism that you will get where you are going and ultimately learn a thing or two, have some laughs, have some tears, have some moments of "holy shit I can't believe I overcame that" and "I can't imagine my life without them."

Let life break your heart without letting it break YOU. Let yourself feel the full range of human emotions, and let that process of overcoming be your masterpiece. Let your fucking LIFE be your masterpiece, and let it be your greatest source of inspiration. Let it mold you, shape you, create you, break you, and build you up again. Then share that masterpiece, that inspiration, with those who appreciate true beauty and art for what it is: raw beauty and honest art.

The most riveting, interesting, and captivating stories have plot twists and turns you don't see coming, and I think when you embrace that as a fact, it's easier to take it all in stride.

Life isn't perfect, but the way in which we come to see and understand it's imperfections is what makes it more so. Be captivated by it and notice all the little details thrown in for the express purpose of honing your unique gifts.

The following is what healing looks like:

Forgiveness. Compassion. Water under the bridge. Walks by the beach, daily. Yoga. Crying. Breathing. Laughing out loud and often at my own jokes. Singing a lot. Cuddles. More patience for things being different than I planned. Family. Friendships—the quiet and understated kind. A knowing look from someone who gets it. Surrender. Tacos. The ritual of coffee. Working from home. Understanding my value. Standing in my truth. Loving big. Clinging to every word. Fucking up and moving on. Writing, so much writing. Dog envy. Assuming it works out better than I can imagine. Caring less and loving more. Going braless. Inner peace. Solitude. Making time to go outside. Watching the waves. Feeling sunshine. Turmeric tea. Dancing in the kitchen. Feet up on the couch. *The Office* seasons one through five, on repeat. Baking. Receiving. Reading. Sparkling water in champagne flutes. Dad jokes. More laughing. Less pressure. Feeling anger. Releasing it. Keeping perspective. Tuning in. Listening. Letting it go. Watching things unfold. Vulnerability. Trust. Honesty. Helping others. Accepting help. Going to bed early. Windows down, music up, seat warmers on. Scarves. Grace. New looks. More lipstick. Vitamins, but not too many. Buttered pasta and parmesan cheese with my babies. Cozy blankets and *Ultimate Beastmaster*. Dim lights. Saltwater baths. Lunar rituals. Alchemy. Spirit animals. Faith. Connection. Looking up. Hats. Three-step skin care. Sweatpants and sneakers. NLP. Phone calls. Waiting. Dreaming. Relaxing. Green juice. Chocolate-covered pretzels. Popcorn. Movie night. Vision boards. Praying. Tarot cards. Rumi. Naïve optimism. Empathy. Big smiles. Meaning it. Consciousness. Feeling awake. Staying grounded. Washing dishes by hand. Brunch. Vinyl. Slowing down. Stretching. Going to bed with a grateful heart; waking up like that too. Understanding, and not needing to. Complete love and respect for who I am. Feeling 100 percent secure and safe.

We are all healing; it looks and feels so good. What does it look like for you? Hold space for someone you love, and for someone you don't know you love yet.

Can you love yourself enough to heal, heal deeply, and heal some more?

Yes, you fucking can.

P.S. You are loved. Pinky swear

This section, simply, is a note from me to you, to inform you, reassure you, hold you into knowing that you are loved.

I pinky swear.

You are more than the sum of your parts.
You have value just by existing.
Your worth is unconditional.
You have everything you need inside you right now.

It is totally possible to love yourself the way you want to be loved. If I can do it—and face my deepest and darkest fear of lovability and embrace with grace and confidence that I alone am enough—so can you.

If you have come this far and are still having feelings that this message just isn't for you? That you are the one person who isn't loved? I have news for you.

Leisse Wilcox

You *are* loved; I pinky swear.

Still don't believe me?

Well, I know for a fact that you've already taken major steps toward loving yourself. Just by reading this book, you've already agreed to love yourself enough to:

1. take time, cultivate patience, and teach yourself to see the big picture as a sum of its moving parts
2. come home to yourself, and learn to call yourself beloved
3. dig in and expand your emotional awareness
4. do this foundational emotional work
5. trust me to guide you through that process
6. make this your own
7. believe that this kind of healing is possible for you
8. try
9. get started
10. see things differently
11. *give yourself* that kind of unconditional love and acceptance, tenderness and affection
12. treat yourself with loving kindness, respect, and adoration
13. be the parent you really wanted
14. find *yourself* in these pages
15. just be you
16. say yes
17. find clarity in what you want
18. listen to the parts of you that are calling out for that love and attention

19. go into your dark and shadowy places and bravely turn on the light
20. take your healing to the next level
21. feel your feelings
22. follow through
23. take the time to figure out the what and allow the *how* to come more easily to you
24. discover your core values
25. observe and question the story you're telling yourself
26. now find confidence in who you are
27. stop apologizing for how you feel
28. look at what is being reflected back to you
29. accept that which is not about you
30. appreciate that every day is healing you in new ways
31. shift into gratitude
32. be grateful for the air in your lungs
33. live your life with grit and grace
34. trust the process
35. reframe your own "failures" as stepping-stones to your success
36. face your fear of failure
37. face your fear of getting what you want
38. feel worthy of receiving it
39. act as if you are already the person you aspire to be
40. shine, confidently
41. take up space and use your voice without guilt or shame
42. trust your damn self
43. see *your* best as your only competition
44. keep choosing love over fear
45. be loving with yourself

46. write your own story
47. love and accept yourself exactly as you are
48. find the courage to stay true to both
49. live with intention
50. speak kindly to yourself
51. trust your ability to affirm what you want in your life
52. choose gratitude
53. find the joy
54. honor your own feelings
55. take accountability for your life
56. choose acceptance
57. forgive yourself
58. forgive others
59. let go of the past and move on
60. find compassion for others
61. look up
62. have faith
63. choose an optimistic outlook
64. have hope
65. be patient
66. practice Emotional Alchemy in your own life
67. set healthy, loving boundaries
68. have a bad day and carry on
69. appreciate that adversity brings you to strength
70. believe it and *then* see it
71. heal, heal deeply, and heal some more
72. choose happy
73. celebrate the little things

That's seventy-three ways in which you already love yourself; can you love yourself enough to write down twenty-seven others that brings you to an even one hundred?

Yes, you fucking can.

TACO TIVITY 24

Yes, you fucking can

You didn't come this far to only come this far.

Write out twenty-seven more ways in which you commit to loving yourself.

That gives you one hundred ways you already love yourself. And more begets more, so if you love yourself this much, think about how that is amplified by the ripple effect you've created in the energy and dynamics around you.

TACO TIVITY 25

Love bomb, pass it on

Reach out to someone right now and let them know they are loved.

Text.
Tweet.
DM.
Instagram.
Phone.
Visit.
Carrier pigeon.

Whatever way you choose, let the first person who comes to mind right now know how much they mean to you, even if that means starting with "hello." We are all connected, and it's essential to our inner peace to see and be seen. Share this love with someone in your world that you know you have a connection with—and take the time to tell them.

EPILOGUE

Phoenix rising

My kids and I read before bed every night and recently went through a serious *Harry Potter* phase. One of the most visual scenes—from an already incredibly visually written series—is the description of Dumbledore's phoenix, Fawkes, as he withers, dies, and rises again. The picture painted is one of this regal, majestic, proud, confident, almost untouchable bird becoming sallow, withered, gray, fragile, weak, wasted away, and invisible until he bursts into a cascade of flames and is born anew from his own ashes.

Hashtag relatable.

I will be brutally honest with you: There have been moments, months, and even years of my life that have brought me to my mother-fucking knees. I'm talking about reaching deep lows that I am not proud to have experienced—and sometimes came completely out of the blue.

I'd have moments so good it felt like I was sitting on the beach, enjoying a beautiful sunny day, sipping cocktails in sunnies and listening to vintage reggae while eating tacos right off the grill, when suddenly a tsunami of pain, trauma, triggers, and grief, all wrapped in a shiny brand new package I had never seen before, *would come out of nowhere.*

The momentum I had felt gathering slowed. The path I thought I was on veered. The emotions I thought I had processed and filed under "healed" came hurtling toward me, bringing anxiety and insomnia that left me reeling and lying in a fetal position for more time than I am comfortable sharing. The emergency phone calls to my person were made, the radical levels of self-care were upped with much snacking and sleeping, and the tuning out of the rest of the world (beyond cuddles with my delicious family and calls with my amazing clients) was made a priority.

And it passed (as it always does). I let myself feel all the things, as well as cry, scream, rage, wallow, and listen to a steady diet of *The National* until the heaviness subsided and things felt like they were getting back to normal.

Because things always do level out, and the intensity you feel will lighten if you let it.

Surrender to the push and pull of the things beyond you that you cannot control. What I can control is, as I said, ensuring that I am well cared for, that my immediate connections stay strong, and that I surrender to the comfort of trusting and not knowing.

This is a time of rebirth and of growth, which means that this—for so many of us—is a time of transition. And transition is hard AF. If you've ever given birth, or witnessed a beauty in your life giving birth, you know intimately that transition is when it's no holds barred. You can't tell if you're going to throw up, shit the bed, or both (and you are praying it doesn't happen at the same time). You feel like you've lost control over your body, no longer quite sure if this body belongs to you anymore anyway. You are sweaty, shaky, and are desperate for answers to questions like: "What do I do?" and "What happens next?" and "For the love of all that is good, how long does this LAST?!"

And then, blessedly, just when you think you can't go on anymore, your baby is born; your tiny, perfect, pink baby is ready to be held and nurtured and, above all, L O V E D. By you.

And miraculously, you forget about the terror of transition— and the fear and the pain and the spiraling out—because now you are holding love and joy in your arms, and love and joy are far more powerful than any degree of chaos and crazy.

This is a call to action to constantly do what feels right and true in the face of the hardship and adversity that come with navigating that transition.

Lovely, before you can be the phoenix rising, you have to set yourself on fire. You have to set yourself on fire before you can rise up from the ashes. So let go. Burn up. Surrender to the weight that has come crashing down and allow yourself to close your eyes and crumble under it as it does.

Then pause, take your first breath, and rise up.

Can you love yourself enough to rise up?

Yes, you fucking can.

OUTRO

To Call Myself Beloved

Every bad decision I've ever made was made from a place of having low self-worth.

I didn't recognize this fact until my late thirties; before then I'd believed that each of those bad decisions—each of which taught important lessons in their own way—were unique, isolated, and completely independent of one another. But in using that powerful mega lens, it hit me one day that every single one was made from an old place in which I didn't value, appreciate, or even really respect myself the way I do now. In fact, it was in part the realization that led me to valuing, appreciating, and respecting myself to this degree today.

It's funny because the clues were there; there was even a pattern or script feeling to relationship dynamics that I think I'd glossed over as they were happening until I was ready to not just hear the message but listen to it and let it fully sink in.

"I thought you were worth it at the time, but now I'm not so sure."

And there comes a time when it's met with "enough."

I took that good hard look when I was finally ready to do so and realized that each of the relationships whose closure included those fateful words had been structured around and built upon a toxic "rescue narrative"—you know, "I was struggling and he/she saved me from myself." There's such a romantic notion to that idea, and I think it comes from being spoon-fed, force-fed, overfed that narrative—particularly as girls and women—since we are oh so tiny.

It comes to us in the messaging that we inherently need to be saved and that one day—ONE DAY—someone will finally come along, sweep us off our feet, and fully and completely understand us. There's a kernel of truth in this belief; we each have the desire to be seen and heard. But waiting for and holding on to the vision that we'll only feel whole once someone else, someone external to ourselves, comes to rescue us from whatever our previous problem or affliction is, is dangerous.

And it's not romantic—it's codependent. It implies that until we have that person, that savior, we will remain incomplete and flawed. The problem there is that in subscribing to that narrative, and in adopting that storyline for ourselves, we internalize the actual belief that we will never be whole on our own. Uh-oh.

It took me a long time to understand and integrate that concept, and I wasn't ready to do so until I was really ready to do so. I lived the first thirty-seven years of my life believing that I would never be good enough as I was and that my existence only counted if someone else was there to validate it and to validate me and to approve of me and accept me.

I lived trapped by the lies I was told as a kid. I stayed a little too long in a relationship that looked perfect on the outside but felt lonely on the inside. I worked my ass off for—and lent thousands of dollars to—a megalomaniac who never intended on paying me. I almost forewent a lifesaving treatment *for fear of how it would make me look.* I almost ignored the risks of reconstruction for fear of how I'd look and the massive fear that wow, without hair or breasts, I REALLY wouldn't find a man to love me.

I asked myself some really hard questions about my identity as a very feminine woman and where that femininity comes from. While I believe that worth and femininity were tightly tied together for me, and I misunderstood the fundamentals of both, it was cancer that really forced me to remove the many masks I'd been hiding behind for decades of my life.

I never wore a wig or had reconstruction or wore a prosthetic. I felt like, in the spirit of removing the metaphorical masks, I was also being forced to remove the physical masks of my appearance as well.

Now, I had *nothing* to hide behind.

When I shaved my head, and when I went bald, I felt more beautiful; instead of feeling like I had to do or prove anything, I just led with my light, and I've never had more compliments (particularly ones telling me how beautiful my eyes and magnetic energy are).

Two nights before my final chemo treatment, one of my six-year-olds said, "Mummy, you are beautiful. You look beautiful; you look like a strong and confident woman." Mind. Blown.

The mastectomy, too, drove it home for me that nothing is finite; we expect our bodies will stay the same, but that's an illusion. Just like our bodies change in puberty, and again in second puberty in our twenties, and again during pregnancy, and again after kids, and again after menopause, I realized that this surgery was just the next iteration of my physical self. I could detach from what I had looked like and still feel like me and also confront some dark demons about my own lovability.

Our bodies, like our lives, are designed to evolve.

During the decision-making process over both chemo and a double mastectomy, I had many conversations with friends, family, and my own self about what made me feel like me; much of my initial resistance to these lifesaving treatments was centered on fear of the unknown, and much, to be very honest, was centered around the thought of "Oh my God, I am single now, with beach-wave hair and perfect tits; how will I ever find my guy when I'm bald and scarred?"

Am I proud of that? No. But I'm self-aware enough to understand where that thinking came from. And it was in that process when it kind of came "out of nowhere," the feeling that I am more than the sum of my parts. I am the pastiche of those parts, held together by the core of being me. And being me means living a life that is rich in love for my family, generous in kindness, joy, laughter, and levity, relentless in optimism and keeping things grounded and real, and guided by love and grace—and always having gratitude for it all.

That core, that essence, that essential me-ness isn't touched by anything external to me. It can be enriched, of course, but at my core I am who I am and that is 100 percent my responsibility to uphold. And I uphold it because now, after all those years, after all that trauma, after all that disbelief and doubt and anger masked as sadness, I did it. I did the simple, the profound, the life-shifting Emotional Alchemy work of coming home to myself and of calling myself beloved.

When people go through a massive physical transformation, they have some proof of the change in their body—this is what I looked like before, and this is what I looked like after.

With emotional work, you can definitely see evidence of that inner change, often through the eyes or the way we carry ourselves, but there's no real metric to demonstrate the old you from the new you.

But you know what I hope? I hope this book acts as a catalyst for you to do just that, to find the inspiration for the you before (the one who pleased all the people, put up walls, had no boundaries, determined your worth from something or someone external to you) and the you now, the you to come (the one who stands confidently in her authentic truth and genuine light).

My favorite poem is four lines long and was my second of my twenty-two tattoos. It's inked on my right forearm and in my own handwriting, like a note to self. I found it at the perfect season of my life, just as I was leaping into making radical life changes, and when I read it, it really hit me in my soul.

It feels like a woman at the end of her life, having an exit-style interview with God, asking her the big questions. As soon as I read it, I knew it to be true, and I knew it to be my raison d'être for doing the big work of coming to terms with the life I had and the life I wanted to have.

Did you get what you wanted in this life?
I did.
And what was it that you wanted?
To call myself beloved; to feel myself beloved on the earth.

~"Late Fragment" by Raymond Carver

Author bio

Leisse Wilcox is a transformational mindset + success coach who helps high-potential women courageously become the vision of themselves they can't stop dreaming about. A passionate (and TEDx) speaker, dynamic thought leader, author, NLP practitioner, top podcast host, cancer survivor, mom of three, and taco enthusiast, her entire experience has been about coming home to her truest self and to call herself "beloved," knowing intimately that changing the world starts by making the changes we want to see within ourselves first. Featured on ABC and in *Forbes*, *Toronto Star*, and *Thrive Global*, Leisse's intention is to guide people to come home to themselves, giving them permission to live authentically. You can watch her on Season 2 of Amazon Prime's *The Social Movement* and contact her via LeisseWilcox.com for online courses and to work with her privately.

@leissewilcox

LeisseWilcox.com

To Call Myself Beloved: The Podcast with Leisse Wilcox

Acknowledgments

Anyone who tells you they are self-made is lying; it takes a village—even of unwitting antiheroes—to shape us into becoming the fully realized vision of who we are. This book, as a physical expression of who this woman is behind the pages, is living proof of that. A lot of gratitude lives in these pages. "Thank you" doesn't quite say it, but it's a start. To my aunt Corrie for being graciously unwavering in her support. To Katherine for all but insisting I write this book for three years; to Sabrina, Letitia, and the YGTM team for being the bridge that took this from "one day" to THIS day. To Sarah Nicole for the invitation to show my scars and to Emily D. for making it safe, and absolutely beautiful, to do so. To my aunt Hilda for four months of unconditional care, and then some. To my uncle Carl for the cogent insights that made a lot of scary things feel a lot less so, and to my uncle Stewart for listening as I talked out a lot of shadowy stuff. To Bubbles for being the indelible catalyst of a mother figure. Thank you to John, John, Dwayne, Bradley, Jeffrey Dean, and Ben for being unsuspecting celebrity crushes that have brought a lot of levity through some tough times. Thank you to the many coaches and spiritual advisors who've helped the healing. Thank you to the 22,000 (mostly) random people for listening and helping me cultivate my voice and purpose through truthful passion.

And thank you to Mia, Grey, and Clara for treating laughter like a hobby and teaching me what unconditional love feels like.

I am grateful for all that has come before, and all that is yet to.

For we walk by faith, not by sight. 2 Corinthians 5:7

Author's note

What we know about memory is that each time we remember something, we remember it differently—even if the difference is that we remember remembering it. We also know that trauma affects our ability to remember. Every word of this book is recalled to the very best of my ability; interestingly, I don't remember much about my childhood, save for these intense flashes of clarity I've shared here with you. Many of these memories were repressed until I was in the depths of my own healing, which allowed me the safety to revisit and feel them . . . healing as I went. Intense, I know. The mother wound, the father wound, the sense of safety, security, and attachment—these are real-deal pain points and vulnerabilities for most people. Having the courage to be honest about that is the first step in healing forward.

If you take one thing away from this book, let it be this:

In 2019 my kids and I were standing in the kitchen, and while I don't remember exactly what started our conversation, I remember that I started into one of my (cough, many) mini-lectures on why it's so important to just be yourself. My youngest (then six) responded (after I said something along the lines of "When I was a kid, my parents always made me feel that . . .") with "Yes, mummy, and you turned out pretty awesome."

Life has a funny way of working itself out.

Works cited

Prologue

Obama, Michelle. 2018. *Becoming*. New York: Crown.

Pablo Picasso: https://www.brainyquote.com/quotes/pablo_picasso_108723, accessed June 24, 2020.

Part Two: Introduction

Confucius: https://www.goodreads.com/quotes/950577-we-have-two-lives-and-the-second-begins-when-we, accessed June 24, 2020.

Chapter 16

Anaïs Nin: https://www.goodreads.com/quotes/5030-we-don-t-see-things-as-they-are-we-see-them, accessed June 24, 2020.

Chapter 19

Doyle, Glennon. 2020. *Untamed*. New York: The Dial Press.

Chapter 25

Maya Angelou: https://www.goodreads.com/quotes/7273813-do-the-best-you-can-until-you-know-better-then, accessed June 24, 2020.

Theodore Roosevelt: https://quotefancy.com/quote/33048/Theodore-Roosevelt-Comparison-is-the-thief-of-joy, accessed June 24, 2020.

Chapter 27

Nayyirah Waheed: https://www.goodreads.com/quotes/910906-i-love-myself-the-quietest-simplest-most-powerful-revolution-ever, accessed Jun 24, 2020.

Chapter 28

Carrie Fisher: https://www.goodreads.com/quotes/8166730-take-your-broken-heart-make-it-into-art, accessed June 24, 2020.

Chapter 29

John Steinbeck: https://jgdb.com/quotes/author-john-steinbeck/page-38, accessed June 24, 2020.

Mahatma Gandhi: https://www.brainyquote.com/quotes/mahatma_gandhi_121411, accessed June 24, 2020.

Chapter 32

Maya Angelou: https://www.goodreads.com/quotes/904289-you-only-are-free-when-you-realize-you-belong-no, accessed June 24, 2020.

HELPING WOMEN BIRTH THEIR BRAIN BABIES

At YGTMama Media Co., we help women bring their visions to life.

Through a collaborative and supportive community, we truly value the idea that it takes a village as we bring your Brain Baby into this world. We are a unique and boutique publisher and professional branding company that caters to all stages of business around your book and personal brand as an author. We work with seasoned and emerging authors on solo and collaborative projects.

Our authors have a safe space to grow and diversify themselves within the genres of nonfiction, personal development, spiritual enlightenment, health and wellness, love and relationships, motherhood and business as well as children's books, journals, and personal and professional growth tools. We help motivated women realize dreams and ideas by breathing life into their powerful passions. We believe in women's empowerment, community over competition, and equal opportunity.

JOIN OR CONNECT WITH THE MAMA TEAM

🌐 YGTMAMA.COM

📷 @YGTMAMA | @YGTMAMA.MEDIA.CO

📘 @YGTMAMA | @YGTMAMA.MEDIA.CO